An Archivist's Guide to Copyright

An Archivist's Guide to Copyright

Navigating Risk Management

William J. Maher

BLOOMSBURY ACADEMIC
NEW YORK • LONDON • OXFORD • NEW DELHI • SYDNEY

BLOOMSBURY ACADEMIC
Bloomsbury Publishing Inc, 1359 Broadway, New York, NY 10018, USA
Bloomsbury Publishing Plc, 50 Bedford Square, London, WC1B 3DP, UK
Bloomsbury Publishing Ireland, 29 Earlsfort Terrace, Dublin 2, D02 AY28, Ireland

First published in the United States of America 2026

Cover design by Chloe Batch
Cover image © iStock.com/natrot

Library of Congress Cataloging-in-Publication Data

Names: Maher, William J. author
Title: An archivist's guide to copyright : navigating risk management /William J. Maher.
Description: New York : Bloomsbury Libraries Unlimited, 2026. | Includes bibliographical references and index.
Identifiers: LCCN 2025040550 (print) | LCCN 2025040551 (ebook) | ISBN 9798881801670 hardback | ISBN 9798881801687 paperback | ISBN 9798881855086 pdf | ISBN 9798881801694 epub
Subjects: LCSH: Copyright--United States | Fair use (Copyright)--United States | Archives--Law and legislation--United States | Archivists--United States
Classification: LCC KF2995 .M34 2026 (print) | LCC KF2995 (ebook)
LC record available at https://lccn.loc.gov/2025040550
LC ebook record available at https://lccn.loc.gov/2025040551

ISBN: HB: 979-8-8818-0167-0
PB: 979-8-8818-0168-7
ePDF: 979-8-8818-5508-6
eBook: 979-8-8818-0169-4

Typeset by Integra Software Services Pvt. Ltd.

For product safety related questions contact productsafety@bloomsbury.com.

To my wife Terry, who ended up learning more about copyright than she ever really wanted to know.

Contents

Preface

Figure 0.1 Image created by author from public domain elements. © William J. Maher.

Does the very sight of a "C" in a circle, this symbol of copyright, send shivers down your spine? Are you often afraid that anything you do as an archivist will end with you tumbling down a copyright rabbit hole, at the bottom of which is a letter threatening you with a lawsuit? When it comes to copyright, are you the type of archivist who is quite happy because you don't know much about it? Or are you the type of archivist who knows a bit about copyright and finds it all quite depressing?

Either way, this book is written for you. It is written to help you find a middle ground between those two extremes, and to explore the middle ground between those two types of archivists. Its goal is to expand the number of archivists who know enough about copyright to have confidence to focus on their primary mission of selecting, caring for, and making available records to serve their communities without getting trapped in the copyright maze.

As yellow hazard signs warn, we cannot avoid the fact that US copyright law applies to a large portion of the materials held in our archives, or that it covers many of the activities we and our users pursue. That means that we, as archivists, need to be prepared to take on the role of copyright managers. We need to know what the law declares, but that doesn't mean we must chain ourselves only to those parts of the law that prohibit or impede action. Instead, this book looks at the law in its entirety and surveys related rights so that archivists can be sufficiently comfortable with the complexity of copyright law. It should help you focus on the core responsibility of scientific management of archives—to preserve records and make as many of them as possible available to users without creating legal problems or disrespecting the rights of those who created or are documented in the records we hold.

There is no avoiding the fact that the copyright law was written to provide market regulation of cultural or intellectual property works. It is unfortunate that the law also unintentionally covers not just works in commerce, but also a wide swath of other works that archives preserve and make available to users. Unfortunately, many of the works your archives holds are copyright orphans. According to the law, they have been covered by copyright from when they were created, and they will remain in copyright for many more years even though their copyright owners are unknowable or untraceable. Technically much of what we and our users will want to do with these orphans might be contrary to copyright, but giving priority to strict adherence to the law will undermine our mission. As much as we would like this to not be the case, there is no way to achieve zero risk of liability for basic things an archives needs to do.

To create breathing room, this book builds a framework for an informed and deliberative risk management approach to copyright in archives. No doubt, risk management may involve taking actions that do not always fit within the letter of the law or may at the least rely on rather "liberal" interpretations of some of the law's exceptions and limitations. However, by first presenting a detailed summary of a substantial part of the US Copyright Act and an overview of other or related rights, this book should prepare you to construct your own risk management approach for the specific copyright challenges you and your archives encounter.

To get beyond the paralysis that might come from just a cursory awareness of the law's exclusive rights and penalties, this book provides a rather extensive survey of the statute as well as of court cases that tell us what the law means. To say that Chapters 4 and 5 are dry and complex may be an understatement. However, your patience in reading them will give you the essential foundation for administering copyright, understanding risk factors, and applying risk mitigation steps so you can become your own risk manager.

Caveat. The author is not a lawyer, and this text should not be considered legal advice. Instead, this book should be understood as archival management advice on:

- how to understand what copyright is and what its rules are
- how it affects the materials you curate
- how it might constrain the activities expected of you as an archivist
- how it may affect what uses you and your researchers make of the copyrighted works in the archives.

This book is *not a license* to ignore the law, nor is it a substitute for seeking and obtaining professional legal advice when necessary. It should, however, help you to communicate better with legal counsel about the relation of the distinctive nature of the archival mission to those specific aspects of the law that are relevant to archives. It is hoped that when, and if, you contact counsel, you will find this book helps you explain both your copyright "problem" in terms counsel will understand, and how the archival mission and your professional standing need to be factored into counsel's work to represent you well and effectively.

Before you embark on this book's journey through copyright, it may be helpful to know about its provenance and sources of inspiration. The author is an archivist with over four decades of experience in the archives of a large research university—an archives centered on institutional records but one that also acquires, preserves, and makes accessible sizeable and diverse "manuscript collections" and records of external organizations for an active local and global user community. As my career progressed over 47 years, I increasingly encountered copyright challenges in acquisitions, outreach projects, and especially in serving the needs of students, scholars, and the public. The enormity of these challenges became only more apparent as the law changed and copyright control became longer and tighter in the 1990s and 2000s. This was despite the best efforts of our archival profession to seek legislation and court rulings to acknowledge the important societal role of archivists and our users.

In addition to being an archivist, I am also trained as a historian. Thus, the book reflects my belief that societal context is essential to understand the past and the present. Thus, you will find a modest amount of historical background to explain why the law is what it has become, as well as some of the more curious stories behind the law. Likewise, because law and policy cannot be divorced from structural economic and political conditions, the book also touches on those influences that have given us the law we must live with.

Finally, I believe that part of my initial engagement with copyright law was driven by the sense that more archivists and more archives users need to better understand the law so that, as citizens, we can advocate for legislative changes and work against further constraints from the courts. That's why this book closes with recommendations for how individual archivists and our professional organizations can play a role in public policy changes.

Good luck.

Acknowledgments

Archives and acknowledgments share more than just the same first letter. They are both about origin stories of a sort. The inspiration for this book comes in two ways from Maynard Brichford, founder of the University of Illinois Archives. First, he taught me that the archivist should be passionate in working for the widest possible use of archival materials.

Second, it was through one of his exam questions that I was thrown into the copyright labyrinth. His question was simple: "Define or identify the doctrine of fair use." That ended up being the only question I got wrong on his final exam. In my defense, that was 48 years ago, when the words "fair use" were just on the verge of their first appearance in the copyright statute.

Still, it created an interest that was rekindled nearly two decades later. That was when I was on the Council of the Society of American Archivists (SAA), and SAA's Executive Director, Susan Fox, inspired us to understand that archivists should be following the rapid changes being proposed to copyright law, including a set of professional fair use guidelines. Susan was also the one who asked me on short notice, in the summer of 2000, to teach a day-long workshop on copyright for archivists.

The workshop's 26-year run has required that I dig deeply into copyright, giving me the opportunity to progressively learn how to explain the law and provide tools relevant to archivists. So, it is really to the hundreds of students at dozens of workshops that I owe thanks for the challenging questions that drove me to explore the many nooks and crannies of the law and its relation to the endless variety of archival collections. Likewise, I must thank my own archives staff for providing many invaluable opportunities to learn more about solutions to archival problems created by copyright law.

Of course, I owe profuse thanks to Erinn Slanina, acquisitions editor at Rowman & Littlefield, now Bloomsbury Publishing Inc, for being inspired by an announcement for a recent copyright workshop. That's when she approached me about doing this book about copyright for archivists. It took some persuasion, but Erinn persisted, and she has been extremely supportive throughout the writing, review, and production phases. Her vision is most appreciated.

I am particularly fortunate for colleagues and friends who have made many contributions to the writing and scope of the text. Archival copyright specialists and seasoned authors Aprille McKay and Peter Hirtle offered many pages of advice and corrections on the first draft of the manuscript. They made sure I was aware of my oversights and when my efforts to summarize wandered into misstatements. Bryan Whitledge provided perceptive advice on cultural property issues and brought his particular skills in public policy advocacy to bear on the final two chapters. On a very tight deadline, John Franch did a thorough proofreading that caught the numerous typos, missing words, and leftover words that beleaguer word-processed documents. He also caught more than a few places where my style got in the way of clarity.

It is to my wife, Terry Maher, that I and you the readers owe a particular debt. As a professional editor, she rose again and again to wield her ax ruthlessly to my turgid early drafts. Always thinking of the readers first, she patiently, but pointedly, reconstructed narratives that suffered from my having spent too much time reading the law and court rulings that were chock-full of technical terminology, not to mention heavily larded with dependent clauses. If your reading encounters difficult passages, it's either because I didn't follow her advice, or as Charles Dickens' Mr. Bumble opined, "the law is an ass."

Ultimately, as much as I have many people to thank for advising and guiding me on this book, its content is my sole responsibility. I thank you, the reader, for bearing with me as, together, we try to understand copyright so we can best serve our archives and our public.

1 Archives and Archivists: Does Anyone Understand Us?

Pity the poor archivist. Our field may be one of the most misunderstood jobs in the world. Tell someone you're an archivist, and routinely the response is something like "you're an architect?" We also hear archaeologist, activist, anarchist, etc. So, it's no wonder that those who make copyright law and policy don't understand what we do, why we do it, and why copyright needs to change to give us breathing room. Combine that with the fact that different kinds of archives have different rules and missions, and you have a perfect storm of misunderstanding and misperceptions that can make dialogue difficult even among archivists.

That's why this book starts with a chapter on the nature of archives, so we all embark on this copyright journey together with a baseline understanding of how copyright law relates to the kinds of archival deposits and documentary collections we curate. My experience may not be universal, but I believe my 45 years of professional work with institutional records, external organizational records, and subject-matter "manuscript collections" has revealed the many challenges and frustrations archivists face when navigating copyright law.

That experience has been greatly supplemented by the many copyright questions I have encountered at national, regional, and special-format archives conferences and workshops over the years. More than a decade of attending copyright treaty meetings at the World Intellectual Property Organization (WIPO) in Geneva, Switzerland, has given me experience in trying to make the archivist's needs for exceptions to copyright persuasive to those who set policy for what WIPO calls "copyright and the creative industries." Over the course of the past three decades, these experiences collectively have made only more acute the recognition that policymakers as well as those in collateral professions lack understanding of what archivists do and why we do it. So, let's start our journey by establishing a foundation of some baseline definitions and basics for understanding copyright's relevance to our work and how we can cope with it.

1.1 Definitions and Basics

Eighty years ago, when the National Archives was only 10 years old, the then Archivist of the United States, Solon Buck, quoted an assistant as saying that when many people encountered the word "archives," they didn't know whether to eat them or douse them with bug spray.[1] Today, the word "archives" has gained ground in common parlance, but it's still usually used without the meaning and understanding of our increasingly sophisticated profession. Nevertheless, the expansion of the field has seen the professional meaning of "archives" grow from one, two, or three to now twelve definitions that often overlap.[2] The variations among the current meanings reflect increased sophistication among archivists and the greater complexity of records in the electronic era. All of that is fascinating but beyond the scope and purpose of this book and chapter.

When confronting copyright, however, we need a common basis for understanding the relation of archives to copyright law. Therefore, the working definition of "archives" for this book is:

> *Non-current documents that provide a record of the activity of an entity such as government, institution, corporate entity, family, or person, and that have been systematically maintained both during their original creation and subsequent retention after they have fulfilled their original purpose.*

Classically, "archives" has been seen as referring narrowly to the contextually based documents that provide evidence of actions of an official body (e.g., government, business, university, etc.). However, especially in American practice, "archives" has come to include privately and personally created material (e.g., "personal papers"), generally of an unpublished nature and managed by libraries, museums, and historical societies in ways that follow the practices of organizational archives. Thus, in the context of this book, "archives" should be seen as referring to cultural archives as a whole, rather than solely to the records of enduring value of a specific organization or agency.

"Archives" throughout this book should also be considered in this broad sense regardless of whether the holding repository is called an archives, library, museum, history center, or special collection. "Archival materials" will be used to refer to a breadth of documentary formats: paper, digital files, photographs, sound recordings, motion pictures, or virtually any other medium in which information can be stored and retrieved. "Archivist," for the purposes of this book's concern with copyright, refers to any repository employee with assigned responsibility for the care of archival materials. "Archivist" is also used loosely and inclusively to include staff below the level of archives director, chief archivist, or other title who has overall program responsibility. This assumes that copyright advice and decisions will be referred to whichever higher-level authority there is within the archives unit for review.

Most definitions of archives also emphasize that, regardless of physical format, the archetypical content for which we are responsible is documents created for short-term transactional purposes and not for broad public dissemination. This transitory nature shows how copyright law is a very poor fit for archives. In addition, the vast bulk of archival material consists of unpublished works created for internal business or personal use. They are generally not created with the intention of securing the economic value that copyright would provide for widespread distribution in multiple copies. No wonder copyright seems to come from some alternate universe.

The problem is that, whereas archives are a systematic way to preserve and make available documents for the purposes of accountability and heritage preservation, copyright is inherently a matter of market regulation that establishes a monopoly over creative works. Some archives may contain or even specialize in creative works from authors active, or aspiring to be active, in markets where copyright controls make sense. In these limited cases, such works and authors present little copyright ambiguity because these authors are much more identifiable and discoverable than is the case for the more typical archival materials created without a commercial purpose. In other words, this smaller category of works with a market intent is a more efficient fit for copyright rules than the larger quantity of archival orphan works created primarily for internal uses.

Overall, then, archives and the bulk of archival materials are not so much a dysfunctional market, but not a market system at all. The fact is, the non-commerce world of archives leaves most archival materials orphaned from their creators and the market, despite the fact that they have value and usefulness for purposes of education, research, and heritage.

Unfortunately, the law makes copyright ownership automatic on the creation/fixation of a work, even one of minimal creativity. That's why so much of what is held in archives has been swept into an alien copyright universe controlled by rules that are often ill-fitting for purposes of our archival mission.

1.2 Archives Functions and Intersections with Copyright

Despite the variety of institutional homes for archives, multiple physical formats of archival materials, diverse subject scopes, or even the very specifics of the definition of "archives," there is a unity of purpose to the collecting and administration of archives. It is best expressed by the preamble of the International Council on Archives/UNESCO 2011 *Universal Declaration on Archives:*

> *Archives are a unique and irreplaceable heritage passed from one generation to another. Archives are managed from creation to preserve their value and meaning. They are authoritative sources of information underpinning accountable and transparent administrative actions. They play an essential role in the development of societies by safeguarding and contributing to individual and community memory. Open access to archives enriches our knowledge of human society, promotes democracy, protects citizens' rights and enhances the quality of life.*[3]

To fulfill this lofty mandate, archivists must apply professional standards and best practices in seven interrelated, functional domains that enable us to deliver evidential and information value to our publics:

- Establishment and authorization to provide a clear mandate and reporting line for: documentary scope; constituencies to be served; retention and disposal authority.
- Authentication: policies and practices to ensure integrity of records received as genuine and free from tampering.

- Appraisal: evaluation and selection of records for retention on the basis of their value as evidence and information.
- Arrangement: ensuring that records acquired retain their evidential context by documenting their provenance and maintaining their original order.
- Description: creation of finding aids and access tools to provide intellectual control and facilitate discoverability of content by known and prospective user communities.
- Preservation: ensuring the continued viability of archival materials by applying standards for facilities and environmental systems and by reformatting materials via analog or digital copying, and by providing active management of digital files to avoid obsolescence.
- Access and Use: promotion and facilitation of direct and indirect use by multiple diverse communities.

Although preservation and use are the domains that are the most obviously impeded by copyright's monopoly, it is important to understand the scope and control of copyright in relation to the entire array of archival functions in order to achieve effective archival management. For example, best practices would call for a repository's authorizing mandate to clarify the archivist's ability to issue copyright permission letters or to make copies of institutionally authored documents available to the public. Appraisal of born-digital files, e.g., hard-drives of administrators' records, may require the archivist to make a number of copies of the files merely to review and select which file directories or file types merit retention. The appraisal function is even more challenging from a copyright perspective if any of that digital content is in proprietary formats or locked behind technological measures that control access. Arrangement work for digital files might even require revamping the file directory structure to reflect provenance, and that could similarly intrude on the copyright owner's exclusive right of making derivative works.

Meanwhile, preservation, which may be the function the public most commonly associates with archivists, cannot be accomplished without the ability to make copies of works to serve as substitutes for fragile or deteriorating originals. However, both the analog and digital means used to make the copies can conflict with the copyright owner's exclusive right of reproduction. In the case of software-dependent digital files, the exclusive right of making derivative works could be infringed if digital preservation standards call for changing the file format from obsolete software to something that will continue to be supported by the preservation system. Furthermore, creating regular preservation backups or migrating files when servers are replaced inevitably involve making further reproductions, which could require authorization from the copyright holder.

Facilitating and promoting the use of archival materials, however, is likely to be the most common function that raises copyright issues for archivists. Whether it is to make a limited number of photocopies of letters for use by a visiting class; to scan a photograph for display in an exhibit or website; or to provide lengthy quotes from, or complete copies of, a document for a researcher in another state or country—these are all at odds with a strict reading of copyright law.

These copyright constraints are regrettable because use—the seventh archival domain—is the ultimate archival function. Use is the preeminent purpose, whether for internal administrative support, outside scholarship, substantiating grievances against the archives' parent institution, or other social justice purposes. Without the possibility of making archival materials usable either on site or by remote users, there is little point in acquiring, caring for, or preserving archives. When Solon Buck troubled himself about a 1940s *Washington Post* characterization of archives as "dead files," he noted: "The belief that archives are dead files is responsible for the theory that they should be stored in warehouses with no provision for making them available for use, though why they should be preserved at all if they are really dead is difficult to see."[4] Forty years later, the primacy of use was emphasized by the SAA Task Force on Goals and Priorities when it wrote, the "use of archival materials is the goal to which all other activities are directed."[5] Even if twenty-first-century changes have called into question some of the thinking from prior generations of the American archival profession, it's difficult to argue with the underlying logic of Buck's statement. Clearly, the expense of resources to create and maintain archives cannot be justified if archives cannot be put to whatever practical use is needed for present and future generations, especially when future topics and activities may not have been imagined when the documents were first created, acquired, and preserved in the archives. Most uses of archives, especially those supporting access by and for remote users, require acts contrary to copyright's exclusive rights of reproduction and distribution. As a result, pursuing the ultimate function of archives can put us at odds with the law.

Luckily, as we will see in this book's discussion of copyright law's exceptions and limitations and of the utility of a risk management strategy (Chapter 4 Sections 4.1.7 through 4.1.9, Chapter 8), this tension need not preempt our professional work. Rather, the centrality of our mission to serve users can be an ameliorating factor that gives us room to work. So, as archivists, we shouldn't despair. Just stay focused on our professional mission. Don't become servants indentured to the copyright industry. Our mission does not give us a free pass on copyright, but our mission still needs to remain our professional goal. Focusing on that goal is what will inspire our institutions and our publics. We need to remember that as we make copyright decisions.

2 Conceptual Overview of Copyright for the American Archivist

Since the first US Federal copyright act in 1790, the copyright statute has grown from a mere 1,309 words to a 336-page behemoth that has been amended over sixty times since its last major revision in 1976. Any archivist needing to understand how the current law's 106 sections relate to a particular archives question inevitably must face digging into the statute itself. Unsurprisingly, it is not organized in a way that reflects archives documents, functions, or users. How to read the law and learn to navigate its important but complex provisions regarding archives will be covered in detail in Chapter 4, but it is best to start by gaining an understanding of the basic concepts of US copyright law and how they relate to each other.

2.1 What Is Copyright?

Copyright is a special type of property ownership that encompasses products of the mind that have been captured in works such as texts, images, diagrams, time-based media, and music. Similar to laws for real or movable property, copyright law confers on the author of creative works certain exclusive rights that effectively give the creator a monopoly over what might be done with their works.

2.2 What Is Covered by Copyright?

Because the focus of copyright is the intellectual/creative content of a work rather than the physical object, the actual scope of copyright is fundamentally separate from the medium in which a work has been embodied (e.g., letter, book, photograph, etc.). Copyright's scope is better understood in term of genres that may be found in an archives–textual, graphical, sound, images, video, and even three-dimensional objects, any of which may possess informational, evidential, or intrinsic/artifactual value for archival preservation and use.

2.3 What's Not Covered by Copyright?

Some of the information content found in an archives might be categorically excluded from copyright: facts and ideas, processes and methods, and unfixed expression (e.g., oral tradition). The law has a low threshold for the amount of creativity that a work must have for it to be eligible for copyright, but the above listed exclusions are considered such common building blocks for creative works of expression that they are not, per se, eligible for copyright protection. Similarly, access to the texts of works created by the U.S. Federal government is so important for citizen rights that they are outside the scope of the copyright monopoly. By practice and judicial rulings, the laws and court rulings of state and local governments are also outside of copyright, although the specifics of which state and local works are in or outside of copyright will vary from jurisdiction to jurisdiction.[1]

2.4 Who Owns the Copyright?

The initial owner of a copyright is the person who first created it and fixed it in a tangible medium of expression, whether a design chiseled into stone, words penned onto a page, or sentences typed into a computer. Regardless of how a work is fixed into a tangible medium, ownership of copyright is attached to the creative expression or the intellectual nature of the work, not to its embodiment in any particular form, even if the author may give away the object containing the creative work. Nevertheless, it is possible for the copyright owner to transfer ownership of their copyright in the creative work to another person or corporate entity, provided the transfer is documented in writing. Absent any formal transfer of copyright ownership, the creator remains the owner whether they maintain custody of the physical embodiment or whether or not they remember they wrote the work or that they are the owner.

2.5 What Rights Does Ownership Bestow?

At the center of copyright is the fact that it provides exclusive, or monopoly, rights over activities that only the owner can do or grant permission to do. Thus, without permission of the owner, no one else may copy the work; distribute the work; adapt, translate, or transform it into a derivative work; perform the work publicly; display the work; or perform a sound recording publicly by digital audio transmission.

2.6 What Is Copyright Infringement, and What Are Its Consequences?

Infringement occurs whenever anyone, without permission of the copyright owner, engages in one of the acts listed above as exclusive rights. An infringer is subject to civil and sometimes criminal legal action that could result in penalties, including impoundment, destruction of infringing products, and especially monetary damages and assessment of legal fees.

2.7 How Long Does Copyright Endure?

Although the precise term of copyright can vary depending on the type of work, publication status, and nationality of author, copyright lasts a long time—effectively decades beyond the current US life expectancy. As with much of copyright, the term of any particular work can vary depending on specific circumstances. Fortunately, there are tools to be able to assess when the work will enter the public domain, i.e., when copyright expires.

2.8 What Room Does the Copyright Law Provide for Archivists to Accomplish Their Mission?

Copyright's broad sweep, exclusive rights, and long term present a challenge for basic archival work, but it does contain some exceptions and limitations to those rights, thus providing some legal space for archival work. Most important are the library and archives exceptions in the law's § 108 and the general fair use exceptions in § 107.[2]

2.8.1 § 108 provides some "bright line" exceptions to enable libraries and archives and their employees to make copies for preservation purposes and to supply users with copies for private study and research. The actual text of the law includes qualifying conditions for these exceptions as well as some limitations on their scope. These will be discussed in detail in Chapter 4.

2.8.2 § 107, Fair Use, provides much broader copyright exceptions for both archivists and users but without the legal certainty that archivists and our users need. It is prominently contested in relation to commercial uses of copyrighted material in the entertainment and publishing world. Still, fair use can provide legal room for archives work, including that related to research, education, private study, and news reporting. The final determination whether something is a fair use only comes from a court in a response to an infringement claim. Thus, it is not a certain exception for archives use. Nevertheless, there are four factors the law calls for courts to consider in deciding whether a particular use is fair. Careful consideration of these factors can give the archivist confidence in proceeding with many types of copying needed to meet the archival mission.[3]

2.9 International Concepts and Issues

There may be no per se international law of copyright, but US law is guided by several concepts and standards in international copyright treaties. As a result, some parts of US law affect what we can do with works created by persons and entities outside the United States. There also may be implications for us in the laws of other countries when our use of digital global networks "crosses borders" to reach users outside the United States.

With full awareness that for every copyright rule there may be many variables, our fundamental rule should be that the law we must follow is US copyright law. Still, it is important to remember there are times when our archival actions may have differing consequences if the rights for the works in question are held by a person or entity outside the United States. Major problems, thankfully, are rare enough, so rather than getting into such detail, this chapter will instead note general international dimensions.

Especially important is the 1886 Berne Convention for the Protection of Literary and Artistic Works, most recently amended in 1979. It was first adopted by several European countries and now includes 181 member

Box 2.1 Changes in US Law to Comply with the Berne Convention

- Make copyright automatic on the creation of a work.
- Remove formalities for a copyright to exist, i.e., eliminate requirements for publication with notice and registration.
- Restore rights in foreign works that had been in the public domain because lack of formalities.
- Change the term of protection from a fixed number years plus option for a renewal to a single term based on life of the author plus 50 years.
- Expand scope of eligible works, based on an itemized list, to include "works of authorship."
- Eliminate exclusion of unpublished works.

states. It created principles and standards for the protection of rights of authors of creative works in order to guide the implementation of specific laws in member states to secure those rights. The United States extended copyright protections to some foreign works in 1891, but it did not move to join Berne until the 1970s, and it did not complete the adoption of Berne until 1989, by making amendments to the US copyright law. Complying with Berne required a number of changes to our law, summarized in Box 2.1. Even with those adjustments, there remain some philosophical differences in American law versus those of several other countries, especially relating to so-called "moral rights" (see Chapter 6, section 6.6).

The fact that amendments to the US law enabled us to accede to Berne underscores the above-stated rule of "when in doubt, just follow the US law." That should be sufficient for most of what American archivists need to do. Indeed, § 104(a) states that unpublished works "are subject to protection under this title without regard to the nationality or domicile of the author" (see Chapter 4, section 4.1.4); § 104(b) indicates that published works are also covered by our law if published in the United States or in a treaty partner or authored by a national or domiciliary of the United States or of a treaty party. That scope includes all but a handful of the world's countries.[4]

To address issues beyond the scope of Berne, the United States has acceded to a few other international treaties, most importantly those of the World Intellectual Property Organization (WIPO).[5] They include the 1996 WIPO Copyright Treaty (WCT) and the 2013 Marrakesh Treaty to Facilitate Access to Published Works for Persons Who Are Blind, Visually Impaired or Otherwise Print Disabled.

The focus of the 1996 WCT was "protection of works and the rights of their authors in the digital environment," and it called for legal protections of electronic systems that provide security to digital access mechanisms. This led Congress to make changes to our law, mainly in § § 1201–5 (see Chapter 4, section 4.12). For persons with visual and other impairments, the 2013 Marrakesh Treaty created additional exceptions to those already in US law. This led to amendments as seen in the current § 121 and § 121A. Although adjusting our law to standards of other countries may seem like forfeiting distinctive aspects of American law, for archivists the practical result is to merely reinforce the above rule of "follow the US law."

Although following the US law may sound simple, some of the rules added for treaty compliance create differences in how US and foreign works are treated. One example is relevant to this book's discussion of risk management. There is a bit of a safety buffer in § 411(a)'s requirement that an unpublished work must be registered with the Copyright Office before a suit can be initiated (see Chapter 8, section 8.3.3.2). That buffer creates room for you to take risk mitigation steps. However, to be consistent with the premise of Berne that copyright should be automatic on creation of a work, § 411(a)'s registration requirement applies only to what are known as United States works—essentially ones where all authors "are nationals, domiciliaries, or habitual residents of the United States." The difference is not that dramatic, but it does point to the need to watch the details.[6]

Thus, there is some comfort or at least predictability provided by the basic rule in the law's statement that unpublished works "are subject to protection under this title [i.e., the copyright law] without regard to the nationality or domicile of the author."[7] Of course, a copyright owner in another country could take an action against you or your institution in US courts, based on US law, but that kind of action is limited and reinforces that the rules to follow are those in the US law. Not surprisingly, there are hypothetical circumstances where that rule may not be the guarantee you would like it to be. In the digital environment, there's the theoretical possibility that your website might make content available that is owned by a foreign rights holder in their home country. That could put you or your institution at odds with that country's laws. If your institution has assets or conducts business in that country, there may be liability under their laws, and the defenses in US law, e.g., fair use, would be irrelevant.

Don't let the many variations among the laws of other countries paralyze you. A risk management approach (see Chapter 8) in planning digital and web projects will show how forethought about the presence and extent of prospective content from high-profile authors or copyright owners can help you take appropriate remedial steps. No archival action will ever be risk-free. That's why this book's emphasis is on the importance of pursuing your archival mission based on a solid understanding of the law and a deep knowledge of your holdings.

3 Holy Cow! Even Saints Have Infringed! Landmarks of Copyright History

3.1 Early History of Copyright

Yes, that's correct—even saints have infringed. According to historical tradition, the first copyright infringement case was brought in the middle of the sixth century by Finnian of Movilla, later known as St. Finnian, against his former student Colmcille, now known as St. Columba. According to legend, Columba was discovered late one night in the Movilla monastery's scriptorium copying out a psalter that belonged to Abbot Finnian, who demanded that Columba turn the copy over to him. When Columba refused, Finnian appealed to King Diarmid, and the king ruled in Finnian's favor saying, "To every cow, her calf. To every book its copy."[1] The account of this event was not chronicled until several decades later, so the exact words may not be certain. However, the case has long been noted as establishing a fundamental rule about ownership of works of authorship.[2]

Whenever we have one of those moments where we find ourselves scratching our heads with a puzzled look on our faces because this copyright rule just doesn't make sense, it's always worth looking back at history. Some of the time, the historical oddities we find in copyright's peculiar history help explain how our modern copyright law developed. This chapter cannot demystify all the seemingly counterintuitive bits of copyright law, but it can outline the social and technological conditions that gave rise to the law we have today. If nothing else, it may help you fill awkward silences at dinner parties by recalling any one of the anomalous statutory provisions or court rulings from centuries past.

Regardless of its age or factual accuracy, the story of Columba and Finnian reveals some threads that constantly reappear in copyright history: Infringement can be claimed even when it is only one copy that has been made. Serious attention to copyright infringement was less likely without mechanisms or technology that can exacerbate unauthorized copying or facilitate distribution. If you want to enforce your copyright, you need a strong civilian authority.

First, regardless of the available technology or the righteousness and sanctity of authors or prospective users, Finnian's seeking out the nearest king to enforce his claim demonstrates that governmental authority and power are essential to securing the copyright monopoly. With that in mind, let's look at how the mix of authors, governmental authority, technology, and the consuming public has played out while the copyright world changed so much since the time that Irish legends were born.

3.2 State Interest in Learning During the Renaissance

The sixth-century's technological limits on the means of creating, reproducing, and distributing works remained substantially intact for 900 years after the case of *Finnian v. Columba*. Over that time, European cultural production, or at least that which has survived, was largely the product of a hierarchical society in which patronage, whether ecclesiastical or secular, provided the basis for creating new works, whether produced by hand or by mechanical device. In this pre-modern society, copyright emerged from the practice of governments granting "privileges" to private citizens to supply a product or service. This was common throughout decentralized Renaissance Italy, especially in the independent city-states, such as Florence and Venice. In some cases these privileges took the form of a patent, for example, the 1421 privilege the Florentine republic granted for the design of a specific type of boat. Such government-conferred privileges, or exclusive rights, were well established on the eve of the technological innovation that would have given Finnian nightmares—a machine that could produce exact and nearly innumerable printed copies.

Throughout the Middle Ages and early Renaissance, there was an active trade in copying and distributing copies of manuscripts, but it was Johannes Gutenberg's *c.* 1450 invention of movable type that quantitatively changed the conditions from which copyright's exclusive rights ultimately developed.[3] By 1469, Venice had granted a five-year privilege to a printer, and in 1486 it granted what is considered to be the first copyright—Marc Antonio Sabellico was given exclusive control over the printing and distribution of a history of Venice. Ten years later, Aldus Manutius received a 20-year privilege for the printing of all works in Greek, and in 1502, Venice also gave Manutius exclusive rights for use of the Italic typeface that he had invented. Meanwhile, as printing technology spread in Northern Europe, similar privileges were granted to printers in Germany, France, and the British Isles.[4]

3.3 Protestant Reformation and Centralization of the English State's Authority

The circulation of printed works in the early sixteenth century contributed to the early spread of the Protestant Reformation in continental Europe. In England, even before King Henry VIII's interest in divorce and remarriage put him at odds with the Roman Papacy, the early stirrings of religious dissent raised his regal eyebrows. Royal proclamations in 1529 and 1530 effectively banned books and created controls on printers to prevent the importation or printing of works that were deemed undesirable.

A key element for state control of printed works was the Stationers' Company, whose members, on payment of a fee, were entitled to print books. In 1538, following the formal break from Rome, a royal proclamation established a system requiring printers to acquire a license to print any book—a license available only by going through a governmental review.[5] The Company's authority was significantly expanded in 1557, when Henry's Catholic daughter, Queen Mary Tudor, granted a charter giving the Stationers' Company a monopoly over all printing, provided they publish nothing that was offensive to the government. The Charter required the printers to register the works they intended to print and prevented a printer from publishing a work that had already been registered as the "copy right" of another printer. Importantly, the Stationers' Company itself had the power, without having to go to the Crown, to deliberate on and enforce complaints that came before it. It thus wielded significant control over printing and publishing throughout the rest of the sixteenth and well into the seventeenth century.

3.4 English Civil War and Dethroning of the Stationers' Company

Following the 1642–1651 English Civil War, the Licensing Act of 1662 expanded the Stationers' Company monopoly by limiting the number of master printers, limiting the importation of foreign books, and giving the Company search and seizure authority. Nevertheless, discontent at their monopoly and their censorship had been long-standing and had grown by 1695 to the point that Parliament allowed the Licensing Act to expire. That left the company without legal means to enforce its monopoly as rival printers stepped forward to meet the growing public demand for books.[6] In the debates that followed about what might replace the licensing act, authors Daniel Defoe and John Locke focused attention not just on censorship, but also on the need for rights to protect authors, not printers. Out of this mix, the printers and publishers came forward with a proposal to vest ownership of works in the authors who could then confer rights for publication to printers. Although their proposal was not accepted in whole, Parliament passed and the Crown approved the "Act for the Encouragement of Learning and for Securing the Property of Copies of Books to the Rightful Owners Thereof" in 1710.

Now commonly known as the Statute of Anne, the law focused more on the book trade than on the authors per se, but its central idea was that the authors were the first owners of a work who could then transfer those rights.[7] The Statute also established that the rights of printers and publishers were no longer perpetual, but only for a term of 14 years that could be renewed for a further 14 years, and then only if the author were still alive. It also required that one copy of each book published be deposited in nine libraries in England and Scotland. The new law also established penalties for infringement at the same time that it lifted prohibitions on the importation of Greek, Latin, or other foreign language books printed overseas.

3.5 Queen Anne's Legacy

The long saga from the appearance of the printing press and printing privileges in Italy and Northern Europe to the sweetheart deals among printers, publishers, and governments resulted in a law that remains the foundation for the copyright law of today. The length of copyright term and the registration and deposit regulations found in the Statute of Anne may now seem quaint, but the radical inventions of that statute remain central today—copyright belongs to the author, it will eventually expire, and the law's purpose is not censorship, but promotion of learning. A further constant is that the exclusive rights in works, whether held by authors or publishers, exist only through the force of sovereign governments.

3.6 American Copyright Emerges

The English experience and the Statute of Anne set the terms for the origins of US copyright law. Once the thirteen colonies succeeded in gaining independence from Great Britain in 1783, they needed to develop their own legislation to encourage the creation of domestic literature to support education and development. What emerged was influenced by the ideology behind the American colonists' drive for independence. That carried with it a disdain for the centuries-long aristocratic model of patronage prevailing in Europe for the production of writings and other creative works. Not surprisingly, the former colonists also had strong objections to censorship and monopolies.

Furthermore, the great distance across the Atlantic created a need to advance the publishing industry within the newly created United States. Legally this was difficult. A decentralized government under the Articles of Confederation meant that Congress's 1783 call for states to adopt copyright laws resulted in different laws in each of the various states, with the resultant laws requiring travel to each of the states in order to register one's copyright. Because this problem paralleled other governance challenges, leading to the 1787–9 Constitutional Convention, it should be no surprise that a national solution was developed. Thus, the Constitution included a clause to empower the new federal Congress "To promote the progress of science and useful arts, by securing for limited times to authors and inventors the exclusive right to their respective writings and discoveries."

Almost as soon as it was convened, the first Congress received a number of individual requests to be granted a federal copyright for specific works. However, rather than responding with a number of separate bills, Congress took the pragmatic step of enacting a law based on the Statute of Anne. The title of the copyright law adopted in May 1790 clearly reflected its provenance: "An Act for the encouragement of learning, by securing the copies of maps, Charts, and Books, to the Authors and Proprietors of such copies, during the times therein mentioned" [variant use of upper case in the original]. Its provisions tracked those of the 1710 British law: US citizens or resident authors or their assigns were the ones entitled to a copyright; the term was 14 years and renewable for a further 14 years; securing copyright required deposit of the work with a District court and the US Secretary of State; and neither importation, printing, nor distribution of foreign works were prohibited by the act.

3.7 US Copyright 1800 and Beyond

The law, of course, has evolved in the more than two centuries since the first US copyright act. Despite the original narrow scope of the 1790 law, covering only maps, charts, and books, subsequent revisions of the copyright act followed the basic principles of the original act until the fourth major revision in the late 1970s. Up to that time, and as a reflection of the expansion of cultural interests and the development of new technologies, other materials were progressively made eligible for copyright: prints (1801); dramatic works in public performance (1856); photographs (1865); translations, dramatizations, statuary, models, and designs (1870); motion pictures (1912); sound recordings (1971); and computer software (1983). Length of copyright's term was changed in 1831 to 28 years for the initial term, and in 1909 to 28 years for both the initial and renewal term. In 1976, term was changed to life of the author plus 50 years, later amended in 1998 to life of the author plus 70 years. The 1909 law added work-made-for-hire provisions, whereby copyright ownership in works made by employees in the course of their work duties would be owned by their employer.

Although procedures for registration and deposit evolved over the nineteenth century, it was not until the 1976 law that copyright became automatic on the creation of a work. The requirement for a copyright notice, established in 1801, remained essentially in effect until March 1,1989.[8] There have been many more amendments to the copyright law since the 1976 revision, which went into effect in 1978, but they will not be mentioned here since they are better understood within the context of the current copyright law (see Chapters 4 and 5 for a discussion of details).[9]

3.8 How the Courts Have Made the Law

As much as over two centuries of legislative change explains the expansion of copyright's coverage and counterbalancing exceptions, today's law is also the result of hundreds of court rulings since the US law was first enacted in 1790. Exact statistics on the number of cases are a bit difficult to obtain. A tally of R. R. Bowker's 1912 survey of all British and US copyright cases shows that there were a total of 137 US federal cases in the period from 1828 through 1911.[10] More relevant for today's readers are the data from scholarly studies conducted by Barton Beebe to analyze all the District, Circuit, and Supreme Court cases relating to fair use since that provision was added to the statute. He identified 435 fair use cases, resulting in 579 court opinions for the period 1978 through 2019.[11]

Beebe's empirical analysis led him to caution against the idea that certain "leading cases" might be seen as prescribing how future cases would be decided. With that caveat, archivists wanting to understand major historical trends in the scope and effect of US copyright law should review the following selection of cases for insights into how law has evolved through the resolution of disputes brought before the courts.[12]

3.9 Selected Federal Court Cases

1884 *Burrow-Giles Lithographic Co. v. Sarony*. Supreme Court upheld the constitutionality of Congress's inclusion of photographs in the scope of copyright.

1903 *Bleistein v. Donaldson Lithographing Company*. Supreme Court made clear that copyright could apply to advertisements and commercial art, not just fine art. The Court opinion asserted that judges should not be assessing artistic value and it disassociated authorship from genius. Thus, even non-artistic administrative records are within copyright's scope.

1973 *Williams & Wilkins Co. v. United States*. Medical publisher sued the National Institutes of Health and National Library of Medicine for violating copyright by on-demand photocopying of articles from scientific journals and distributing them to research staff as part of an interlibrary loan program. The Court of Claims ruled that the circumstances of the copying fit within the judicial doctrine of fair use. On appeal, a tie vote by the Supreme Court left the fair use finding in place, but the case brought attention to the potential of library copying to be infringing.

1984 *Sony Corp. of America v. Universal City Studios, Inc.* In this case, otherwise known as the "Betamax case," the Supreme Court established that the manufacturer of technology to enable an individual to copy audiovisual broadcasts was not liable for contributory infringement. Important for copies archives make for their users, the case supported copying for personal use as a fair use.

1985 *Harper & Row v. Nation Magazine*. Supreme Court rejected *The Nation*'s fair use claim that its status as a news magazine justified its publication of portions of the unpublished manuscript of President Ford's memoir. See Chapter 5 for further discussion, especially re how unpublished status of a work weighs against fair use.

1986 *Maxtone-Graham v. Burtchaell*. After Burtchaell sought and was denied permission for use of quotations from Maxtone-Graham's interviews of women about unplanned pregnancies, he used about 7,000 (of about 37,000) of Maxtone-Graham's words in his book opposing abortion. Second Circuit Court of Appeals found for fair use and dismissed case based on factual nature of the material and the commentary and criticism purpose of the use.

1987 *Salinger v. Random House*. Second Circuit Court of Appeals rejected biographer's fair use defense for his use, in a biography, of unpublished correspondence and writings of J. D. Salinger. See Chapter 5 for further discussion and related fair use cases, e.g., *Wright v. Warner Books, Inc.* (1991), where fair use was allowed for unpublished materials.

1989 *Community for Creative Non-Violence v. Reid*. The Supreme Court ruled that a sculptor was not acting as an employee when he created a 3-D display for use by a community organization raising funds to benefit services for unhoused individuals. The court used the common law principles of agency to determine that Reid was not an employee. The case is useful for understanding threshold requirements for something to actually be a work made for hire. See discussion of works made for hire in Chapter 4, Section 4.2.

1991 *Feist Publications, Inc., v. Rural Telephone Service Co.* In a case involving dispute about Feist having copied telephone listings from Rural Telephone's directory, the Supreme Court ruled that facts could not be copyrighted, no matter how much labor is involved in their collection and presentation. This rejected the long-held notion of "sweat of the brow" being sufficient basis for copyright to exist, and affirmed that facts are not subject to copyright.

1994 *Campbell v. Acuff-Rose Music, Inc.* Supreme Court ruled Campbell and 2 Live Crew's use of the Roy Orbison classic "Oh, Pretty Woman" in a rap song was a fair use because it was a parody. The case established that in deliberations on fair use, a case-by-case analysis must examine all four fair use factors in relation to the purpose of copyright. See Chapters 4 and 5 for a detailed discussion of how the Court sifted through the four factors and the precedent-setting nature of the *Campbell* ruling on the role of transformativeness in determining fair use.

1995 *American Geophysical Union v. Texaco.* Circuit Court ruling that demonstrated that a deliberate effort to avoid an established market mechanism for permissions to make copies of scientific journal articles was decisive in a finding against the plaintiff's claim of fair use.

1998 *Sundeman v. the Seajay Society, Inc.* Circuit Court relied on *Campbell v. Acuff Rose* and the 1992 Fair Use of Copyrighted Works Act to rule as fair use the photocopying, research use, and reporting at a scholarly conference of unpublished literary works of Marjorie Kinnan Rawlings.

1999 *Bridgeman Art Library v. Corel Corp.* District Court ruled that, regardless of the tremendous skill and labor Bridgeman had dedicated to making faithful photographic images of public domain art works, the resultant photographs were not eligible for copyright. Citing the 1991 *Feist* decision, the court described Bridgeman's photographs as "slavish" copies lacking protectable originality. Following *Bridgeman*'s ruling, an archives should not claim copyright over the simple scanning or other copying of works.

2001 *Self-Realization Fellowship Church v. Ananda Church of Self-Realization.* Circuit Court ruled that spiritual writings of guru Yogananda were determined to have been created without any direction of the Self-Realization Fellowship Church, and thus were works of his self-expression or religious beliefs and not works for hire. Appealed to, but denied certification by, the Supreme Court.

2003 *Eldred v. Ashcroft*. Eric Eldred called for the 1998 Copyright Term Extension Act to be declared unconstitutional because it retrospectively extended the term of existing works. Supreme Court rejected Eldred's argument, ruling that in extending the term of copyright, Congress was within its constitutional authority. Parallel results appeared in *Golan v. Holder* (2012), which unsuccessfully challenged the constitutionality of restoring copyright to foreign works that had previously been in the US public domain. The ruling in favor of copyright term extension fueled the fire for attention to the problem of orphan works in archives and libraries.

2006 *Bill Graham Archives v. Dorling Kindersley*. Circuit Court found a publisher's use of thumbnail-size images of concert posters and tickets for a book on the Grateful Dead to be a transformative fair use. See Chapter 5 for further discussion.

2013 *Cariou v. Prince*. Circuit Court found an artist's reuse of a photographer's images to create composite artworks and display them in a gallery, publications, and on a billboard to be a transformative fair use even though the artist's composition did not comment on the original photograph. See Chapter 5 for further discussion.

2014 *Authors Guild et al. v. Hathi Trust et al.* Circuit Court of Appeals upheld District Court ruling that Hathi Trust and the University of Michigan did not infringe when it digitized in-copyright orphaned and non-orphaned works. Fair use was found because the digitization process created a searchable index for the books.

2016 *Authors Guild v. Google*. In 2005, Authors Guild filed suit claiming that the Google Book project infringed copyright because it digitized in-copyright books and made snippets of text available through its search engine. After years of efforts failed to obtain court approval of a settlement, the District Court rejected the infringement claim based on Google having made a fair use. On Authors Guild's appeal, the Circuit Court agreed with the District Court. Authors Guild's subsequent appeal to the US Supreme court was denied certification in April 2016.

2020 *Cambridge University Press v. Patton* (Georgia State E-Reserves). In 2008, a group of publishers sued Georgia State for infringement related to GSU's use of materials in its e-reserves system. Georgia State asserted a fair use defense. In a succession of District and Circuit rulings, remands, and re-analyses of dozens of specific uses, the majority were found to be fair uses. In 2020, GSU was declared the prevailing party and was awarded court costs but not attorney fees.

2023 *Andy Warhol Foundation (AWF) v. Goldsmith*. In 2021, the Second Circuit Court of Appeals ruled against AWF's licensing of Andy Warhol's artistic alteration of a photograph originally made by a professional photographer of the musician Prince. The Warhol Foundation appealed to the Supreme Court in 2022 for review of the circuit court's analysis of the first fair-use factor. The Supreme Court's ruling in favor of photographer Goldsmith significantly scaled back the weight given to "transformativeness," and shifted the focus to assessing the purpose of and justification for a second party's use to be found fair. See Chapter 5 for further discussion.

2024 *Hachette Book Group, Inc. v. Internet Archive*. Circuit Court of Appeals upheld District Court decision that the Internet Archive's (IA) "controlled digital lending" of in-copyright books was infringing. Citing *Warhol*'s warning against an overly broad concept of transformativeness, the Appeals Court found that IA had failed to prove that its secondary use did not compete with the publisher's market.

If nothing else, this chapter's review of copyright's history illustrates the central role of governmental authority across the ages. It has been governmental mandates that still provide the foundation for protecting markets, although governmental actions do sometimes balance the copyright monopoly with the interests of creators and the public. The progression of court cases illustrates the increasing precision in how copyright's monopoly and the public interest intersect. Not surprisingly, these decisions may not on first glance seem related to archives work, but they all contain elements which may sometimes connect with your circumstances, e.g., whether a volunteer or the archives is the copyright owner of a work they prepare for you. Moreover, having a summary view of the centuries of copyright history can help us recognize that the copyright law is more than just a competing set of theoretical concepts and obtuse verbiage. We may not like the results of some of the legislation or court cases, but knowing the legal history behind the laws and decisions can help us understand why copyright law has gotten to where it is today. In other words, it's this history that helps explain why copyright law largely fails to recognize archivists and the world we serve.

4 The US Copyright Act (Title 17 U.S.C.)

Artisan sausage crafted by a succession of sclerotic Congresses!

That may be an archivist's impression when first trying to find anything useful or relevant in the US Copyright Act. More likely, a second look will conjure up images of a Rube Goldberg-designed car made from an odd mixture of old spare parts, resulting in a well-intentioned but ultimately dysfunctional car that's overloaded with needless features. However, like many other laws, the copyright act is the product of a long evolution and many efforts to address changing technology while also satisfying divergent stakeholder interests. Regardless, the Copyright Act as found in Title 17 of the United States Code (hereafter abbreviated as 17 U.S.C.) is the law within which US archivists must work.

Two unavoidable conditions complicate the relation of the archivist's mission with the copyright law. On the one hand, this law is very case-and-fact specific, meaning that general rules rarely apply. On the other hand, archives inherently contain thousands, if not millions, of unique or nearly unique works, each of which reflects highly diverse "facts" of creation and authorship. To bridge the gap between copyright law's myriad specifics and the idiosyncrasies of archival content, sooner or later the archivist will want or need to read the statute itself to determine how to pursue archival objectives without running afoul of the law or neglecting the flexibilities it does include. This chapter is designed to walk through the major portions of the law so that a practicing archivist will be able to find and cite those sections of the law relevant to their particular situation. Its goal is to engender enough confidence so archivists do not let the law's complexity immobilize them into excessive caution.

How to Read the US Copyright Law

The copyright law can be found in Title 17 of the US code, and you can download a keyword-searchable PDF of the full text of the law from the Copyright Office's website, https://copyright.gov/title17/title17.pdf. The Copyright Office also maintains a website (https://copyright.gov/title17/index.html) with the law in a navigable, chapter-by-chapter and section-by-section format. Thus, readers have a choice to have the full text in a searchable PDF at hand as a ready reference or, when occasion requires focusing on particular topics, they can also use the website for quick access to the content of relevant sections. Both versions include footnotes citing specific laws that amended earlier text. Overall, the law is divided into fifteen chapters, but, as the Copyright Office notes, chapters 9 and 13 (Protection of Semiconductor Chip Products and Protection of Original Designs) are not actually considered as copyright. Don't even attempt to figure out why these chapters on related rights are sandwiched into the formal text on copyright. It's just a quirk of the legislative process that shouldn't distract you from looking at the considerable number of other chapters and sections that are relevant to archival work. Meanwhile, note that, to avoid confusion, chapters in the Copyright Act will be referred to as "17 U.S.C. Chapter . . ." whereas "chapter" will refer to chapters within this book.

And yes, you should begin by surveying the law as a whole to get an idea of its structure and functional organization before doing a targeted search for that one topic that just came up in your archives yesterday or before digging into the details of what kinds of works are covered by copyright or how long before those manuscripts you just accessioned will be free of US copyright, i.e., enter the public domain. By starting with an overview, you will find that the function of each of the Copyright Act's chapters is generally apparent from its title. For example, 17 U.S.C. Chapter 2 would be where you would look to learn who can own copyright, whereas 17 U.S.C. Chapter 3 would be where to find the rules that dictate how long copyright remains in force, and 17 U.S.C. Chapter 5 is where to learn about the penalties for infringement of copyright owners' rights.

Similar to the law's general Table of Contents, each Chapter starts with its own table of contents, or in the web version, a sidebar of links listing the Sections (often represented by the § symbol) that deal with the subdivisions of the broader chapter topic. For example, the table of contents or web links for 17 U.S.C. Chapter 1 lists the many numbered sections and subsections that are routinely used to define copyright's exclusive rights, identify types of works covered, and note exceptions to those rights as well as factors used by courts to resolve specific disputes. Another example worth a quick look is the table of contents or web links for 17 U.S.C. Chapter 2's explanation of copyright ownership. It shows how the matter of ownership is subdivided according to differing conditions, such as ownership in joint works, transfers of ownership, and distinctions between ownership of a physical object and ownership of the work itself. In a few instances, the individual sections within a 17 U.S.C. chapter are not terribly long or overly subdivided into subsections. Unfortunately, in too many cases, the legislators seem to have overindulged in every imaginable jot and tittle. This is especially true with newer additions to the law (e.g., 17 U.S.C. Chapter 14's incorporation of the provisions of the 2018 Music Modernization Act). Those subdivisions can be particularly entangling as the law tries to adjust to new technology, such as the 2002 Technology, Education, and Copyright Harmonization (TEACH) Act that attempted to adjust the exception for classroom teaching to apply for online education.

That's why before starting your functional survey of the law, you might want to take a stiff drink. More seriously, a good way to start might be to first look at *one* of the few straightforward sections (e.g., § 102, § 106, or § 107) and do a quick comparison with a more complicated one that has many nested subdivisions (e.g., § 203 or 204, which deal with termination rights).[1]

Now that you have dipped your toes into the copyright whirlpool by contrasting one straightforward section with one of the many truly complex and indigestible ones, you should conclude your high-level survey by randomly flipping through the law and skim the section titles of whichever of 17 U.S.C. Chapters 1 through 5, 12, 14, or 15 catch your eye. Once you have previewed the section titles within your area of interest, select one or two of its sections and try to read at least one in its entirety. Feel free to give up if you land on any particularly obtuse paragraph or set of nested clauses that defy comprehension. If you find the reading confusing or frustrating, congratulations, you are still sufficiently sane and fully competent to proceed through the rest of this chapter!

As a general consideration, when reading the law or even this book's summary of it, note that almost any provision within the copyright statute is no more than a default template for outlining rights and exemptions. Nearly all of these provisions can be overwritten by separate written agreements, otherwise known as licenses. Thus, as the author of this book, I am automatically its copyright owner once it is typed into my computer, but to have it published, I have been asked and have agreed to either transfer my ownership to the publisher or sign a license or contract that assigns to the publisher one or more of my exclusive rights (e.g., to make and distribute copies).

4.1 17 U.S.C. Chapter 1: "Subject of Matter and Scope of Copyright"

Overall, the first chapter of the law is the longest and probably most important with which to become familiar. Here you will find such basics as the meaning of terminology, types of works eligible for copyright, types of exceptions available to facilitate the archivist's work. Be sure to become comfortable navigating its components. The sections on scope of copyright, exclusive rights, and limitations on those exclusive rights define much of the territory an archivist must consider in relation to other 17 U.S.C. Chapters, especially how all of this fits with elements of 17 U.S.C. Chapters 4 and 5 to undergird a risk management strategy.

4.1.1 § 101: "Definitions"

To establish a foundation for the meaning of provisions throughout the entire copyright law, the statute begins with definitions for fifty-four terms. In most instances, the definitions are relatively straightforward. For example, copies are "material objects, other than phonorecords, in which a work is fixed by any method now known or later developed, and from which the work can be perceived, reproduced, or otherwise communicated, either directly or with the aid of a machine or device." However, note that this definition incorporates two other terms—"fixed" and "phonorecord" that are also defined within § 101. The terms most likely to be relevant to archival work are listed in Box 4.1.

To avoid uncertainty or confusion with standard archives, library, or museum terminology, it is always advisable to check § 101 to see whether our terminology is consistent with the law. For example, within archives and libraries, "audiovisual" is frequently used to encompass audio recordings as well as motion pictures and videotapes. However, the definition in § 101 establishes an important difference between sound recordings (sometimes

Box 4.1 Key Definitions in §101 to Read

Architectural work	Pictorial, graphic, and sculptural works
Audiovisual works	Publication
Collective work	Publicly perform or display a work
Compilation	Registration
Created	Sound recordings
Derivative work	Transmit
Display	United States Work
Literary works	Useful article
Motion pictures	Work of visual art
Perform a work	
Phonorecords	

called phonorecords) and audiovisual works, which include only those works where a series of related images are intended to be shown together with accompanying sounds. The difference has practical consequences for the scope of exclusive rights, exceptions, and duration of copyright of each of those different media.

A few of the definitions in § 101 are lengthy and complex enough that they effectively establish the scope and limitations of rights to the point that they otherwise would seem suitable for a stand-alone 17 U.S.C. chapter or section of their own, for example, "work made for hire." Finally, beyond the terms in § 101, some other sections of the law include definitions particularly relevant to the newer provisions of the statute, often made by amendments to adjust to changing technologies. For example, "digital audio transmission" is described in § 114 which was amended in 1995 to cover the scope of exclusive rights in sound recordings.

4.1.2 § 102: "Subject Matter of Copyright: In General"

With the meaning of terminology established, the law moves on to identify exactly what kinds of works are eligible for copyright protection. The preamble sentence of this section establishes that the law's exclusive rights are a matter of US federal protection and that the focus of protection is on works of authorship;[2] that contain originality; and that are fixed in some manner

Box 4.2 Works of Authorship Eligible for Copyright

(1) literary works
(2) musical works, including any accompanying words
(3) dramatic works, including any accompanying music
(4) pantomimes and choreographic works
(5) pictorial, graphic, and sculptural works
(6) motion pictures and other audiovisual works
(7) sound recordings
(8) architectural works

that is technologically neutral. Eligible "original works of authorship" include a mix of genres (e.g., literary, musical, and pictorial) and formats (e.g., sound recordings and motion pictures). In simple terms, the importance of § 102 is that, for a creator to be entitled to exclusive rights of copyright in relation to archival holdings, the work must fit within one of the eight categories listed in § 102 (a) Box 4.2.[3]

The US Constitution's Article I Section 8 emphasizes creative works. Following that principle, § 102 (b) makes clear that ideas, methods, and unfixed expression are outside of federal copyright protection (see Box 4.3).

It should be noted that, based on the Constitution's reference to the protection of "writings" and section 102's emphasis on originality, courts have established that facts by themselves are not eligible for protection. This would apply both to facts in any kind of work, such as names and addresses in a directory or the score of a basketball game reported in a newspaper article as well as "facts" discoverable within highly creative manuscripts.

4.1.3 § 103: "Subject Matter of Copyright: Compilations and Derivative Works"

The scope of copyright includes not only individual original works of authorship but also assemblages of several individual works, whether by the same author or multiple authors. The resultant compilation itself is eligible for copyright, as is common for literary anthologies or "greatest hits" albums and CDs. Meanwhile, if an original work is taken and adapted, as is the case

Box 4.3 Outside of US Copyright Protection § 102(b)

Idea	Method of operation
Procedure	Concept
Process	Principle
System	Discovery

with translations or with the conversion of a novel into a movie script, or the creation of a new arrangement of a musical work, then the secondary, derivative works are themselves eligible for their own copyright. Whether a compilation or a derivative work, the copyright in the secondary work only relates to the new material. Meanwhile, the compiler or adapter/translator gains no copyright or control over the underlying material. That remains with the original author. Further, to create the compilation or derivative work, permission from the original author is necessary. In some cases, if the derivative work is a critical commentary or parody of the original work, the secondary author may be able to claim a fair use exception. However, as we will see, fair use is a matter that ultimately is not determined except by the outcome of litigation.

4.1.4 §104: "Subject Matter of Copyright: National Origin"

For the unpublished materials that form the archetypical core of archives, § 104 (a) establishes that the provisions of US copyright law apply to that material, regardless of where the material or author originated. For the published works that appear in archives, the provisions are a bit more complicated; § 104 (b) provides that US copyright law will apply to published works, if at the time of first publication:

- the author is a national or resident of the United States or of a treaty partner of the United States; or
- the work was published in the United States or a treaty party; or
- the work is a sound recording that was first fixed in a treaty party; or
- the work was published by the United Nations or Organization of American States; or

- if the work is a pictorial, graphic, or sculptural work that is incorporated in a building in the United States or a treaty party; or
- the work is the subject of a Presidential proclamation.

The above is a paraphrase, so when in doubt the archivist is best advised to check the facts of the published item against the specific language in § 104(b).

4.1.4A § 104A: "Copyright in Restored Works"

In the early 1990s, Congress added § 104A as part of the United States joining international trade agreements, such as the North American Free Trade Agreement and the World Trade Organization. The addition of § 104A extended US copyright to cover certain foreign works that previously had been in the US public domain. These were foreign works that had never been covered by US copyright because they had not complied with "formalities" (publication with a copyright notice and registration). Thus, § 104A made those foreign works eligible for US copyright protection, provided they were still in copyright in their country of origin as of the effective date of the law (January 1, 1996). Henceforth, these would be covered by US copyright with the same exclusive rights and for the same duration as works created in the United States.

4.1.5 § 105: "Subject Matter: US Government Works"

Copyright protection is not available for works of the US federal government. It is, however, possible for the federal government to obtain ownership of copyrights in works created by others through a formal transfer, whether by gift or contract. Thus, if an agency of the federal government contracts with a private exhibition or audio video producer, it could obtain copyright in the resultant work and exercise all of the rights of copyright, such as controlling distribution, display, public performance, etc. It is essential to note that § 105's placement of government works into the public domain *only* applies to works of the federal government and not to those created by other units of government such as states, counties, and municipalities.

The copyright status of any non-legislative or non-judicial works from other levels of government will vary from jurisdiction to jurisdiction. By judicially established rules, the major exception to that condition is that laws, ordinances, court opinions, and similar documents have been held as not subject to copyright.[4] That leaves most state and local government publications, such as tourist guides, maps, and photographs, as well as the unpublished material in their archives, subject to the US copyright law. Practices will vary significantly from state to state, but insofar as most states operate with open records laws, the state ownership of copyright does not preclude public access to and use of state-authored works, in some cases even for commercial purposes. To check whether any given state's works are presumptively under copyright, see the detailed references linked from the clickable map at https://copyright.lib.harvard.edu/states/. Of course, the threshold conditions for inclusion in copyright's scope as stated in § 102 (a) and (b) still apply such that the facts, ideas, processes, etc., in an otherwise copyrighted state guidebook would be exempt from federal copyright.

4.1.6 § 106: "Exclusive Rights in Copyrighted Works"

To determine how any particular archival activity could be constrained by the copyright monopoly, the best place to look is Section 106. It contains the core definition of the exclusive rights that the law gives to copyright owners. Because those exclusive rights cover several types of activities that could occur with a single use, these rights are sometimes discussed as a bundle of rights. Fortunately, the text of § 106 is one of the shorter and more concise parts of the statute and is quoted in full in Box 4.4. Also, luckily for the archivist, § 106 begins with a preamble that makes clear that the exclusive rights are "subject to sections 107 through 122." Those are the parts that include important exceptions and limitations that provide some room to work, which will be discussed below.

The center of § 106 establishes that only the copyright owner has the right to do, or allow to be done, six different things with their work. The first three activities apply to all types of works listed in § 102: to reproduce or make copies; to create derivative works from the original; to distribute the work by publication, broadcasting, lending or by placing the work online. Doing any of these activities without permission of the copyright owner is a violation of their rights and entitles them to take legal action.

The remaining three rights in § 106 relate to activities specific to particular types of works where performance or display are relevant, but they are articulated separately from the copying, adapting, and distribution rights.

Box 4.4 § 106 Exclusive Rights in Copyrighted Works

Subject to sections 107 through 122, the owner of copyright under this title has the exclusive rights to do and to authorize any of the following:

(1) to reproduce the copyrighted work in copies or phonorecords;
(2) to prepare derivative works based upon the copyrighted work;
(3) to distribute copies or phonorecords of the copyrighted work to the public by sale or other transfer of ownership, or by rental, lease, or lending;
(4) in the case of literary, musical, dramatic, and choreographic works, pantomimes, and motion pictures and other audiovisual works, to perform the copyrighted work publicly;
(5) in the case of literary, musical, dramatic, and choreographic works, pantomimes, and pictorial, graphic, or sculptural works, including the individual images of a motion picture or other audiovisual work, to display the copyrighted work publicly; and
(6) in the case of sound recordings, to perform the copyrighted work publicly by means of a digital audio transmission.

A careful reading of § 106 (4), (5), and (6) specifying which types of works have or do not have these additional rights should reveal the logic behind the differentiation. For example, it is logical that a pictorial work might have a display right but not a performance right, whereas a motion picture may be performed when it is projected in a theater but individual frames of the motion picture could be selected out for purpose of display in a gallery. Sound recordings would not be displayed but could be performed, although their exclusive right of performance applies only to digital transmission.[5]

4.1.6A "But Wait, There's More . . . " Section 106A "Rights of Certain Authors to Attribution and Integrity"

That telltale uppercase "A" after a section number reveals that Congress was once again trying to either shoehorn new rights into the law or play catch-up with the rest of the world, adding a further aspect to what is eligible for copyright. In compliance with the Berne Convention's recognition of certain

Box 4.5 What § 106A Added to Definitions in § 101

A "work of visual art" is:

(1) a painting, drawing, print, or sculpture, existing in a single copy, in a limited edition of 200 copies or fewer that are signed and consecutively numbered by the author, or, in the case of a sculpture, in multiple cast, carved, or fabricated sculptures of 200 or fewer that are consecutively numbered by the author and bear the signature or other identifying mark of the author; or
(2) a still photographic image produced for exhibition purposes only, existing in a single copy that is signed by the author, or in a limited edition of 200 copies or fewer that are signed and consecutively numbered by the author.

"moral rights," the Visual Artists Rights Act of 1990 created § 106A to provide creators attribution and integrity rights for a narrowly defined group of "works of visual art."

These would be in addition to those rights they already had in § 106 (1–5) (see Box 4.5 for definition of eligible works). These added rights for "works of visual art" would endure only for the creator's lifetime, and only for works created six months or later following its December 1, 1990 enactment. See Box 4.6 for the special "moral" rights that the authors of the these kinds of works have beyond what is in §106.

Overall, the enactment of these special rights reflects first time so-called European *droit d'auteur*, or "moral rights," entered into US federal copyright law.

However, except for repositories with collections focused on visual artists, the attribution and integrity concerns of § 106A are unlikely to be a regular concern for archivists. Of course, there is always the possibility that any given archival deposit could randomly contain a qualifying "print, or sculpture, existing in a single copy, in a limited edition of 200 copies or fewer that are signed and consecutively numbered by the author." If so, careful attention should be paid to maintaining attribution to the creator and to avoid any

Box 4.6 Scope of "Moral Rights" for Visual Artists

Right to:

- Claim authorship in the work
- Prevent use of their name for works they did not author
- Prevent any distortion, mutilation, or modification which would be prejudicial to their honor or reputation
- Prevent any destruction of a work of recognized stature

"intentional distortion, mutilation, or other modification" of the work. "Moral rights," however, are not otherwise in the federal copyright law. The distinction is based on US copyright being an economic and public-good model and not on the natural rights model found in the laws of European countries and many of their former colonies. This will be discussed in Chapter 6.

4.1.7 § 107: "Limitations on Exclusive Rights: Fair Use"

Finally here's a part of the copyright statute that's brief and very readable. The fair use provisions in § 107 are centrally important to how much room archivists have to operate, although they require interpretation as reflected by the fact they are the subject of many books and countless articles that are at the center of major court cases. It is concise enough to fit in the sidebar to this narrative (see Box 4.7).

For archivists it is an all-important exception to, and limitation on, copyright's monopoly. It begins by establishing that *a particular unauthorized use* of a work may not be a copyright infringement when the use is done for purposes of criticism, comment, news reporting, teaching, scholarship, or research. This list of potential permitted fair use seems broad enough to allow much of the copying, distribution, and adaptation necessary for archival work. However, the balance of the preamble of § 107 makes clear that the "fairness" of a use for any of the listed activities depends on the circumstances of the particular case.

Especially important is the notion that the ultimate determination "in any particular case" depends on how a court rules after considering four

Box 4.7 § 107 Limitations on Exclusive Rights: Fair Use

Notwithstanding the provisions of sections 106 and 106A, the fair use of a copyrighted work, including such use by reproduction in copies or phonorecords or by any other means specified by that section, for purposes such as criticism, comment, news reporting, teaching (including multiple copies for classroom use), scholarship, or research, is not an infringement of copyright. In determining whether the use made of a work in any particular case is a fair use, the factors to be considered shall include—

(1) the purpose and character of the use, including whether such use is of a commercial nature or is for nonprofit educational purposes;
(2) the nature of the copyrighted work;
(3) the amount and substantiality of the portion used in relation to the copyrighted work as a whole; and
(4) the effect of the use upon the potential market for or value of the copyrighted work.

The fact that a work is unpublished shall not itself bar a finding of fair use if such finding is made upon consideration of all the above factors.

factors. The balance of § 107 articulates the factors that must be weighed to determine if an unauthorized use (i.e., one of the actions listed as exclusive rights of the copyright holder in § 106) is a qualifying fair use:

1. Character and purpose of the use
2. Nature of the work being used
3. Amount and substantiality of the portion used
4. Effect of the use on the market for, or value of, the original work.

Although the four factors would seem to establish what is or is not fair, when Congress first put the judicial doctrine of fair use into the copyright statute itself in 1976, it explained that "since the doctrine is an equitable rule of reason, no generally applicable definition is possible."[6] Unfortunately, the *House Report* did not anticipate how much weight should be given to the unpublished status of work, and early fair use court cases gave nearly presumptive weight to that factor. Sixteen years after fair use had been made statutory, Congress added what is now the final clause of § 107—"The fact that a work is unpublished shall not itself bar a finding of fair use if such finding is made upon consideration of all the above factors." That provides some breathing room for archivists and our users.

The several fair-use court cases that have unfolded since fair use became statutory in 1976 have only reinforced the Congressional sense that each case had to be decided on its own facts. Even though only one of those cases has involved archival materials, the succession of cases has established several principles for archivists to consider as part of risk mitigation when going about basic archival activities that otherwise would seem prohibited by copyright law.

In thinking about fair use, the archivist needs to accept two key points. First, neither this nor other books nor any of the many online fair-use guides can establish that any particular use is actually "fair." Only a court can decide. Second, any decision on whether a particular use is fair depends not only on any single element, but also on all four factors taken together. For example, as demonstrated in one of the first Supreme Court rulings on fair use, *Harper & Row v. Nation Enterprises* (471 U.S. 539 [1985]), the fact that *The Nation* was a news reporting organization did not preclude a finding against them when the court considered other factors, such as the unpublished nature of the material quoted, the importance of the limited quantity of the material quoted to the core value of the underlying work itself, and the effect that *The Nation*'s publication had on the market for the underlying work.

The fact is that no single factor can by itself ensure a finding of either infringement or fair use. Instead, the rule that decisions are the result of holistic analysis means that the certainty to which archivists seem congenitally predisposed is not possible. Nevertheless, archivists do have a distinct advantage when trying to make sound judgments on potential fair uses as part of their risk management approach to pursuing the archival mission.

Fair use is the ultimate example of how frustratingly fact-specific copyright law can be, but archivists are the experts on the circumstances that lead to the creation and archival deposit of copyrightable works and in an enviable position to assemble the facts any court would need to decide upon a case. Few others are likely to know the nature of those facts better than a research-oriented archivist who has a solid grounding in the many circumstances that could weigh for or against a finding of fair use. While only a court can decide what will be deemed fair, what the archivist can do is to assemble all of the relevant facts and then make an honest assessment of how each aligns with the multiple facets of the four factors the courts will assess. A framework for such data collection and analysis can be found in a number of online tools, but especially in the "Fair Use Checklist" that Kenneth Crews has created based on a thorough review of decisions on copyright infringement cases. It can be found in Appendix 1 and on Columbia University's Copyright Advisory Services at https://copyright.columbia.edu/basics/fair-use/fair-use-checklist.html.

To gain a deeper understanding of the pivotal terms of fair use decisions and of how to apply those results to specific archival situations, a deeper look at many of the cases that have shaped fair use jurisprudence is provided in Chapter 5. Also, in Chapter 8 you will find a risk management model to apply after other limitations and exceptions and other aspects of the law for mitigating risk have been considered.

4.1.8 § 108: "Limitations on Exclusive Rights: Reproduction by Libraries and Archives"

Although rooted in pre-Second World War discussions between publishers and librarians, it was not until 1976 that US law formally recognized that libraries and archives should have clear legal exceptions to copyright.[7] By that time, low-cost photocopiers and sophisticated microfilming equipment had been incorporated as basics in academia, research, and even some public libraries. The 1976 Copyright Act provided archives and libraries with explicit exceptions to enable them to make copies, and in some cases provide users with copies, of copyrighted works to fulfill their missions as heritage, cultural, and educational institutions. Although Section 108 has yet to be updated to reflect twenty-first-century conditions, for a limited number of statutorily defined activities it provides "bright line" rules that can simplify some archives work. Unlike the lack of guidance in § 107's fair use exceptions, § 108's exceptions provide notable detail on what archives and libraries need to do to be eligible for otherwise unauthorized copying. Applying them correctly requires following the conditions as well as the exclusions found within §108 itself.

Three general conditions apply to all Section 108 copying: (1) the library or archives is open to the public or available to "other persons doing research in a specialized field"; (2) the copying should be "without any purpose of direct or indirect commercial advantage"; and (3) any copy made or distributed must include a notice of the work's copyright status.

Libraries and archives also may make three copies of unpublished (§ 108(b)) works for preservation, security, or deposit at another library or archives. Less generous are the provisions for published materials. § 108(c) authorizes, making up to three copies as replacements for works that are damaged, deteriorating, lost, or stolen, or in an obsolete format and only when an unused replacement cannot be obtained at a fair price.

The antique patina of US copyright law is reflected in the fact it was only when this provision was updated in 1998 that the allowance changed from "a copy" in "facsimile form" to "three copies," which brought the law forward at tortoise-speed to the heyday of preservation microfilming of a few decades earlier. In 1998 Congress expanded the allowance from one copy to three, and it authorized digital copies, but it remained oblivious to technology since the limitation to three copies ignored the nature of computer storage and backup practices, which inherently require more—far more—than three copies except in the most constrained situations. Furthermore, it constrained the value of digitization by stipulating that the digital copies could not be made available in digital format outside the premises of the library or archives.

Subsections 108(d) and (e) address the need for libraries and archives to make copies for users, except for non-literary works excluded by § 108(i) (see below); § 108(d) may be less relevant to archives because it is concerned with published material and it focuses on requests for "no more than one article or other contribution to a copyrighted collection or periodical issue." By contrast, Section 108(e) supports copying of an entire work or substantial portion of a work. Therefore, if the library or archives has first determined that a copy or phonorecord of the copyrighted work cannot be obtained at a fair price, that effectively means that an archives can use the § 108 (e) exception to make entire copies of unpublished works. Thus, § 108(e) is of considerable utility to archives, where the majority of unpublished material may consist of isolated single works (e.g., individual letters, photographs, or audio recordings). Although there is some variation in the prerequisites in

108(d) and (e), both of these "user copies" exceptions follow nearly identical principles: (1) the library or archives should have no reason to think that the copies will be used for anything other than private research; (2) the copies must become the property of the user; and (3) notice of the copyright must be provided.

Two further subsections add some important general conditions on the overall library and archives exceptions; § 108(f) provides:

1 libraries and archives do not incur liability for unsupervised use of copying equipment, but they must post a copyright warning notice on any such equipment

2 users of such equipment are not excused from liability for copying that exceeds fair use

3 nothing in § 108 limits the reproduction or distribution by lending of limited numbers or excerpts of audiovisual news programs

4 nothing in § 108 affects fair use right or contract obligations.

Despite all of this good news, please note the concerns and controls in § 108(g). It foresees the possibility of isolated or unrelated copying of the same material over time, something that is quite likely to happen with some of the one-of-a-kind unpublished material that is common in archives. Moreover, it cautions libraries to not engage in any copying that might be part of a concerted or coordinated effort by a group or where "such aggregate quantities" might "substitute for a subscription to or purchase of such work."

In the late 1990s, when Congress was considering what became the Sonny Bono Copyright Term Extension Act (CTEA), a provision was inserted, now identified as § 108(h). It was a concession to the library community to partially mitigate the fact that CTEA added 20 years to the duration of copyright. The § 108(h) provision states that "during the last 20 years of any term of copyright of a published work, a library or archives . . . may reproduce, distribute, display, or perform in facsimile or digital form . . . for purposes of preservation, scholarship, or research. . . ." To take advantage of this exception, the library or archives must first determine that the work is no longer subject to normal commercial exploitation, that a copy cannot be obtained at a reasonable price, and that the copyright owner has not already filed a notice that the first two of these conditions apply. Unfortunately, when this exception was developed, it was limited only to published works which may have tempered library objections to the amendment but did not preclude the strong opposition of the Society of American Archivists to CTEA's adding 20 years to copyright.

A further disappointing note is that the provisions for library and archives exceptions in § 108 close with a subsection that gives special status to particular types of works, thus negating the exceptions for making copies for users (i.e., § 108(d) and (e)) for non-textual works. Specifically, Section 108(i) states that libraries and archives do not have an exception to copy and supply users with copies of musical works, pictorial, graphic, or sculptural works, or motion pictures or other audiovisual works. For these kinds of works, the only bright line allowance for copying is for preservation purposes, as discussed above (§ 108(b) and (c)). This leaves archivists needing to rely on fair use as the only exception to make copies for on-site or remote users of these works.

Overall, Section 108 exceptions do provide some utility in support of archives activities, and they should be tools that the archivist regularly employs, especially since they require less interpretation than the broader, more flexible, but more ambiguous, fair use exceptions in Section 107.

4.1.9 § 109: "Limitations on Exclusive Rights: Effect of Transfer of Ownership of Particular Copy or Phonorecord"

Sometimes described as the first sale doctrine, the § 109 copyright exception incorporates the principle of exhaustion. That is, once there has been the lawful transfer of ownership of a particular copy of a work, the person to whom the copy has been transferred may sell or otherwise dispose of that copy without infringing on the copyright holder's rights. This exception to § 106's exclusive right of distribution means that libraries can loan physical books, and that bookstores and garage sales can sell used books. If the work is a phonorecord (i.e., a sound recording) or a computer program, § 109(b) does allow rental or lending for direct or indirect commercial purposes. Because the exclusive right of display in § 106 (5) would bar display of a work in a physical exhibition, archivists will be pleased with the relief offered by § 109(c). It extends the first sale exception to provide legal clearance to allow the owner of a lawful copy of a work to display that work directly or by projection of one image at a time and in a place open to the public.

4.1.10 § 110: "Limitations on Exclusive Rights: Exemption of Certain Performances and Displays"

"Hodgepodge!" That may be the best way to describe the eleven separate performance and display exceptions in § 110. They focus only on the exclusive rights of performance and display rather than the more inclusive approach of § 107 (fair use), which applies to not just performance and display, but also to the exclusive rights of reproduction, distribution, and adaptation. In addition, the § 110 exceptions center on particular formats, especially musical, audio, and video, and each is tailored to particular audiences and occasions.

Of these eleven exceptions, only the first, § 110 (1) (to be discussed below), is likely to be of much utility to most archival needs. Of course, there's always the possibility, given the great diversity of archival materials and archives users, that you might have an occasion where one of the other § 110 exceptions could be useful. Rather than taking your time to dig into their details right now, Table 4.1 provides a cursory overview of all eleven of these performance and display exceptions. As a comparative chart, it inevitably omits considerable detail that might be important if you intend to rely on any particular one. Thus, if any one of these seems to fit your circumstance, read the full text of the relevant subsection at https://www.copyright.gov/title17/92chap1.html#110.

It would be a mistake to dismiss § 110 entirely just because its many references to audiovisual, dramatic, and musical works in the above chart seem more relevant to a video producer or musical impresario than to an archivist. Doing so would overlook how often you show archival materials in the process of your instructional sessions for students and visitors. When you meet with a class or the public to promote access to the archives, it may be common for you to play that audio clip of Lanston Hughes reading one of his poems or to show that film segment of a young John Kennedy making a campaign stop in your town. Likewise, you may want to read aloud 1920s entries from a diary of a local socialite and display photographs of her in her "flapper dress."

All of these activities fit the definitions of "display" or "perform" that appear in § 101 of the Copyright Act. Absent an exception, your instructional use could touch on a copyright owner's exclusive right. No doubt, the risks of being called out on such actions may be slight and no doubt that fair use may also cover your action. Knowing that §110 (1) provides a performance and display exception for in-person teaching, however, should give you added confidence in doing such presentations and instruction.

Table 4.1 § 110 Limitations on Exclusive Rights: Exemptions of Certain Performances and Displays: Overview

Section	Exempted Actor	Exempt Activity	Audience	Conditions and Limits
§ 110 (1)	Instructors or students in non-profit educational institutions	In-person performance or display of work in course of instruction	Face-to-face teaching	Copy used must be lawfully made
§ 110 (2)	Government body or accredited non-profit institution	Digitally transmitted performance or display of nondramatic literary or musical work or portions thereof	Mediated instruction	11 detailed conditions, e.g., transmit only to officially enrolled students; no retention of digitized materials
§ 110 (3)	Place of worship or religious assembly	Performance of a nondramatic literary or musical work or dramatico-musical work of a religious nature, or display of a work	In course of religious services	Only covers nondramatic literary or musical work or of a dramatico-musical work of a religious nature
§ 110 (4)	Unspecified actors, but proceeds (after expenses) to benefit educational, religious, or charitable purposes	Performance of a nondramatic literary or musical work		No transmission to public; no admission charge; no fee to performers or promoters

Table 4.1 continued

Section	Exempted Actor	Exempt Activity	Audience	Conditions and Limits
§ 110 (5)	Commercial establishments, especially restaurants and bars	Transmission or retransmission of nondramatic musical work originated by a radio or television broadcast station		Establishment size, # of loudspeakers & parking spaces, and size of display screens
§ 110 (6)	Governmental body or nonprofit agricultural or horticultural organization	Performance of a nondramatic musical work	Annual agric./hort. fair/exhibit	
§ 110 (7)	Vending establishment open to the public without admission charge	Performance of nondramatic musical work for promotion of sale of copies or of audiovisual devices for performance		Performance is not transmitted beyond the establishment
§ 110 (8)	Governmental body; or a noncommercial educational broadcast station; or a radio subcarrier	Performance of nondramatic literary work transmitted & designed for and directed to blind or others unable to hear aural signals in a transmission of visual signals		No direct/indirect commercial advantage

Table 4.1 continued

Section	Exempted Actor	Exempt Activity	Audience	Conditions and Limits
§ 110 (9)	Radio subcarrier in the course of transmission "specifically designed for and primarily directed to blind or other handicapped persons who are unable to read normal printed material"	Performance *on a single* occasion of dramatic literary work *published in the last 10 years*		No direct/indirect commercial advantage; only one performance of same work by same performers or under the auspices of the same organization
§ 110 (10)	Social function organized and promoted by nonprofit veterans' organization or a nonprofit fraternal organization	Performance of a nondramatic literary or musical work	Excludes social functions of college/univ fraternity unless for charitable purpose	General public is not to be invited; proceeds (after expenses) must be used exclusively for charitable purposes
§ 110 (11)	Member of a private household or person under their direction	Alterations to render imperceptible limited portions of audio or video content of an authorized copy of a motion picture		No fixed copy of altered version of motion picture may be made

Unfortunately, the performance and display exceptions do not translate well for online or distance education even though § 110 (2) attempts to address teaching via digital networks. This subsection was added to allow the online performance or display of a nondramatic literary or musical work in an amount comparable to what would be used in a live classroom. However, this is a rambling and convoluted subsection that imposes at least eleven specific conditions you must meet to qualify for the exception. That severely limits its usefulness, and explicating those conditions is beyond the scope of this book. Should you be involved in formal online courses for a governmental entity or accredited educational institution, you should look for guidance in the checklist for instructors from the University of Texas's Copyright Crash Course. Its useful guide helps instructors determine if their particular online teaching use might fit § 110 (2)'s requirements, and it reinforces the ever-present availability of fair use for circumstances where § 110 (2)'s conditions are too burdensome. It is available at https://guides.lib.utexas.edu/copyright/teachact

4.1.11 Exceptions in §§ 111 through 122

The balance of 17 U.S.C. Chapter 1 of the copyright statute consists of exceptions that are largely peripheral to archives but worth at least a high-level awareness of their focus. These relate to either specific types of works, specific types of users, or occasions for the creation and use of statutory compulsory licenses (see Box 4.8).

Box 4.8 Compulsory Licensing

For certain types of work, especially music and sound recordings, once a work has been distributed to the public, the law establishes a licensing system that allows the use of the work without the explicit permission of the copyright owner so long as royalties are paid to the copyright holder. The standard fees are set by the Copyright Royalty Judges, a body authorized in 17 U.S.C. Chapter 8. Even a quick glance at one of the sections involving compulsory licensing, e.g., § 115, will show that use of any of the compulsory license exceptions is burdened by many conditions and details.

If you are curious enough to look at §§ 111 through § 119, and § 122, prepare yourself to encounter maddeningly complex syntax because each of these sections was written to respond to changing technology, managing markets, or messy court cases, often with involvement of vested interests.

Because of the generally marginal relevance of the exceptions in §§ 111 to 119 and § 122, their scope will be presented only at a summary level in Table 4.2. If the summary suggests a possible relevance for your archives, please do a close reading of the relevant text and consider conferring with legal counsel. You can find the full text by looking for a link titled "Sections 112–122" that appears on the right-hand side of the display, below the series of links for §§ 101–111 within the web page for Chapter 1 of the Copyright Law (https://www.copyright.gov/title17/92chap1.html).

4.1.12 § 120: "Scope of Exclusive Rights in Architectural Works"

The brevity of § 120 is a welcome relief for tired eyes. At a mere 111 words, it is shorter than any other section of Chapter 1of the law. This section was added when the 1990 Architectural Works Copyright Protection Act extended copyright to the very *design* of a building. That Act inserted a definition of architectural works into §101 and added "architectural works" to the scope of what § 102 considers as eligible for copyright. Fortunately, the 1990 act also included exceptions that would allow the making, distributing, or public display of pictorial representations of an eligible building if it is located where visible by the public, and it allows the owner of the building to destroy or make alterations without permission of the author/copyright owner.

4.1.13 § 121 and § 121A: Exceptions for the Visually Impaired

§ 121 and § 121A "Limitations on exclusive rights: Reproductions for blind or other people with disabilities" and "Limitations on exclusive rights: Reproduction for blind or other people with disabilities in Marrakesh Treaty countries"—the exceptions in § 121 allow accessible copies of previously published literary works to be made and distributed in the United States to meet the needs of those with visual or other disabilities that prevent them

Table 4.2 Exceptions in §§ 111–119, 122 Overview

Section	Scope of Exemption
§ 111 "Limitations on exclusive rights: Secondary transmissions of broadcast programming by cable"	For audiovisual works carried by cable TV systems, § 111 allows the further transmission of a program when necessary to serve multiple locations within a subscriber's building.
§ 112 "Limitations on exclusive rights: Ephemeral recordings"	Broadcasters can make and retain, for a limited term, recordings of transmitted programs for later delivery by the broadcaster. Includes the word "archival," but context suggests it is only for preservation and security purposes.
§ 113 "Scope of exclusive rights in pictorial, graphic, and sculptural works"	When a pictorial, graphic, or sculptural creative work is incorporated into a "useful article," (e.g., a lamp) the author of original creative work retains all the exclusive rights of copyright in the work, but images of the useful article in which creative work is visible may be made and distributed for advertising and news.
§ 114 "Scope of exclusive rights in sound recordings"	Exclusive rights to reproduce a sound recording do not extend to making an independent fixation of the same sounds as in the original recording. § 114's meandering provisions seem more like added exclusive rights than exceptions.
§ 115 "Scope of exclusive rights in nondramatic musical works: Compulsory license for making and distributing phonorecords"	Allows use of compulsory licenses to enable making of sound recordings of previously distributed musical work and distribution of the new recordings to the public. Includes system for payment of royalty fees. Written to resolve issues from 1909 establishment of compulsory licensing for music.
§ 116 "Negotiated licenses for public performances by means of coin-operated phonorecord players"	Creates a system for negotiated licenses for public performances of sound recordings of non-dramatic musical works on devices such as jukeboxes.
§ 117 "Limitations and exceptions on exclusive rights: Computer programs"	Allows legal owners of copies of computer programs to make and retain an "archival copy" of the program or to modify the program for their own use.

Section	Scope of Exemption
§ 118 "Scope of exclusive rights: Use of certain works in connection with noncommercial broadcasting"	Establishes licensing system for public broadcasting programs to provide a middle ground between voluntary and compulsory licensing.
§ 119 "Limitations on exclusive rights: Secondary transmissions of distant television programming by satellite"	Establishes compulsory licensing system for broadcasters using satellites to retransmit programs to non-local audiences.
§§ 120, 121, and 121A	See narrative above at 4.1.12 and 4.1.13
§ 122 "Limitation on exclusive rights: Secondary transmissions of local television programming by satellite"	Establishes compulsory licensing system for local television similar to § 119's allowance for distant programming.

from reading the work. Section 121A provides a further exception, allowing accessible works to be imported from or exported to countries who are parties to the 2013 Marrakesh Treaty.

4.2 17 U.S.C. Chapter 2: "Copyright Ownership and Transfer"

4.2.1 § 201: "Ownership of Copyright"

After the maze of issues and contingencies in the first chapter of the copyright law, the next few chapters provide occasional relief. There may be complications ahead, but at least 17 U.S.C. Chapter 2 on ownership starts off in a promising way. That's a good thing because it is an important part of the law to guide your thinking about who actually owns any works in your archives that you might need to copy for a user or incorporate in a digital project. So, rather than following the numerical sequence of 17 U.S.C. Chapter 2's sections, the narrative below will work from least to most complex of the provisions related to ownership.

Initial ownership. As stated in § 201(a), ownership first belongs to the author or co-author. By using the word "initial," the law reflects the idea that copyright ownership is portable and can be transferred. For that transfer to be valid, § 204(a) states it must be effected either by operation of law or by a written instrument signed by the owner (e.g., a Deed of Gift). While having a signed written instrument is sufficient, establishing formal notice of the facts of the transfer and addressing the possibility of conflicting transfers can be done by a formal recording with the Copyright Office ("recordation") of the transfer as outlined in § 205. Both recordation and registering the change in copyright ownership are voluntary rather than mandatory.

Physical ownership is not copyright ownership. In considering how many copyrighted works your archives actually owns, you should keep in mind that merely having physical possession does not provide copyright ownership, nor can a donor give you copyrights they do not actually own. Section 202 states: "Ownership of a copyright, or of any of the exclusive rights under a copyright, is distinct from ownership of any material object in which the work is embodied. Transfer of ownership of any material object ... does not of itself convey any rights in the copyrighted work embodied in the object ...." Thus, even if a donor transfers their copyrights in writing via a signed Deed of Gift, that transfer would cover only the copyrights in the works that they authored and still owned at the time of the Deed. It would not cover either incoming correspondence they received or any works they had authored but to which they previously had assigned copyright to others, such as publishers of journals and books.

Works made for hire. A further complication are those items that any individual authored but where the copyright belonged to their employer because they were works made for hire. Although first inserted in the law in 1909, a "work made for hire" was not defined until the 1976 revisions. Since then, § 201(b) has read: "(b) In the case of a work made for hire, the employer or other person for whom the work was prepared is considered the author for purposes of this title, and, unless the parties have expressly agreed otherwise in a written instrument signed by them, owns all of the rights comprised in the copyright."

For help understanding the conditions for a work to be a work made for hire, you should turn to the definition in § 101, which identifies two ways for something to be a work made for hire. The first is relatively straightforward: "work prepared by an employee within the scope of his or her employment." By this standard, photographs of university buildings and events taken by a staff member of the campus public relations office presumably would have a copyright owned by the university. By contrast, photographs of campus demonstrations taken by a sociology professor for research on crowd behavior may not be owned by her employer. However, merely because someone is an employee does not mean that everything she does can be considered a work made for hire, as illustrated in the case of *Schmid Bros. Inc. v. W. Goebel Porzellanfabrik KG*. It involved a member of a women's religious order who had created artistic drawings eventually used to make porcelain Hummel figurines.[8] With regard to professional staff such as faculty, case law has often recognized the greater independence and judgment academics have in how they conduct their research and writings so that their works are less likely to be subject to works made for hire conditions, depending on institutional policy. A major copyright treatise notes: "Because of the traditions of independence and judgment that are commonly associated with professional activities, the fact that the individual who prepared the work is a professional, such as an architect or university professor, will weigh heavily toward a finding that he, rather than his employer, is the author of any works that he creates while in the other's employ." Of course, that rule could be reinforced or overwritten by institutional policy.[9]

Works made for hire: Non-employees. The § 101 definition also identifies circumstances where certain works may be considered a work made for hire if done by contract workers. It states that a work made for hire can also be "a work specially ordered or commissioned for use as a contribution to a collective work, as a part of a motion picture or other audiovisual work, . . ." if the parties so agree expressly in a signed, written document. Because the definition includes at least three qualifying conditions and only applies to eight particular types of collective works, do not assume that merely hiring a photographer to take pictures would automatically make the images work made for hire. Nevertheless, such specifics were only added to the law in the 1976 revision, and prior judicial standards used under the 1909 law were more flexible, depending on the notion of agency, as discussed below.

Not addressed are circumstances where the creator is not an actual employee but a volunteer doing work on behalf of some sponsoring organization. For that, one must turn to case law. In those circumstances, courts have examined the twelve factors of agency to determine the extent to which the sponsoring organization provided the creative motive force for the generation of the work (see Box 4.9). It may be easier to think of this as a matter of the extent to which the volunteer's organization was making creative choices about how a work is to be made. It's more than that your archives loaned a camera to have a volunteer photograph a "friends of the archives" event or lecture. However, work made for hire conditions are more likely if you instructed the volunteer where to stand to take the pictures, what kind of poses you wanted them to capture, or how to compose group shots of the officers of the board against specific backgrounds, etc.

Joint works of authorship. The primary clause about copyright ownership in § 201(a) acknowledges that, for joint works, each of the authors is a co-owner in the work. Although these works can present some special issues, you should start by referring back to the definitions in § 101. It says that a joint work is "a work prepared by two or more authors with the intention that their contributions be merged into inseparable or interdependent parts of a unitary whole." Each author is considered a full owner, and this inseparability of copyright may facilitate some of your work as an archivist. If you wish to obtain permission for use of a joint work, you need only have the permission of, or license from, one of the joint owners.[10]

Box 4.9 § 201(b) Works Made for Hire

Is someone an employee?

Relevant factors under general common law of agency: (*Community for Creative Non-Violence v. Reid,* 490 U.S. 730 [1989])

1) skill required;
2) source of the instrumentalities and tools;
3) location of the work;
4) duration of the relationship between the parties;
5) whether hiring party has right to assign additional projects to the hired party;
6) extent of hired party's discretion over when & how long to work;
7) method of payment;
8) hired party's role in hiring and paying assistants;
9) whether the work is part of the regular business of hiring party;
10) whether hiring party is in business;
11) provision of employee benefits; and
12) tax treatment of the hired party.

Licensing can handle a number of such situations. The downside, however, is that no transfer of copyright ownership can happen without a formal written agreement from each and every co-author, thus posing practical limitations on boiler-plate Deed of Gift clauses for transfers of the donor's copyright.[11] Instead, you would need to incorporate customized deed language and addenda signed by each of the individuals who coauthored a joint work with the donor of the collection. Because that would be logistically difficult in most circumstances, it would instead be more effective for the deed to ask the donor to license to your archives the use of any works the donor may have coauthored with others.

Termination of transfers and licenses. It is highly unlikely that the rights of a creator to terminate an earlier transfer or license will arise with most of the materials in your archives. Still, it is useful to have a general idea of the termination rights. To compensate for the unequal bargaining position of aspiring artists and creators when they first seek a publisher or record producer for a work that may or may not realize significant later sales, Congress added § 203 to the law in 1976. By following complex procedures, the author, or in some cases their heirs, can institute a termination of whatever license or transfer of ownership the author agreed to so their book could be published or their song could be produced and released on records for commercial markets.

The right to terminate is inalienable and cannot be waived. Generally speaking, within a five-year period beginning 35 years after the original transfer, the author or their heirs can terminate the grant of rights and then take advantage of any long-term economic value the work may have accrued. Thus, the rights in a song, which a composer sold for $200 in 1980 to pay their rent but which became a hit and was later picked up for use in a movie soundtrack, could be terminated by the composer or their heirs. Future revenue would go to them rather than the major media company holding the original transfer.

This simple explanation does not do justice to the complexity of the rules that § 203 provides or to the related provisions on copyright term in § 304(c). Remember the advice given at the beginning of this chapter about needing a stiff drink? You are going to need more than one if an author who signed a Deed of Gift 35 years ago starts asking you about terminating the rights they gave when you were a novice archivist. However, considering that the underlying purpose of, and thus incentive for, filing termination is related to commercial works, unless your archives holds material relating to such commercial works, it may be more likely that you will have retired before you would need to dig into the intricacies of termination conditions.[12]

4.3 17 U.S.C. Chapter 3: "Duration of Copyright"

As stewards of materials generally held in perpetuity, archivists have a deep stake in the subject matter of 17 U.S.C. Chapter 3. It's here that you'll find the rules to answer this important question: "Ok, I understand the need for authors to have exclusive rights, but for how long?" Seems like a simple question, but as with some other parts of the law, we need to consider three factors even before opening our browser to these pivotal pages of the statute.

First the length of copyright's term cuts to the core of our mission as archivists because until a copyright ends, the latitude we have for our work is greatly constrained. With so much archival content being works for which it's next to impossible to find a rights holder to answer a permission request, only the end of a copyright's term can eliminate the greatest risks we have in making, distributing, adapting, and performing the cultural works we curate. Second, for the mundane administrative records and documentary artifacts of day-to-day life held in our archives, copyright lasts too long! Third, understanding copyright duration in general and determining whether any given work in our collections is still in copyright can be very frustrating, especially if we start by merely reading 17 U.S.C. Chapter 3 section by section.

The broad-brush narrative below will explain the basic function of each of the sections in 17 U.S.C. Chapter 3, but spoiler alert! Ready at hand is something to make your life easier! Thanks to Cornell University Library's Copyright Services, there is an annually updated online tool, "Copyright Term and the Public Domain in the United States," https://guides.library.cornell.edu/copyright/publicdomain. This wonderful and scholarly site helps you to determine whether the term of any particular work in your archives has expired and entered the US public domain, but don't skip to that without at least a general sense of the various parts of 17 U.S.C. Chapter 3.

The reason that this chapter can be so challenging is that this was Congress's best effort to change our law to comply with the Berne Convention. Congress needed to bridge a transition from copyright being based on publication to one with copyright being automatic on creation of a work. From the first federal copyright law in 1790 until the beginning of 1978, US copyright existed only in works that had been published and that conformed to certain formalities, such as inclusion of the copyright symbol and registration with the federal government. Even with an update in 1909, completion of those steps was required to secure an initial term of copyright that could be renewed later for a further term but only by filing the appropriate paperwork at the appropriate time.

Under the 1909 revision (in effect until January 1, 1978), published works that contained a copyright notice and were registered had an initial copyright term of 28 years from date of publication. Unpublished works, if formally registered, had a term of 28 years from date of registration. Despite the option of filing for a second term of 28 years, a significant percentage of those copyrights were not renewed, especially monographs. Also, to comply with Berne, the basis for duration of copyright was changed to one that started automatically with the creation of the work and extended to a minimum of 50 years past the life of the author. In 1978, for the first time, unpublished works were fully brought under federal copyright rather than being subject to various state and common law practices, which generally had meant a perpetual term of protection. For both newly created and never registered pre-existing unpublished works, the transition was relatively simple. Those works went from no federal copyright to having a term of life of the author plus 50 years, later changed to 70 years. However, for all of the works that had been published and registered before January 1, 1978, the effective date of the new law, Congress had to create provisions to bridge from the old to the new systems.

The above capsule summary of copyright duration, even when read together with the Cornell public domain chart, is unlikely to answer all of the questions you have relating to duration. If you find yourself thinking about digging deeper by reading the actual text of the law (always an advisable step whenever you start believing that you are certain about an answer to any copyright question), then the following high-level overview should help you determine which of the 17 U.S.C. Chapter 3's sections need a close look. It provides an overview of the focus and purpose of each section but intentionally leaves out the detailed specifications and internal contingent clauses. That's so you can have the thrill of discovering these nuggets of the law yourself.

4.3.1 § 301: "Preemption with Respect to Other Laws"

A key purpose of the 1976 law was to bring all of the copyright-related practices in the United States under a single federal regime while also moving beyond the ambiguities that had arisen in judicial interpretations of the 1909 law's lynchpin of "publication." Thus § 301 establishes that the new federal copyright statute would preempt any state or other law relating to the exclusive rights or scope of copyright. The "Historical and Revision Notes" in the House Report were quite emphatic: "All corresponding State laws, whether common law or statutory, are preempted and abrogated. Regardless of when the work was created and whether it is published or unpublished, disseminated or undisseminated, in the public domain or copyrighted under the Federal statute, the States cannot offer it protection equivalent to copyright."[13]

Nevertheless, § 301(b) makes it clear that the intent was not to annul or limit those state or common law rights relating to unfixed expression or otherwise outside the scope of the kind of works listed in § 102(a). In addition, although now largely moot, § 301(c) excluded from federal copyright any sound recordings fixed before February 15, 1972. While those recordings will remain outside of federal copyright, the 2018 Music Modernization Act created a parallel system of protection and provisions for use of those early recordings, to be discussed below under § 1401.

4.3.2 § 302: "Duration of Copyright: Works Created on or after January 1, 1978"

For any new work created on or after the law's 1978 effective date, the copyright endures from its creation for a term of life of the author plus 70 years. However, there are a few relatively straightforward exceptions to this rule for "new" works:

- For works of joint authorship, the term endures for 70 years after the life of the last living coauthor.
- For anonymous, pseudonymous works, and works made for hire, the copyright endures for 95 years from publication or 120 years from creation, whichever expires first.
- To address uncertainties that could arise about whether or when an author has died, the Copyright Office is authorized to receive and maintain records relating to the death of authors.

- The Copyright Office is also authorized to issue certified reports, on request, of the presumption of the death of an author 95 years from the publication of a work or 120 years from its creation.

4.3.3 § 303: "Duration of Copyright: Works Created but Not Published or Copyrighted before January 1, 1978"

Unpublished works created before the effective date of the new law have the same term as stated in § 302—thus life of the author plus 70 years, or 120 years if an anonymous work or a work made for hire.

4.3.4 § 304: "Duration of Copyright: Subsisting Copyrights"

To avoid superseding the copyrights of those works that were still in their initial term as of January 1, 1978, or which had already been renewed in conformance with the provisions of the 1909 law, the new statute called for them to have a single term of 75 years, later extended to 95 years by the 1998 Sonny Bono Copyright Term Extension Act. A further lengthy subsection, § 304(c), was added to extend the time that either an author or their heirs would have to exercise their termination rights for copyrights that had been in existence prior to January 1, 1978.

If you ignored my prior advice to not attempt to read or decipher § 203 on termination rights, you will probably find § 304(c) and its shorter companion § 304(d) even more dizzying. Termination rights are an important protection that the law put into place, but they are confusing and have often been criticized for creating too complex a path for authors to follow. If there arises the rare occasion where they do occur in your archival practice, plan to talk with your institutional legal counsel. Meanwhile, an excellent place to preview the nooks and crannies of the rules is the Copyright Office's web page on notices of termination.[14]

4.3.5 § 305: "Duration of Copyright: Terminal Date"

Leading the competition for "Simplest Part of Copyright Law" is § 305. It even meets the "25 words or less" criterion, and it needs no further explanation. It reads: "All terms of copyright provided by sections 302 through 304 extend to the end of the calendar year in which they would otherwise expire." For example: knowing that a never published or registered letter written home from a First World War soldier has a term of life plus 70 years, and knowing that this veteran died on April 15, 1955, you would be able to conclude that the letter would enter the public domain not on April 16, 2025 but on January 1, 2026.

4.4 17 U.S.C. Chapter 4: "Copyright Notice, Deposit, and Registration"

One of the fundamental purposes of both the 1976 copyright law revision and of the Berne Convention Implementation Act of 1988 was to remove the dependence of copyright on "formalities." That makes the very title of 17 U.S.C. Chapter 4 seem a bit odd. Why talk about notice, deposit, and registration if they are not needed for a copyright to exist?

In fact, a full reading of 17 U.S.C. Chapter 4's sections, especially 401, 402, and 408, reveals passages restating that notice, deposit, and registration are indeed *not* necessary for copyright to exist. However, 17 U.S.C. Chapter 4 explains how complying with some or all of those steps will provide benefits to the copyright owner, including the ability to file an infringement case. Some copyright hardliners cite such provisions as showing that the United States is non-compliant with the Berne convention, but until court rulings or legislation create a change in the law, the details throughout all its sections, especially §§ 411 and 412, are helpful in thinking about risk management when you consider planning projects involving copying, distributing, and preparing derivative works from items, especially unpublished works from your archives.

Much of 17 U.S.C. Chapter 4 is focused on regulations and details for the copyright owners and the Copyright Office to follow in relation to notice, deposit, and registration. While some of its sections may be lengthy or contain tiered sets of rules, most of it is quite readable. Here are the key points to know about from those sections:

- When a work eligible for copyright is published, it should carry a copyright notice. That notice should contain the symbol © or the word "copyright" or its abbreviation, the year of first publication, and the name of the copyright owner. If a notice is present, defendants in suits cannot claim innocent infringement (§ 401). If the work is a sound recording, parallel provisions apply but instead of calling for the © it calls for using the symbol of ℗, a "P" in a circle. (§ 402).

- Individual contributions to collective works, such as articles in a journal or chapters in an edited volume, may carry their own copyright notice that is independent of the copyright notice for the overall collective work (§ 404).
- Although it is not a condition of copyright, the owner of a copyright of a work published in the United States is still required to deposit two complete copies of the work in the Copyright Office for the use or disposition of the Library of Congress (§ 407).
- Although not a condition of copyright, the owner of any copyright may register their copyright claim. To register, one must also deposit one copy (for unpublished works) or two copies (for published works) in the Copyright Office (§ 408). The Copyright Office's regulations do allow group registration of multiple unpublished works, but they must be from the same author and listed by their separate titles on a single application. Submission of digitized copies is required rather than originals. Details may be found in the Copyright Office *Circular 24 Group Registration of Unpublished Works*.[15]
- The Copyright Office has the authority to establish regulations, application forms, and fees relating to registration (§ 409). It also has the authority to determine if the work qualifies for copyright (§ 410(a)) or is ineligible for copyright (§ 410(b)), e.g., a photograph taken by a monkey.[16]

There is an important relationship between registration and what responses to infringement the copyright holder can bring and what relief might be obtained. This can result in notable benefits for the archives if followed carefully. First, note that § 411(a) connects registration with infringement actions: "no civil action for infringement of the copyright in any United States work[17] shall be instituted until preregistration or registration of the copyright claim has been made in accordance with this title."[18]

Furthermore, not only can an infringement action not begin without the registration process authorized by 17 U.S.C. Chapter 4, but § 412 ties registration to what remedies or damages may be available to the copyright holder, and it does not limit this requirement only to "United States works." It states:

> " . . . no award of statutory damages or of attorney's fees, as provided by sections 504 and 505, shall be made for—
> (1) any infringement of copyright in an unpublished work commenced before the effective date of its registration; or
> 2) any infringement of copyright commenced after first publication of the work and before the effective date of its registration, unless such registration is made within three months after the first publication of the work."

Because the registration requirements for litigation can require time and attention of the copyright holder, the provisions in § 411 and § 412 can abate some of the risk the archivist might face in launching projects that involve digitization of many types of the unpublished materials in your holdings (see Box 4.10 for the amount of time and costs required for registration). Unless the materials you want to digitize and put online have notable commercial value or unless they are of a highly creative nature (e.g., fictional literature,

Box 4.10 Registration Requirements May Buy Time for Archives

Once an online registration application and electronic deposit is completed, processing time can be from 1 to 2.6 months if no correspondence is needed; less than 1 month to 8.3 months if correspondence is needed (21 percent of eService claims) with digital deposit); or less than 1 month to 19.1 months with mail-in physical deposit.*

Common fees are $45 for a basic electronic registration of a single work; $85 for up to 10 unpublished works with "Group of Unpublished Works" (GRUW) application if all are unpublished, all by same author or co-authors, and each is separately titled. The full array of fees can be seen in *Copyright Office Circular 4 Copyright Office fees*. Note that if litigation is prospective or pending, a Special Handling fee of $800 would apply.

---

* Library of Congress, Copyright Office, "Registration Processing Times," accessed May 26, 2025, https://www.copyright.gov/registration/docs/processing-times-faqs.pdf.

poetry, art photography, etc.) there is a reasonable chance that the lack of prior registration, combined with the costs and logistics of registering, could reduce the risk of an infringement suit. However, by themselves, the 17 U.S.C. Chapter 4 registration requirements do not provide a complete buffer against litigation. When combined with how they could mitigate the amount of monetary damages and attorney fees (see § 504 and § 505 below), however, they should be considered as one of the elements useful for risk mitigation. Additional project management steps to employ based on the registration requirement will be discussed in this book's Chapter 8 on risk management.

4.5 17 U.S.C. Chapter 5: "Copyright Infringement and Remedies"

This chapter is where the rubber meets the road—that point where copyright's meaning becomes real, where there's weeping and gnashing of teeth, and where the lawyers earn their keep. While it's true that actual federal cases against archives and archivists are exceedingly rare, that may only be because archivists have been very cautious, maybe even overly cautious. It also helps that the monetary stakes may be so low for the largely out-of-commerce works found in US archives that it's not worth it for potential plaintiffs to pursue a federal suit. However, this does not mean that you shouldn't take seriously the consequences that 17 U.S.C. Chapter 5 outlines. Further, knowledge of the types of penalties as well as the potential loopholes is important to your overall risk management practices. These elements should be treated as constants along with the variables that are fundamental to how you do risk calculations.

As § 501 makes clear, violating a copyright owner's exclusive rights makes one an infringer and thus creates cause for federal civil or possibly criminal action.[19] If you violate the law, §§ 503 and 504 further identify the remedies available if just cause for infringement is sustained by the courts. So, it's important to understand the penalties you may face if your use is found to be an infringement. At the same time, important for archivists is the fact that § 501(b) requires that for a copyright holder to institute an action they must first comply with the registration and deposit requirements in § 411(a). That process can buy some time when the material in question is a "United States work" and is unlikely to have been exploited previously by the authors for commercial purposes. Regardless of whether you are called to account, infringement is a violation of federal law and not to be dismissed.

Remedies available to the copyright holder are outlined in §§ 502, 503, and 504. They include temporary and final injunctions to prevent or restrain infringement until the case is settled. These remedies can take the form of a court injunction to stop the sale of infringing items or to turn off a website while action is pending on an infringement claim. The court may also impound the offending copies as well as records related to the sale or distribution of the infringed works. Once a final judgment of infringement is declared, the court can also order the destruction of all copies and masters by which the infringing copies have been made (§ 503(b)). In other words, pretty strong stuff!

Not surprisingly, the remedies for infringement that receive the greatest media attention are those that deal with monetary damages and lost profits. These remedies/penalties are of two basic types. First, "Actual damages and profits" (§ 504(b)) include both the revenue the copyright holder lost because the infringer had undermined their market and any profits the infringer may have made on the illegal activity. Alternatively, there are "Statutory damages" § 504(c). If it is complicated to establish the dollar amounts of the actual lost revenue and the improperly gained profits, the court may instead award an amount to avoid going through those calculations. The copyright law states that if the copyright holder requests statutory damages, the court may award not less than $750 and not more than $30,000 for all infringements of any one work (§ 504(c)(1)). If the copyright holder can prove that the infringement was willful, the statutory damages can increase to not more than $150,000. By contrast, if the infringer can convince the court they had no idea their acts constituted infringement, the statutory damages can be reduced to not less than $200 (§ 504(c)(2)).

Lest any readers look for refuge in the $200 cap on damages for innocent infringement, the fact that you have read this far in the book and paid attention to its emphasis on the centrality of the exclusive rights in § 106 could make it difficult to have a credible defense that you did not know you were infringing. I suspect an energetic counsel for the plaintiff would argue that you had indeed lost your innocence. Nevertheless, this same subsection (§ 504(c)(2)) contains one very important safety valve for conscientious archivists. That passage is:

> *The court shall remit statutory damages in any case where an infringer believed and had reasonable grounds for believing that his or her use of the copyrighted work was a fair use under section 107, if the infringer was: (i) an*

> *employee or agent of a nonprofit educational institution, library, or archives acting within the scope of his or her employment who, or such institution, library, or archives itself, which infringed by reproducing the work in copies or phonorecords. . . .*

The possibility that a court might remit (i.e., refrain) from imposing statutory damages can significantly reduce the incentive for a copyright holder to resort to a suit, since their remedies would be limited to injunction, impoundment, and calculated actual damages. Where archives are working with material that has largely been out-of-commerce and where the purposes for copying are more educational than commercial, this provision could be a safety valve, but it requires that the archives employee has some basis to believe that use might qualify as a fair use. This provision has not been tested in court, but it stands to reason that you might be asked to demonstrate on what basis you believed it to be a fair use. Thus, it is essential that you document your decision making when managing projects, for example via the Columbia University Library's Copyright Advisory Office's "Fair Use Checklist" found in Appendix 1 and at https://copyright.columbia.edu/content/dam/copyright/Precedent%20Docs/fairusechecklist.pdf, showing how you weighed all four factors leaning for and against the use being fair. Note also that for nonprofit educational institutions, libraries, and archives, the language of the statute seems to limit this safety valve to the first of the exclusive rights, i.e., reproduction of a work in copies or phonorecords, whereas a parallel provision, also in § 504(c)(2) relating to public broadcasting entities, provides this safe harbor only in regard to the exclusive rights of performance and reproduction via transmission of a program. Without any case law on the provision, it is not clear how likely it would be for the abatement of damages to apply to the violation of the exclusive rights of distribution or derivative works.

A further bad news/good news condition arises out of § 505, which provides that the court may award costs and attorney fees to the "prevailing party" regardless of whether that party is the plaintiff or the defendant. In other words, if you are not the prevailing party, you or your institution can be on the hook for a significant amount of money. However, if careful risk management has left you with a fair use defense that is strong enough to convince the court that you had a reasonable basis to believe you were compliant with § 107, there's reason to think that you or your institution would be able to have your legal fees covered. Legal fees can be substantial enough that the prospect of securing them can figure into the incentive of pursuing the case. In fact, Paul Goldstein's treatise notes: "The prospect of paying the defendant's attorney's fees should also deter copyright owners from seeking, through litigation, to extend their rights beyond their proper bounds."[20] This makes clear that if a user's analysis gives them reasonable grounds to believe they have fair use, the prospect of being awarded attorney's fees could figure into their risk-management assessment. (See Box 4.11 on fees awarded in the case of a successful fair use of Barbie dolls in art photographs.)

If the thought of possible monetary damages assessed against you in a civil infringement case is not intimidating enough to make you thoughtful and deliberative about using a work without the copyright holder's permission, then § 506's review of when criminal offenses apply should do the trick. Indeed, the very term "criminal" should be daunting enough. For a review of what § 506 (a, c, d, e) cite as the basis for criminal liability, see Box 4.12 on what makes a criminal offense. It's hard to imagine that you would get into this kind of trouble if you use a combination of common sense and adherence to basic professional archival practice. Otherwise, please peruse § 506 to see what exactly constitutes the basis for federal criminal prosecution.

Meanwhile, § 507 outlines the statute of limitations for when civil or criminal action must be initiated. For archives projects that put entire collections or record series online you might take into account that a copyright holder

Box 4.11 Defendant Awarded Legal Fees

Mattel Inc. sued artist/photographer Tom Forsythe for his use of Barbie dolls in photographs showing the doll in provocative poses, often with kitchen appliances, to make a statement about consumerism and objectification of women. After the court had found that his work was a transformative fair use, it ordered Mattel to pay Forsythe more than $1.8 million in legal fees and court costs (*Mattel Inc. v. Walking Mountain Productions*, 353 F.3d 792 (9th Cir. 2003)). "Judge Says Artist Can Make Fun of Barbie," *New York Times*, June 28, 2004.**

** See also "Significance: Mattel, Inc. V. Walking Mountain Productions," Artist Rights, accessed May 26, 2025, https://www.artistrights.info/mattel-inc-v-walking-mountain-productions.

Box 4.12 How to Be a Copyright Criminal

Committing an actual criminal offense in copyright would seem to require unprofessional behaviors that are avoidable with reasonable care.

Criminal offences might arise for willful infringement for:

- commercial advantage or personal gain; or
- electronic reproduction or distribution within a 180-day period with a total retail value of more than $1,000; or
- distribution via computer networks of work that is being prepared for commercial distribution; or
- inserting false information into a copyright notice; or
- distributing or importing works with copyright notices known to be false; or
- removing, with fraudulent intent, a copyright notice from a work; or
- making a false representation in an application for copyright registration.

has only three years to bring a suit. As the section states, any *civil* action must be "commenced within three years after the claim accrued" (§ 507(b)). Meanwhile, *criminal* proceedings must be "commenced within 5 years after the cause of action arose" (§ 507(a)). With regard to civil action, the language would seem to suggest that someone wishing to sue your archives for having posted their mother's otherwise unpublished memoirs would need to do so within three years of when you placed the item online.

Unfortunately, case law has been inconsistent as to whether the statute of limitations clock starts ticking when the infringing act occurred (e.g., when it was put online) or when the copyright holder discovered or could have reasonably discovered the infringement. If the former, your legal exposure for online content would be only for the three most recent years of online postings. If the latter, your exposure could extend for many years before an aggrieved party discovers the posting.

A 2024 US Supreme Court case of *Warner Chappell Music, Inc. v. Nealy* tangentially touched on this issue in relation to the date for calculating damages, but it stood clear of resolving the question of whether the rule of the date of infringement or the rule of the date of discovery should apply.[21] The question for the high court's specific consideration was whether the three-year limit also meant that the monetary damages were to be based only on the three most recent years or to extend as far back as when the infringement first happened. Instead of answering that question, the majority opinion stated that, since the lower courts had accepted the case on the basis of the discovery rule, then the award of damages had to follow the discovery rule time scale. My impression is that this case was not a good one for clarification of what the law has left ambiguous about when the statute of limitations starts. Until another case or amendments to the law clarify whether the infringement rule or the discovery rule should prevail, the more conservative approach would be for archivists to assume that their liability would start from when the plaintiff discovers or could reasonably discover the infringement. This 2024 case underscores that the infringer will face a greater monetary liability if the discovery rule is applied. Thus, it would be wise to assume that your archives will remain exposed to suits for far more than just the first three years after a work has been copied or distributed/published online without the owner's permission unless you can make a solid case for one of the statutory exceptions in § 107 through 122.

Two further sections of 17 U.S.C. Chapter 5 (§ 511 and § 512) merit brief attention, but do not be lulled into thinking that they provide clear-cut additional safe harbors for your archives' digital projects. Those of you working in archives that are part of state agencies or state-operated research and educational entities may know that the US Constitution's 11th amendment provides sovereign immunity to states from being sued in federal court, such that a state or one of its institutions could be spared from court action imposing statutory damages. However, insofar as the text of the copyright law is concerned, § 511 explicitly denies this immunity. Some have questioned the constitutionality of this part of the law, and immunity has been sustained in a few cases. Still, there has been no high court ruling on immunity from action in federal court, and even if states and state institutions did have immunity, it seems unlikely that an employee would be able to sustain such a claim. Thus, the prudent archivist in a state agency or state instrumentality should pay less attention to the 11th amendment's broad statement and more attention to the specific language in § 511.

Finally, you should not read too much into the title of § 512—Limitations on Liability Relating to Material Online. Many institutions of which archives are a part of may meet the qualifications to register as Internet Service Providers (ISPs) with the Copyright Office.[22] Be aware that the immunity offered by § 512 is a narrow one. It does not provide immunity for everything an institution does via its technology network and websites. Instead, ISP immunity is more directed at the content posted or transmitted by individuals acting as individuals rather than as institutional actors, e.g., by their blogs or emails. Nevertheless, § 512 does provide an important side benefit to archives. If your parent institution has already registered with the Copyright Office as an ISP, then it will be able to benefit from § 512's notice and takedown provisions, meaning that you could be in a position to get an early notice that a copyright owner believes the content you have posted is infringing. You can then take immediate action to remove that from an online site, then investigate the situation. In reasonable circumstances you might even be able to reach an agreement that avoids a suit.

4.12 17 U.S.C. Chapter 12: "Copyright Protection and Management Systems"

A purist reading 17 U.S.C. Chapter 12 might logically conclude that, technically, this is not copyright per se. Instead, 17 U.S.C. Chapter 12 uses the power of Congress to effectively electrify a razor wire fence built around digital means to store and deliver copyright works. This chapter is the result of how the United States used the 1998 Digital Millenium Copyright Act (DMCA) to implement the WIPO Copyright Treaty (WCT), and the WIPO Performances and Phonograms Treaty (WPPT), both of 1996.

The idea behind the WCT and WPPT, and thus the DMCA, was that copyright needed to be updated for the digital age. The emergence in the early 1990s of graphical browsers and the World Wide Web made possible new ways of communicating and using books, magazines, images, and, especially, music and video media. Unfortunately, in the view of those industries, digital technology's ability to copy and disseminate these media also made them vulnerable to unauthorized copying and distribution which could undermine the economics of entire industries. Digital technology, of course, also could be used to create technological protection measures (TPMs) to prevent copying. Conversely, in the 1990s' brave new world of expanding technology and communications, astute members of the public were able to hack and circumvent those TPMs, thus creating a global challenge for major industries.

The evolution from the concerns of industry and civil society in the early 1990s about problematic aspects of the new technologies led to the 1998 adoption of the DMCA—a story that underscores deeper problems about how US law is created. For the purposes of this book, however, we need focus solely on what the result—17 U.S.C. Chapter 12—mandates. It merits noting, however, that the United States sought to implement the 1996 international treaties more aggressively than other WIPO Member States.[23]

The basic effect of the DMCA, as incorporated in 17 U.S.C. Chapter 12 and referenced in some other sections of the copyright statute, was *not* to create a new format, literary genre, or art form that could join the others in § 102's list of the scope of copyright. Instead, it aimed at providing legal enforcement for locks on the means by which people can access copyright works and other information in digital systems. This fundamental idea is captured in the opening sentence of § 1201(a) which states: "No person shall circumvent a technological measure that effectively controls access to a work protected under this title [i.e., Title 17-the copyright law]." § 1201(a) also prohibits the manufacture, importation, providing to the public, or trafficking in technology, products, services, or devices for circumventing TPMs.

The law does offer a few exceptions that sound like kindred spirits of those we saw in § 107 through 122 but which are so circumscribed by the dense, industry-drafted language that, once deconstructed, range from the useless to the silly. For example, § 1201(d) provides libraries, archives, or educational institutions an exception to gain access to technologically protected copyrighted works, but *only* to determine whether to acquire a copy of that work. This makes no sense. Why would an archives or library go through the technically difficult process of hacking a TPM in order to purchase the work? If copyright were part of a logical world, any vendor wanting to sell the work would be prepared to offer access on a trial/preview basis for a limited-time evaluation period. No vendor of course would welcome prospective customers trying to hack their access control system. Thus, § 1201(d)'s library and archives exception is mere window dressing.

What's worse is that the law provides no legal avenue for anyone to access public domain works or non-copyrightable material locked behind TPMs in a digital format. Similarly, the public cannot exercise § 107's fair use of still-in-copyright works held in such computer-mediated systems. For archivists needing to appraise, accession, process, and preserve born-digital content, 17 U.S.C. Chapter 12 provides no clear legal path.

Section 1202's excessively long (over 1,000 words) text serves as a digital parallel to what we saw in § 506(c) and § 506(d), which prohibited making false copyright claims or fraudulently removing a copyright notice. Here, reflecting the progressive complication of copyright law, it invents one further technical phrase, "copyright management information." This is supposed to describe the not unreasonable need for some additional ownership identification elements within 17 U.S.C. Chapter 12-technologically protected copyrighted works.

Civil remedies are provided in § 1203 for circumventing a TPM as well as importing or trafficking in any device or software that could circumvent a TPM. Similar to the penalties and remedies in 17 U.S.C. Chapter 5 for conventional infringement, § 1203 covers violations relating to access control measures. "Any person injured by a violation" of what § 1201 and § 1202 seek to protect may bring a legal action and receive either actual or statutory damages. As in 17 U.S.C. Chapter 5, the calculation of actual damages can be complicated, and that is even more the case with materials in the digital environment. Thus, statutory damages, rather than actual damages, would likely be the preferred route for any successful plaintiff.

However, the amounts involved with 17 U.S.C. Chapter 12 violations would be significantly higher and could mount quickly, given how readily digital content can be copied and distributed.

> *§ 1203(c)(3)(A) provides "damages for each violation of section 1201 in the sum of not less than $200 or more than $2,500 per act of circumvention, device, product, component, offer, or performance of service . . ."*
>
> and
>
> *§ 1203(c)(3)(B) states: ". . . a complaining party may elect to recover an award of statutory damages for each violation of section 1202 in the sum of not less than $2,500 or more than $25,000."*

Criminal penalties also are significantly higher; § 1204 states that for violation of either § 1201 or § 1202, willful violation for commercial purposes will result in a fine of not more than $500,000 or imprisonment for not more than 5 years, or both. That's for the first offense. A subsequent offence results in the doubling of those numbers. For criminal proceedings, § 1204(c) states a statute of limitations of 5 years "after the cause of action arose."[24] The only good news is found in § 1204(b) which states that these criminal penalties do not apply to any nonprofit library, archives, educational institution, or public broadcasting entity.

4.14 17 U.S.C. Chapter 14: "Unauthorized Use of Pre-1972 Sound Recordings"

The 2018 Music Modernization Act (MMA) finally addressed the century-old problem that bedeviled twentieth-century judges and legislators—the conundrum of sound recordings. For the longest time, they could not imagine that a creative work might take a form that would not be visible in a way similar to words on a page or images on film. It wasn't until late 1971 that the 1909 law was finally amended to include sound recordings in the scope of copyright law, but only for sound-recordings made after February 14, 1972. That left pre-1972 recordings out of the scope of copyright, a status that was left unchanged during the major revision of the law in 1976. There was one point at which the 1976 law touched on these older sound recordings—it deferred any federal preemption of the state and common law protections for these recordings until 2047. That period was later extended to February 15, 2067, at which point they will be covered by neither state law nor federal law. In other words, they will finally be in the public domain.

This has meant that the federal law could neither provide protection against unauthorized copying and distribution nor require exceptions and limitations for fair use, library and archives preservation, first sale lending, or educational performances. Instead, rights holders or persons wanting to protect their ownership rights or make fair uses had to navigate the variety of state laws to enforce their rights and take their chances that courts would follow common law principles of equity to address what otherwise would have been allowed under federal fair use provisions.

Calls, including from the Copyright Office itself, for solving this problem went unanswered until the 2018 MMA. The Act fell short of actually moving pre-1972 recordings fully under federal copyright, but it created a parallel system whereby the courts and the Copyright Office could supply rules and remedies for infringements. Importantly, it also provided clarity that the exceptions and limitations within the existing copyright act would be available for users, including libraries, archives, and educational institutions.

Although 17 U.S.C. Chapter 14 consists of only one section, it does include enough of the tiered clauses and multiple internal contingencies to require careful reading. Still, it brings good news to archivists, especially in relation to unpublished recordings and published commercial and non-commercial recordings from this earlier period. First, § 1401(a) establishes a term of 95 years for all pre-1972 published recordings, except that:

- All pre-1923 published recordings were to enter the public domain after a transition period to end 3 years after the enactment of § 1401, i.e., January 1, 2022;
- Recordings published 1923 through 1946 were given a term of 95 years plus a further 5-year transition period;
- Recordings published 1947 through 1956 were given a term of 95 years plus a 15-year transition period; and
- All remaining recordings fixed prior to February 15, 1972, whether published or not, are to remain under control of the provisions of § 1401 until February 15, 2067, when they would be free of US copyright. In other words, they would then be in the US public domain.

If one does the math, it might at first seem that the MMA failed to provide much of a benefit to archives and their users. However, three further provisions of the MMA provided significant relief.

First, § 1401(c) creates a process for anyone to make non-commercial uses of any sound recording fixed before February 15, 1972, if it is not being commercially exploited by the rights owner. This allowance is subject to three manageable conditions:

- the user must make a good faith, reasonable search to determine if the recording is not being sold or streamed;
- the user must file a Notice of Non-Commercial Use (NNU) with the Copyright Office; and
- the rights holder does not file an "opt out" notice within 90 days of when the Copyright Office has "indexed" the NNU.

Second, § 1401(f)(1) explicitly indicates that the exceptions and limitations found in § 107, § 108, § 109, § 110, and § 112(f) apply for any sound recordings fixed (i.e., whether published or unpublished) before February 15, 1972. Of course, all of the threshold conditions of those exceptions would apply just as they would for any conventional print, manuscript, or graphical or pictorial work, but this is an enormous step forward for archivists because it means we no longer have the ambiguity created by the variety of state laws, which has been a barrier to moving forward with mission-centric work related to older sound recordings.

Third, § 1401(f)(A) and (C) resolved a gap that continued to exist when Congress neglected in 1976 to bring the older sound recordings fully within the copyright law. As noted above when discussing copyright notice and registration, § 411 and § 412 provide a partial safe harbor for archival projects because they require copyright registration before litigation can begin and before attorney fees and statutory damages can be awarded. However, § 1401(h)(1)(B) states that the § 411 registration requirement does not apply for taking legal action related to pre-1972 sound recordings. To fill this gap, the MMA created a system parallel to registration. It added § 1401(f)(5)(A)(I), which mandates for the initiation of an action for infringement, the rights holder must have submitted to the Copyright Office "schedules" that specify the title, artist, and other information as practicable about the sound recording whose rights they own. This creates not just a step that a potential plaintiff needs to complete before litigation starts but also has resulted in an eminently useful database of information that anyone wishing to make a use of a published recording can search to determine if a rights holder exists. If such a search yields no information about a rights holder, the user should be relieved of most worries about being sued for statutory damages and attorney fees.

Overall, the MMA's response to the longstanding problem of pre-1972 sound recordings may be less than ideal, but for archives it is the most valuable legislative change since the 1992 Fair Use of Unpublished Works Act.

4.15 17 U.S.C. Chapter 15: "Copyright Small Claims," OR " . . . and You Thought All You Had to Worry About Was Being Taken to Federal Court!"

If your institution has already preemptively "opted out" of the copyright small claims process, then you may not need to read further. To find out if your institution has opted out, check the "Library and Archive Opt Out List."[25] If they are not listed as having opted out, soldier on because even though the best risk management practices may reduce the incentives for someone to take you to court, the 2020 Copyright Alternative in Small Claims (CASE) Act provides claimants a means to secure restraining action and monetary awards without needing an attorney and without going to federal court.

Managed by the Copyright Office, the Copyright Claims Board (CCB) serves as a non-judicial tribunal that can award successful claimants up to $30,000. The CASE act and the CCB are intended to make redress of infringement more accessible for those who are not just large publishing or media corporations. CASE's small claims option effectively raises the risk for archivists when treading on the exclusive rights of the low- to non-profile authors that predominate in so many of our collections. Fortunately, the act includes procedures not just for opting-out, but also for the steps a claimant must follow. The overall effect of these can reduce the challenge this section might seem to pose on first glance.

Compared to the dense and contorted language Congress uses at the least provocation, 17 U.S.C. Chapter 15 is relatively approachable. Its guiding principle is to make obtaining effective action on claims more accessible and equitable for individuals, small businesses, and organizations. It does this by creating a process separate from the court system. The following bulleted list provides highlights of the law with section, subsection, and paragraph rubrics so you can check the full text in the law.

§ 1501: "Definitions"

- The process uses alternative terminology. Rather than "plaintiffs," "defendants," and "judgments," it refers to "claimants," "respondents," and "determinations."

§ 1502: "Copyright Claims Board"

- The CCB, a component of the Copyright Office, is comprised of three full-time Copyright Claims Officers nominated by the Copyright Office and approved by the Librarian of Congress.

§ 1503: "Authority and duties of the Copyright Claims Board"

- CCB is empowered to render determinations on civil copyright claims, counterclaims, and defenses.
- CCB can award monetary relief and require that activities be ceased or mitigated (§ 1503(a)).

- Determinations are to be based on records submitted and in accord with © law, judicial precedent, and applicable regulations, but not precedents from prior CCB cases (§ 1503(b)(1)).

§ 1504: "Participation is voluntary, and the claimant may instead pursue action in federal court"

- The statute of limitations is the same as with court cases—3 years from "when the claim accrued."
- Types of claims and counter claims on which the CCB can act:

(1) claim for infringement

(2) claim for a declaration of non-infringement of an exclusive right

(3) claim for misrepresentation in a notification of claimed infringement as referenced in § 512(f).

- Excluded: claims pending in or decided by a competent court; claims against Federal or State agencies; claims against a person or entity outside the United States.
- Permissible remedies
- Actual or statutory damages and profits up to $30,000 (with conditions),
- Agreement to cease certain activity (§ 1504(e)(1)(i)).
- Awards to cover attorney's fees arise only in the case of bad faith.

§ 1505 "Registration requirement"

- Initiating a claim or counterclaim requires either registration or a completed application for registration, a deposit of the work, and the required fee.
- Registration must be completed before claim can be determined or monetary award made.

§ 1506: "Conduct of Proceedings"

- CCB follows judicial precedent when deciding claims.
- Either party may be represented by an attorney or qualified law student.
- Respondent has 60 days to opt out of CCB (§ 1506(i)).
- If respondent does not opt out, they lose opportunity to go to federal court.
- CCB's determination is based on preponderance of evidence (§ 1506(s)).
- Either party may request reconsideration of the determination (§ 1506(w)).
- CCB has a streamlined process for smaller (up to $5,000) claims (§ 1506(z)).[26]

§ 1507(a) Once the CCB has made a determination, it may not be relitigated by the CCB or a court, with minor exceptions.

§ 1508 If a party to a determination has failed to pay damages or otherwise comply, the other party can take the matter to a federal district court.

Because the small claims option was enacted only recently, and this forum was not launched until June 2022, it may be too early to understand much about its effectiveness or what challenges it could pose for archivists (there have been barely three dozen "determinations" by the CCB as of this writing). Based on the guiding principle of the copyright small claims process that participation should be voluntary, archivists should take seriously the law's authorization of pre-emptively opting out. Deep within § 1506 is the relevant provision specifically directed at archives and libraries that allows them to preemptively opt out of the CCB's claims process (§ 1506(aa) (1) and (2)). Procedures for doing so can be found in the Federal Register.[27] In theory, an institution could decide that it would prefer to opt out on a case-by-case basis (§ 1506(I)), and that requires adhering to opt-out regulations within 60 days.[28] It would also mean taking a chance that claimant would decline to take the more cumbersome but potentially more lucratively rewarding route of a federal court ruling. Doing so, however, would require prompt action in case someone initiates a CCB claim. Regardless, if your institution has not opted out preemptively, it should decide quickly when it learns of a CCB complaint.

5 Understanding Fair Use
Four Factors and Relevant Cases

5.1 How Do We Know What's Fair: A Deep Dive into Fair Use

As least as far back as 1841, there were court cases ruling that there may be times when it could be acceptable to make an unauthorized use of a copyrighted work for certain purposes. This common-law recognition of the possibility of fair use was made a federally recognized right in the mid-1970s revision of the copyright law.

Case law and the new statutory fair use were based on the principle that the author's property rights should not hinder creative endeavors of society. Fair use is thus an important way in which copyright mediates between private ownership and public interest. As Justice Souter has noted: "From the infancy of copyright protection, some opportunity for fair use of copyrighted materials has been thought necessary to fulfill copyright's very purpose 'to promote the Progress of Science and the Useful Arts.'" Souter went on to cite Justice Story's comments in the 1841 case: "in truth, in literature, in science and in art, there are, and can be, few, if any things, which in an abstract sense, are strictly new and original throughout. Every book in literature, science and art, borrows, and must necessarily borrow, and use much that was well known and used before."[1] Those principles seem reasonable enough, but the very nature of fair use means that its actual practice may seem to vary. No wonder that fair use has occupied more of the legal literature than just about any other aspect of US copyright.[2]

5.2 The Four Factors

The statutory fair use provisions are essential to archivists. However, because actual decisions are "a matter of equity" for which "no generally applicable definition is possible," decisions must be made through case-by-case analyses to determine whether your intended use might be judged as fair.[3] In the important 1994 case of *Campbell v. Acuff-Rose Music* (also known as the 2 Live Crew or "Pretty Woman" case), the Supreme Court stated the fair use doctrine "permits and requires the courts to avoid rigid application of the copyright statute when, on occasion, such application would stifle the very creativity which that law is designed to foster" (*Campbell v. Acuff-Rose Music*, 510 U.S. at 577).

Regardless of whether fair use is considered a right or merely a defense against claims of infringement, it is indisputable that fair use is a copyright "exception" (see Box 4.7 for the full text of § 107). It is unlike §108's "bright line" exceptions for library and archives because of the all-important last sentence of § 107's preamble paragraph that states: "In determining whether the use made of a work in any particular case is a fair use the factors to be considered shall include. . . ."

To decide if your particular case really is a fair use, the courts must investigate the facts of the work and of your use and weigh those facts against the four factors. Unfortunately, some of the court case rulings, made in the first 15 years after fair use became statutory, over-emphasized some factors more than others. The 1994 *Campbell v. Acuff-Rose Music* case, however, returned balance to the system. Its approach has been a touchstone for how later courts have interpreted the meaning of each of the four factors even if some commentators have warned against over-focus on "blockbuster" cases.[4]

Importantly, *Campbell* stated that the four factors may not be "treated in isolation, one from another. All are to be explored, and the results weighed together, in light of the purpose of copyright."[5] Thus, no single factor can serve as an automatic "in" or an automatic "out" to fair use. Further, the four must not be treated in isolation. Instead, they must be considered holistically so that any given factor (e.g., amount used) can be considered in how it interacts with other factors (e.g., the greater the amount used or the greater the effect will be on the market).

To guide you in your own understanding of whether something you might do as an archivist could fit with existing fair use cases, the following is a review of each of the four factors, with references to how actual cases explored the meaning of what § 107 lists as the four factors. Following that, you will find a table with a "high-level" summary of fair use cases related to unpublished materials. There is also a table outlining the extent that the "transformativeness" of use has weighed enough to qualify for the first factor to be considered "fair."

5.2.1 *First Factor: Character and Purpose of Use*

The preamble of § 107 specifically mentions categories of use that would be deemed "fair"—criticism, comment, news reporting, teaching, scholarship, or research. However, to understand how the courts assess the fairness of a given use for one of these activities, the first factor is subdivided into two components:

5.2.1.1 Character

Does the new work merely supersede the original work or instead does it add something new with a further purpose or different character, thus altering the original with new expression, meaning, or message? That is, to what extent is the new use *transformative*? Does the use add new material, new aesthetics, and new understanding? Transformative use is not absolutely necessary for a finding of fair use, but it is close to the constitutionally stated purpose of copyright, to encourage the creation of new works.

Over the past quarter century, "transformativeness" has been hailed as a foundation for considerable use of works for educational and cultural heritage purposes. Nevertheless, it may not be quite the magic bullet imagined by some proponents in the popular press and professional literature. One of the most influential legal commentators has noted that, during the last decade, there had been a blurring of lines between doing something "transformative" and doing something that effectively creates a derivative work—that is, something that by the terms of §106 is the exclusive right of the copyright holder.[6] In 2023, the US Supreme Court touched on, but did not resolve, the point in the case of *Andy Warhol Foundation for the Visual Arts, Inc. v. Goldsmith*, 598 U.S. 508 (2023). The Court's decision emphasized that the amount of difference of the new use from the original creator's use was central to justifying the new or secondary use. In particular, the purpose of new use needs to be distinct from the original, for example by commenting on or criticizing the original. (See below for the important role commerciality played in this decision.)

5.2.1.2 Purpose

Non-commercial use of a work is more likely to be accepted as fair, but cases have recognized the possibility of a mix of commercial and scholarly interest. The mere prospect of commercial benefit to the user cannot itself preclude a finding of fair use.[7] Rather, it is more a matter of whether the use is exploitative, i.e., the unauthorized secondary use results in something that could function as a "market substitute" for the original.

Market substitution was central to the 2023 *Warhol Foundation* decision. Its center was the interaction of the *character* and *purpose* aspects of the first fair-use factor. The court found that the transformativeness of the Warhol Foundation's secondary use was insufficient to overcome the commercial nature of the purpose of the use, and thus the first fair-use factor weighed against a fair use. That was because the court focused their decision on the fact that the Warhol Foundation's use competed in the same marketplace as Goldsmith's original work. At the same time, the court's majority declined to base its decision on whether Andy Warhol's original 1984 artistic silkscreen modification of Goldsmith's professional photograph of the musician Prince had been a transformative fair use. Unfortunately, taking that route left all of us with insufficient clarification regarding the relation of such uses to an author's exclusive right to make derivative works.[8]

The commercial nature of an unauthorized use arose earlier in the 1985 decision in the case of former President Gerald Ford's memoir. There, the first factor analysis touched on how *The Nation* magazine's scoop in publishing key parts of the book ended up supplanting what the court noted as the copyright holder's commercially valuable right of first publication.[9]

5.2.2 *Second Factor: Nature of the Work*

The first part of the analysis for this factor recognizes that it is the expressive or the creative nature of a work that is most central to the purpose of copyright. Thus, uses of heavily factual works, or uses of fictional or other creative works but focused only on the factual elements within those works, are more likely to be found fair use under the second factor.

Meanwhile, the other half of a second factor analysis relates to whether the original work being considered is published or unpublished. The factor is likely of great concern to archivists because if the work used is an unpublished one, it is less open to fair use. In the Gerald Ford memoir case, the Supreme Court drew on the tradition of common law when it stated, "The law generally recognizes a greater need to disseminate factual works than works of fiction or fantasy." Also stating "the scope of fair use is narrower with respect to unpublished works."[10]

Unfortunately, this statement regarding unpublished works was seized upon in a 1987 Second Circuit appeals court decision that ruled against a biographer who wanted to use selected quotes and paraphrases from unpublished letters of author J. D. Salinger. The Second Circuit Court argued that the unpublished nature of the works also tilted against fair use when it came to review the third factor (amount) and fourth factor (effect on the market). The Second Circuit went even further in a later decision relating to the use of unpublished works in a biography of Scientology founder L. Ron Hubbard. In this case the court explained its finding in *Salinger* as based on the theory that the Ford memoir case had conveyed the idea that unpublished works normally enjoy complete protection against copying, and it was "bound to follow that rule absent an en banc review" in relation to the Hubbard biography.[11] A few years later, the Second Circuit backed away from this hard line in a parallel case involving unpublished works being used in a biography of author Richard Wright. Here it stated, "Neither Salinger, Harper & Row, nor any other case, however, erected a per se rule regarding unpublished works."[12]

Fortunately, Congress rendered the Second Circuit's musings moot in 1992 when it passed an amendment in response to concerns about that court's interpretations. To § 107, Congress added: "The fact that a work is unpublished shall not itself bar a finding of fair use if such finding is made upon consideration of all the above factors." Nevertheless, since the time of that amendment, it is relatively common for later courts reviewing fair use claims to make passing references to the fact that the unpublished nature of a work may weigh against a fair use. Indeed, both the amendment to § 107 and the *Wright* statement about there being no per se bar have been referenced in subsequent cases where the subject matter included works considered to be unpublished.[13]

5.2.3 *Third Factor: Amount and Substantiality*

As with the first three fair use factors, the third should also be understood as having two components—quality and quantity.

5.2.3.1 Quality

The substantiality or quality of the copying relates to whether what is being copied and used might be considered as the "heart of the work." That would weigh against a finding of fair use. In the presidential memoir case, for instance, what Ford had to say about his rationale for pardoning Richard Nixon was clearly at the heart of the value of his memoir, both on its own terms and in terms of the discontinuation of its serialization in *Time* magazine, a $12,500 opportunity that was withdrawn from Ford once *The Nation* "scooped" the story.

However, as with the other factors, substantiality does not serve as an absolute bar on a fair use. In one of the few cases actually involving archival manuscripts—those of author Marjorie Kinnan Rawlings—the court stated, "If all quoted material were deemed significant enough to preclude a fair use just because it was significant enough to be quoted, no one could ever quote copyrighted material without fear of being sued for infringement."[14]

5.2.3.2 Quantity

Although there are no fixed amounts that define what is fair and what is not, copying an entire work would weigh against a finding of fair use, but it does not preclude a finding of fair use depending on other facts relating to the purpose and character of the use.[15] In connection with the other factors, the quantity of permissible copying will vary with the purpose and character of the use (that is, the amount used should be proportional to what is needed to fulfill the character and purpose of the new use). However, the more material copied, the less that transformativeness may be seen as a justification for fair use.[16] In the case of archival materials, such as individual letters, photographs, or video recordings, the quantity factor could weigh against many uses, but the context or purpose of the use could mitigate the negative weight. For example, being able to place online the complete image of a letter of resignation penned by an institution's president may be essential to demonstrating the fast-moving events surrounding why they were being forced out.

5.2.4 *Fourth Factor: Effect on the Market*

Since American jurisprudence on copyright has so often centered on the commercial basis of the creation, distribution, and adaptation of creative works, it should not be surprising that market issues figure significantly among the fair use factors. In fact, as early as the Supreme Court's rulings in *Sony v. Universal Studios* (1984) and *Harper & Row v. Nation* (1985), their decisions as well as those of lower courts have often referred to the fourth factor as most important. Fortunately, lest any single factor seemed to preempt the others, in 1994 the Supreme Court tempered its comments on market effect and emphasized that all four factors have to be weighed together to make a fair use determination. The court said the four statutory factors should not "be treated in isolation, one from the other. All are to be explored, and the results weighed together, in light of the purposes of copyright."[17] Although some other decisions have been cautious about whether factor four should preempt the other three, market effects are referenced in how the other factors are weighed, often yielding sensible results.

Effect on the market can be subdivided into three components of market effect:

5.2.4.1 Impaired marketability

(e.g., neither Ford nor Harper & Row could market the memoir for serialization purposes).

5.2.4.2 Market substitute

(e.g., in *Basic Books, Inc. v. Kinko's Graphics Corp.*, the course packs that Kinkos produced could substitute for sales of the books copied).

5.2.4.3 Derivative markets

(e.g., a book with detailed retelling of the plots of episodes of the "Twin Peaks" television program negatively affected the market for derivative works from the program).[18]

However, in relation to the effect on the market for derivatives, the *Campbell v. Acuff-Rose Music* case makes clear that "there is no protectible derivative market for criticism," meaning that 2 Live Crew's parody of the song "Oh,

Pretty Woman" (owned by Acuff Rose Music) was considered to be critical commentary on the original song, so it did not infringe on the derivative market for the original song. That standard was later applied in a 2001 ruling in favor of Alice Randall, whose book *Wind Done Gone* was deemed a fair use because it was a critical recasting of Margaret Mitchell's *Gone With the Wind.*[19]

For a considerable amount of archival material, the fourth factor can also play an important role in risk management for digitization projects. If, after evaluation of the first three factors, the proposed use is tipping towards fair use, and the original is out of print or otherwise unavailable, or there is no ready market for permission, or the copyright owner is unidentifiable, then factor four would lean toward fair use. For manuscript letters from individuals other than those who may have worked as writers for publication, there may be little to no market for their works. Thus, a use's "effect on the market" may be marginal at best, meaning the fourth factor could tip a decision in the fair use direction.

5.3 What Archivists Can Learn from the Courts

After making it through the explanations of the fair use factors, to say nothing of having slogged through Chapter 4's summation of large parts of the copyright law, it all probably seems quite abstract. You're probably thinking, "When is this guy going to talk about what happens in real cases involving real archives and archives materials?" So, let's look at an actual case that, at first glance, may not seem relevant, but it really is.

Can copyright's fair use provision allow the use of the entirety of an unpublished tell-all autobiography? Surprisingly, yes! But how can that be when it involves at least two factors that would weigh against using it: the unpublished nature of the work and the copying of the entire work? Wouldn't those facts weigh heavily against fair use? Not in the case of a son's murder of his father and a later child custody dispute. Here's a summary of what happened in the case of *Bond v. Blum.*[20]

When William Slavin learned of the marriage of his ex-wife to a man who had changed his name to William Bond, Slavin began a custody battle over their three children. Thanks to the work of a private investigator hired by his ex-father-in-law, Kenneth Blum, Slavin was able to obtain Bond's unpublished autobiography. In the autobiography, Bond detailed how he had gotten away with murdering his own father two decades earlier. Slavin then had the unpublished work introduced as evidence for consideration in the custody hearing. The judge had it placed under "seal" as evidence, but that wasn't enough for Bond, who immediately registered his autobiography for copyright. Once it was registered, he sued Blum and Slavin for infringement for the few copies they had made of the complete unpublished work, and Bond asked for a temporary and permanent injunction against use of the work, including in the child custody case. The District Court examined the facts of the case and ruled that the copying and use of the work for the custody hearing constituted a fair use. Bond appealed to the Federal Circuit Court, which did its own four-factor analysis and ruled that the District Court had applied the four factors correctly and thus the use had been fair. Then Bond appealed to the US Supreme Court, but it declined to accept the case. That is, it "denied *certiorari*."

How could these courts rule fair use when what was involved was the use of the *entirety* of an *unpublished* work, two conditions that sometimes are described as clearly disqualifying for a fair use exception? It's because just one factor, or even more than one factor, by itself does not suffice to determine a fair use case. That's why this case provides an excellent lesson in how the fair use analysis requires an integrated or cross-factor weighing of the four factors.

For this case, let's start with the first factor—character and purpose of the use. The District and Circuit courts noted that the ex-husband's purpose for using the autobiography was not related to its creative expression, but to its role as evidence in the custody case. Further, when looking at the interrelationship of the four factors, both courts considered that the ex-husband's purpose was non-commercial and that his use of the entirety of this unpublished work was in support of a legal proceeding. Thus, it could have no adverse effect on the marketability of the manuscript.

Although the *Bond v. Blum* circumstances may seem more than a bit removed from your archives, the fact is that the work in question was unpublished, just as is the bulk of archival material. Also, the ex-husband's intent involved use of the entire work, which is what we archivists often wish to do. Two of the four factors in this case are much like what we would encounter with many uses of archival materials, making fair use a possibility once the relationship to the other two factors is explored. Thus, *Bond v. Blum* is not only evidence of truth being stranger than fiction, but also a good way to set the stage for this chapter's review of how fair use analyses have operated and to suggest the lessons archivists can draw from major fair use copyright cases.

So what are the guiding principles that courts actually apply to weigh the four factors when deciding on fair use claims? What follows are two charts showing archivally relevant threads that have appeared in fair use litigation since the 1980s—the first (Table 5.1) on the use of unpublished works when assessing the nature of the work, and the second (Table 5.2) on the weight given to transformativeness when assessing the character and purpose of the use.

5.4 Fair Use Case Grids

The fair use exception in § 107 is a principal tool for archivists wanting to take a risk management approach to maintain focus on our mission. The unpublished status of a disputed work has generally not been the decisive factor in fair use cases, but references to the unpublished nature of a work have arisen regularly and at one time were given heavy weight in a decision.

Two grids provide thumbnail descriptions of important fair use cases that may provide important lessons for archivists wanting to make sure they understand the squishiness (as well as the usefulness) of fair use when trying to build an overall risk management strategy. When reviewing either the grid for unpublished works (Table 5.1) or the grid for transformativeness issues (Table 5.2), some cautions are in order:

- The grid format is used because it enables easy, high-level comparison of the functional aspects of different cases in a way that might not be as easy to see in a succession of narratives for each case.
- The grids provide a summary of central elements of each case. As such, granular case details are missing that could be relevant to your specific needs. If you want more details, check out the more detailed summaries found in the Copyright Office's online Fair Use Index.[21] Before writing a policy or adopting a course of action based on what you see in these grids, start by reading the formal opinions/rulings issued by the court(s)—they can generally be found on one or more open access websites. Give those documents priority over news articles or Wikipedia case narratives, even though both of those can help you pick your way through some technical details of cases.

Table 5.1 Overview of Cases Where Unpublished Works Played a Role

Case and Year	Work	How Infringed	Result	Justification/Four Factors
Harper & Row Publishers, Inc., v. Nation Enterprise, 471 U.S. 539 (1985)	Unpublished presidential memoir	*The Nation* published story on Gerald Ford's pardon of Richard Nixon in 2,250-word article quoting some 300 words from Ford's manuscript. The newsworthiness of the quoted material undermined interest of publisher and the licensing of the book for serial publication in *Time* magazine.	On appeal, the Supreme Court ruled that use of unauthorized excerpts was not a fair use.	Factor 1: News reporting by itself not sufficient to justify a fair use. Factor 2: Unpublished nature in this case tended against fair use because use affected ability to profit from right of first publication. Factor 3: While quantity quoted was limited, it was clearly the "heart of the work." Factor 4: *The Nation*'s use directly competed with the market, resulting in loss of revenue to Harper & Row and Ford.
Salinger v. Random House Inc., 811 F.2d 90 (2d Cir. 1987)	Unpublished letters of noted author J. D. Salinger	For a work on the reclusive author, a biographer used several portions of Salinger's unpublished letters as found in three research libraries. Salinger sought injunction on publication.	District Court ruled that biographer's scholarly use of letters, including many paraphrases, was a fair use. On appeal, the Second Federal Circuit Court rejected claim of fair use.	Factor 2: Citing *Harper & Row*, appeals court said unpublished works had more limited scope of fair use. Factor 3: Amount used was excessive given the works quoted were unpublished. Factor 4: Court accepted Salinger's argument that paraphrases harmed his market because anything worth paraphrasing would have cited all of the passages that would have made his own publication of the letters worthwhile.

Table 5.1 continued

Case and Year	Work	How Infringed	Result	Justification/Four Factors
New Era Publications International v. Henry Holt & Co. 873 F.2d 576 (2d Cir. 1989)	Unpublished writings of Scientology founder L. Ron Hubbard	For a work on Hubbard, a biographer quoted extensively from Hubbard's published and unpublished works. New Era Publications sought injunction against publication of biography.	District Court denied injunction because lack of timeliness, and it held that the use of the unpublished works was not fair use. Circuit Court upheld that denial. However, it disagreed with District Court's rationale for its denial of fair use for the unpublished works.	Circuit Court: Factor 1: Purpose and character of biography's use weighed fair. Factor 2: Unpublished nature of works meant no fair use here. Factor 3: Extent of the use of unpublished works weighed against a fair use. Factor 4: Overall, the use had a negative effect on the market because New Era was planning an authorized biography.
Wright v. Warner Books Inc., 953 F.2D 731(2d Cir. 1991)	Unpublished writings of noted author Richard Wright.	Unauthorized biography of Wright used quotations and paraphrases of some of his unpublished writings.	District Court found biographer's use to be fair. On Appeal by Wright's widow, Circuit Court agreed that it was a fair use.	Circuit Court: Factor 1: Biographer's research added value to the original works. Factor 2: Unpublished nature not a per se rule when fair use examined as a whole. Factor 3: Amount and substantiality were minimal and appropriate to the use. Factor 4: Biographer's use did not supplant market for publication of letters.

Table 5.1 continued

Case and Year	Work	How Infringed	Result	Justification/Four Factors
Sundeman v. The Seajay Society, Inc., 142 F.3d (4th Cir. 1998)	Unpublished fictional work (*Blood of My Blood*) of noted author Marjorie Kinnan Rawlings.	Unauthorized complete copy made of work and provided to a Seajay Society officer and a scholar. Scholar wrote critical review of the book and presented it orally to the Marjorie Kinnan Rawlings Society, quoting 4 to 6 percent of the book.	District Court ruled distribution of copies and use of quoted material was fair use. On appeal, the Circuit Court agreed with fair use.	Circuit Court: Factor 1: Transformative scholarly work. Purpose of quotes and paraphrases was to comment and criticize, and copy was made to preserve fragile original. No commercial gain since scholar declined to publish without permissions. Factor 2: Unpublished nature does not bar fair use as per amended § 107. Scholar's purpose was not to usurp right of first publication. Factor 3: Fair because did not quote more than needed for her purpose. Factor 4: Fair because minimal effect on market or potential market.

Table 5.1 continued

Case and Year	Work	How Infringed	Result	Justification/Four Factors
Bond v. Blum *317 F.3D 385*, (4th Cir. 2003), *cert. denied* 540 U.S. 820	Unpublished tell-all autobiography	Unauthorized copying of Bond's autobiography telling how, at age 17, he "got away with murdering" his father in 1981. In 2001, William Slavin (ex-husband of Bond's wife) had a copy of the manuscript submitted as evidence in a child custody proceeding to challenge suitability of the Bond couple to have custody of the three children from wife's prior marriage.	District Court ruled the making of a copy and submitting it to the Baltimore court as evidence for the custody hearing was a fair use. On Bond's appeal, the Circuit Court agreed with the District Court that Slavin's use of the work was a valid fair use. On further appeal, US Supreme Court refused to take up the case.	Circuit Court: Factor 1: Slavin's use was narrow and related to the unpublished work's content. Factor 2: Bond's manuscript contained creative expression, but focus of Slavin's use was only on its "historical facts." Factor 3: Use of the manuscript in the custody proceeding involved all or nearly all of it, but the use was not for its expressive content but to obtain Bond's admission of facts showing his home would be unsuitable. Factor 4: Admitting the unpublished work into evidence would not adversely affect its marketability.

Table 5.1 continued

Case and Year	Work	How Infringed	Result	Justification/Four Factors
Society of the Holy Transfiguration Monastery, Inc. v. Gregory, 689 F.3d 29 (1st Cir. 2012)	Unpublished translations of ancient religious texts	Unauthorized web posting of English translations of ancient Greek manuscripts.	District court rejected arguments that the works had been in public domain, and it found that copying and distribution were not fair uses.	Circuit Court agreed: Factor 1: Copies were essentially verbatim and thus lacked transformativeness, and distribution was for same purpose as that of the author of the translations. Factor 4: Market for further translations would be harmed if this instance were deemed fair.
Monge v. Maya Magazines, Inc., 688 F.3d 1164 (9th Cir. 2012)	Unpublished photographs	Unauthorized publication by a gossip magazine of wedding photographs of celebrities.	District Court ruled fair use Circuit Court rejected fair use defense on all four factors.	Circuit Court Factor 1: Photos were newsworthy, but minor cropping and captioning did not make their use transformative. Use was clearly commercial. Factor 2: Unpublished photos were not highly artistic but more than just factual. Factor 3: "Heart of the work" was used. Factor 4: There was a market for photos such as these, and it was substantially harmed.

Table 5.1 continued

Case and Year	Work	How Infringed	Result	Justification/Four Factors
Diversey v. Schmidly, 738 F.3d 1196 (10th Cir. 2013)	Draft doctoral dissertation	Without authorization of author, two copies of an unpublished draft dissertation were made available to the public by deposit and cataloging in university library.	District Court ruled Diversey's claim was untimely because of passage of three-year statute of limitations in § 507(b) from when Diversey was informed the university had sent a copy to the library. On appeal, the Circuit Court ruled that Diversey's claim was timely because it was less than three years from when the work appeared in the library's catalog [i.e., the moment at which the university made it available to the public].	Circuit Court ruled not a fair use: Factor 1: Addition of a work to a library was a non-commercial educational use, and thus weighed toward fair use. Factor 2: Because work was unpublished, weighed against fair use. Factor 3: Entire work was used, weighing against fair use. Factor 4: Court accepted Diversey's argument that because the library continued listing the draft dissertation in its catalog, he could not succeed in a review and defense of his dissertation elsewhere. Thus, he had been deprived of the value of the dissertation, causing Factor 4 to weigh against a fair use.

Table 5.1 continued

Case and Year	Work	How Infringed	Result	Justification/Four Factors
TD Bank, N.A. v. Hill District Court, New Jersey (Civil No. 12-7188 (RBK/JS) 2016 and 928 F.3d 259 (2019)	Unpublished book	Defendant Hill co-authored an unpublished manuscript in 2007 on customer service while an employee of a bank. After separating from the bank, he published a book in 2012 with a similar title, using portions of the manuscript.	Hill's original employer was merged into TD Bank. When book was published, TD Bank claimed infringement of the original, arguing it had been a work-made-for-hire created while Hill was employed. Hill claimed that even if the manuscript were a work-made-for-hire, his published book was a fair use. District Court ruled that it was a work-made-for-hire. On appeal, the Third Circuit rejected claim of a work-made-for-hire, but stated TD owned work "by assignment." Agreed with District fair use analysis.	District Court: Not a fair use: Factor 2: Hill's verbatim copying of portions was more than just facts and ideas. Factor 3: Weighs both ways–the 2012 publication used only 16 percent of 2007 work, but excerpts played key role in telling the story. Factor 4: Hill's 2012 book provides some impairment to the market if TD Bank wishes to publish the 2007 work.

Table 5.1 continued

Case and Year	Work	How Infringed	Result	Justification/Four Factors
Corbello v. DeVito Nevada District Court Case, 2017 Ninth Circuit, 2020	Unpublished autobiography of Tommy DeVito, a founding member of "The Four Seasons."	Widow of DeVito's co-author claimed infringement for use of quotes and "incidents" from the unpublished work as basis for content in Broadway play *Jersey Boys*.	District Court found the use of the autobiography to be a fair use. On appeal, Ninth Circuit affirmed based on fact that *Jersey Boys* did not infringe on the DeVito autobiography because the play's elements claimed as infringing were no more than basic historical facts. Ninth Circuit did not revisit fair use question.	District Court's fair use finding: Factor 1: Weighed against fair use because a commercial use. Factor 2: Weighed for fair use. The work had remained unpublished because copyright owner had chosen not to make it available. Factor 3: Very little of the work was taken by the play, and what taken was factual. Factor 4: No effect on the market because before *Jersey Boys* opened the autobiography did not have a viable market.

Table 5.2 Overview of Cases Where "Transformativeness" Received Significant Attention

Case and Year	Work	How Infringed	Result	Justification/Four Factors
Campbell v. Acuff-Rose Music, Inc., 510 U.S. 569 1994	Music and lyrics	Use of Roy Orbison's "Oh, Pretty Woman" by 2 Live Crew to create a parody was an unauthorized derivative work.	2 Live Crew had requested but was denied a license from Acuff-Rose Music to do the parody. After the hip hop song was released, Acuff-Rose sued for infringement. District Court ruled that it was a fair use. On appeal, Circuit Court overruled, noting commercial nature and factors 3 and 4 weighed against fair use. 2 Live Crew appealed to Supreme Court resulting in a landmark decision in favor of fair use.	Supreme Court: Fair use Factor 1: Commercial nature of use is not a presumptive bar against fair use; character of 2 Live Crew's use transformed and provided commentary on original work. Factor 2: Deemed not relevant because nature of parodies requires use of artistic characteristics of original. Factor 3: Despite 2 Live Crew parody's touching near "heart of the work," it did not use more than necessary for their purpose. Factor 4: Parody cannot be considered a market substitute for original. Because a copyright owner cannot be expected to license works critical of their own, there is no derivative market for parodies. This case emphasized two key principles: (1) fair use judgments require examination of each factor separately as well as in relation to the other factors; (2) the extent to which the secondary use transforms the original into something new should carry weight in how the other factors are assessed.

Table 5.2 continued

Case and Year	Work	How Infringed	Result	Justification/Four Factors
Kelly v. Arriba Soft Corp., 336 F.3d 811 9th Circuit 2003	Photographs	Arriba Soft's indexing and display of thumbnails of Kelly's online photographs in response to users' search terms claimed as infringing.	District Court granted summary judgment for Arriba Soft's use as a fair use. Kelly appealed to Ninth Circuit, and it agreed with the lower court on it being a fair use.	Circuit Court: Factor 1: A commercial use that was transformative (posting only thumbnails) that provided a public benefit. Factor 2: Leans to Kelly because photos were creative works. Factor 3: Leans neither way: entire works were copied, but that was necessary for purpose of Arriba Soft's new work. Factor 4: Low-resolution thumbnails did not negatively affect market for Kelly's images.

Table 5.2 continued

Case and Year	Work	How Infringed	Result	Justification/Four Factors
Bill Graham Archives [BGA] v. Dorling Kindersley [DK] Ltd., 448 F.3d 605 2nd Circuit 2006	Posters/ poster art and concert tickets	For a pictorial history of the Grateful Dead, DK used thumbnail-size images of promotional posters and tickets for the band's concerts. After negotiations for permissions hit an impasse, DK proceeded with publication of the book.	BGA sued for injunction against further sales and for destruction of unsold copies, and statutory damages. District Court granted summary judgment for DK based on fair use. BGA's appeal to the Second Circuit Court was unsuccessful.	Circuit Court: Factor 1: Although BGA had claimed that DK's mere arrangement of the images of the posters was not transformative, Court noted that the posters were used in the timeline for a different purpose—historical documentation of the occurrence of a concert, making the use transformative. Factor 2: Circuit Court acknowledged posters were primarily creative, but this factor did not weigh much because DK did not exploit the expressive value of the images. Factor 3: Favored fair use because the reduced size of the images was consistent with DK's use as transformative use. Factor 4: DK's use did not harm market for BGA's artwork.

Table 5.2 continued

Case and Year	Work	How Infringed	Result	Justification/Four Factors
Blanch v. Koons, 467 F.3d 244 2nd Circuit 2006	Photos	Fashion photographer's image of sandals on a woman's legs were incorporated into one of Koon's collages exhibited at a museum.	District Court granted summary judgment for Koons based on fair use. Blanch's appeal to Second Circuit was unsuccessful.	Circuit Court: Factor 1: Collage was a transformative (commentary) use and museum exhibition was noncommercial. Factor 2: Because Blanch's photograph had been published, factor 2 weighed for fair use. Factor 3: Neutral. Factor 4: The "market" in which Koons used the image was not one that this photograph by itself could have captured.

Table 5.2 continued

Case and Year	Work	How Infringed	Result	Justification/Four Factors
Perfect 10, Inc. v. Amazon.com, Inc., 508 F.3d 1146 9th Circuit. 2007 [Note: Google was the original defendant, but as the case proceeded, Amazon was added and ultimately became the more central party for court review of alleged infringements.]	Photographs on a subscription website	Claim of infringement by Google using images to create an index. After appeals court determined that Google use would likely succeed as a fair use, the importance of Google's actions diminished. Case then focused on Amazon because it used images from the Google search. Note: Google's results were from sites that had posted Perfect 10 images without authorization.	Perfect 10 requested District Court to grant preliminary injunction claiming direct, vicarious, and contributory infringement. District Court granted partial injunction (against display of thumbnail images but not against hyperlinking). District Court found that claim for contributory infringement was unlikely to succeed because of fair use. Vicarious infringement claim unlikely to succeed because Google did not have power to stop the third-party infringement. Perfect 10 appealed to Ninth Circuit, and Amazon was added to the case.	Circuit Court: Agreed with District Court that hyperlinks did not infringe Perfect 10. Google's providing an inline link to images was not same as hosting the images. Overturned District Court's ruling that Google's thumbnail images were infringing but were a fair use. Factor 1: Highly transformative because rather than copying the images for aesthetic content, the search engine transformed the image into a pointer directing a user to a source of information, thus providing a social benefit. Factor 2: Citing *Kelly v. Arriba Soft*, this factor favored Perfect 10 because photos were creative works, but only weighed slightly because images were thumbnails. Factor 3: As with *Kelly v. Arriba Soft*, leans neither way. Factor 4: Weighs for fair use: Google's use of thumbnails for search engine purposes was considered highly transformative, so market harm could not be presumed.

Table 5.2 continued

Case and Year	Work	How Infringed	Result	Justification/Four Factors
Cariou v. Prince, 714 F.3d 694 2nd Circuit 2013	Published photos	Photographs taken and published by Patrick Cariou were appropriated by visual artist Richard Prince for paintings and collages that he then exhibited at a gallery and had reproduced in the gallery's catalog. For his gallery works, Prince made a number of modifications of the original images (adding color, adding content, combining a number together, etc.).	District Court found Prince's uses were infringing. They were not transformative because they did not comment on the originals. Prince appealed to Second Circuit, which rejected District Court's finding that they had not been transformative. Importantly, it said: "Prince's work could be transformative even without commenting on Cariou's work," thus greatly expanding the scope for a finding of fair use based on transformative. Note: The Circuit Court's broad brush use of transformativeness beyond just the first factor has been called into question, most recently in the 2023 *Warhol Foundation* case noted below.	Circuit Court: Factor 1: Favors fair use because Prince's uses were transformative. "… a secondary work may constitute a fair use even if it serves some purpose other than … criticism, comment, news reporting, teaching, scholarship, and research …." Factor 2: Weighs against fair use because Cariou's works were highly artistic, but this factor may be of limited use when art is being used for a transformative purpose. Factor 3: Prince did use key portions of Cariou's images, but he transformed them so this weighs heavily toward fair use. Factor 4: Cariou has not actively marketed his images for use in derivative works, and his prints appeal to a different sort of collector than Prince. It also noted: "… the more transformative the secondary use, the less likelihood that the secondary use substitutes for the original…."

Table 5.2 continued

Case and Year	Work	How Infringed	Result	Justification/Four Factors
Authors Guild v. Hathi Trust, 755 F.3d 87 2nd Circuit 2014	Published books	Consortium of libraries that had collaborated with Google in the Google Books project established the Hathi Trust Digital Library containing millions of works. Hathi used the digital content to: 1) create a database for public searching; 2) provide access to full text for persons with "print" disabilities; and 3) enable libraries to obtain replacement copies of lost, damaged, or stolen originals.	District Court: Rejected plaintiff's argument that libraries are governed by§ 108 and thus fair use rights were not applicable. Ruled that each of the three uses Hathi made were transformative and thus fair. Authors Guild appealed to the Second Circuit Court.	District Court findings Factor 1: Uses were transformative by creation of a search engine, providing works to an audience not intended by initial publication, and preservation copying was non-commercial. Factor 2: Not dispositive because use was transformative Factor 3: Using full amount was necessary to accomplish purposes of making the books searchable and accessible for persons with disabilities. Factor 4: Transformative uses (making works searchable and accessible for disabled) did not provide a market substitute. Court declined to rule on Authors Guild's hypothetical of harm to a potential market they might consider in the future. Circuit Court agreed with District Court except disagreed that providing works to the print-disabled was transformative. It also did not accept the lower court's view on the making of replacement copies. It remanded (sent back) that question to the District Court.

Table 5.2 continued

Case and Year	Work	How Infringed	Result	Justification/Four Factors
Graham v. Prince, 2023 U.S. Dist. LEXIS 83267 2023	Unauthorized incorporation of photographs into artworks. (District Court combined claims to assess fair use claims because of the similarity of claims against Prince by photographers Donald Graham and Eric McNatt).	Noted appropriation artist Richard Prince took screenshots of images found online that originated in photographs made separately by Graham and McNatt. With some modifications of the screenshots, Prince printed them on canvas to create artworks that were included in gallery exhibits, catalogs, books, etc. Both Graham and McNatt named not only Prince but also exhibition galleries and others as defendants infringing their rights.	District Court denied defendant's motions for summary judgment (May 11, 2023) based on judge's review of all four factors. With the denial of summary judgement, the case was set to go to a jury trial. However, Prince agreed to settle according to terms contained in the January 25, 2024, "Final judgement" in favor of plaintiffs. It enjoined infringing activities and required defendants to pay substantial damages and fees.	District Court: Factor 1: Weighed against fair use. Prince's works were not transformative in purpose or aesthetics because changes to the images and commentary on them were minimal and use was commercial. Factor 2: Weighed against fair use because both Graham and McNatt's photographs were creative, not factual, works. Factor 3: Weighed against fair use. The extent of the work copied, despite some cropping, was too great given the lack of transformativeness (by contrast with DK's use of Grateful Dead concert posters). Factor 4: Weighed slightly in favor of fair use because primary or derivative markets for original and secondary works do not overlap.

Table 5.2 continued

Case and Year	Work	How Infringed	Result	Justification/Four Factors
Andy Warhol Foundation [AWF] for the Visual Arts, Inc. v. Goldsmith 143 S. Ct. 1258 2023	Licensing for publication of artistic silkscreen of a photograph without permission of the original photographer.	Celebrity photographer Lynn Goldsmith had taken professional photographs of musician Prince (Prince Rogers Nelson) in 1981 for use in a magazine. In 1984, *Vanity Fair* licensed the image for artist Andy Warhol to use as "reference" print in making silkscreen art. It was to be used only one time, which the magazine did in a 1984 article. In 2016, after Prince died, publisher Condé Nast obtained license from AWF to use one of Warhol's Prince silkscreens as a cover illustration on a special tribute issue.	After Goldsmith informed AWF that she believed the 2016 use was an infringement, AWF filed suit for declarative judgment that it was fair use and not infringing. Goldsmith counterclaimed infringement. District Court considered all four factors, granting summary judgment of fair use. On Goldsmith's appeal, the Circuit Court overturned District Court finding, saying that all four factors favored Goldsmith. AWF then appealed to US Supreme Court asking for a review of only the first factor.	In examining the first factor, the Supreme Court shifted the focus from how much a defendant's use may have transformed a plaintiff's work to whether an allegedly infringing use has a further purpose or different character. It contended that transformativeness was a matter of degree that should be weighed against considerations such as commercialism. New expression or meaning might transform a work, and give it a different purpose, but by itself that is not sufficient to settle the first factor. The purpose of both AWF's 2016 use of the image and Goldsmith's photograph was the same– licensing for use in a magazine. Thus the first factor favored Goldsmith.

Table 5.2 continued

Case and Year	Work	How Infringed	Result	Justification/Four Factors
Hachette Book Group, Inc. v. Internet Archive, No. 23-1260 (2nd Circuit, 2024)	Print books from which Internet Archive (IA) made digital copies available by digital loans.	IA infringed copyright in publishers' books by IA's Controlled Digital Lending (process whereby only one digital copy is being used at one time). The 127 books at issue were titles publishers offered as e-books.	District Court ruled in favor of publishers and rejected IA's claim of fair use. On IA's appeal, Circuit court agreed that IA had not made a fair use. It lacked transformativeness and was commercial.	The Appeals court ruling emphasized that IA's use did not add new expression or meaning, and it usurped the market for the originals. In so doing, the Appeals Court cited and closely followed the Supreme Court 2023 *Warhol* ruling. *Hachette*, quoting the caution against an "overbroad concept of transformative use" suggests a narrowing of what qualifies as fair use.
Jana Romanova v. Amilus Inc. No. 23-828 (2nd Cir. 2025)	Photograph made by professional commercial photographer.	Amilus infringed copyright when it posted a copy of one of Romanova's photographs on its paid subscription website. Note: Amilus neither responded to Romanova's takedown notice nor did it respond to or appear in either the District Court or Circuit Court of Appeals.	With no response from Amilus, District Court asked Romanova to show why Amilus' use was not a fair use. District Court then dismissed the case saying this had been a fair use. On Romanova's appeal, the Circuit Court rejected the fair use argument as faulty. It directed the District Court to enter a default judgment for Romanova.	Circuit Court determined that all four factors weighed against fair use. It paid particular attention to the lack of transformativeness in Amilus's use. It paid particular attention to the *Warhol* ruling's emphasis on the need for the secondary use to communicate a message differing from the original, and on the need for justification for the secondary use, e.g., criticism of or comment on the original.

- The grid format is intended to reflect the diversity of facts on which particular cases were decided as well as the divergence of decisions possible, even from quite similar-seeming circumstances.
- Feel free to use these grids as broad guides for components to build your own matrix to support risk management-based decisions but avoid using them to create specific rules.
- By mentioning or describing any one of these actual cases, this book does not endorse or condemn the works involved, the behavior of the litigants, or the behavior of the courts. These cases range from the quite profane and exploitative to the cerebral and sacred.

As noted throughout our discussion of fair use, the transformativeness of a defendant's use has played a major role in many decisions that have shaped what may or may not be accepted as a non-infringing fair use. This second grid (Table 5.2) illustrates key points of cases in the 30-year evolution of what transformativeness really means and how decisive it should be.

5.5 Takeaways from the Fair Use Cases

The meaning and legal force of fair use may seem to be as amorphous now as it was nearly a half-century ago. Then Congress could not define it in the legislative history for the 1976 copyright act in any more specific way than saying it was "an equitable rule of reason." Nevertheless, the serial Rorschach impressions we have from these include elements that should help you when thinking about what's reasonable in pursuing your archival mission in a world where copyright has such a vast reach. Here are some conclusions we can draw from the unpublished and transformative cases noted above.

- Fair use decisions are highly fact-centered. That means archivists should use their distinctive research skills and unique access to the works in their collections, as well as documentation in the collection on the creation of those works, to aid in identifying both the risks and safeguards that would be important should a complaint arise.
- When there are similar facts relating to the work, its creator, the user, and the use made of the work, there may be different results, especially as the courts seem poised to move away from formulaic to cross-factor evaluations of any one aspect of the four factors.

- Even judges and courts cannot always decide or agree on the meaning and weight to be given to their prior decisions.
- The economic value of a work and the effect of a user's action on that value seems likely to remain a foundation of much of the litigation and many of the court decisions. Clearly, the presence of economic value will continue to be crucial to who has the incentive to invest in the extended legal action that can be required to obtain a judgment.
- The 2023 *Graham*, *Warhol*, *Hachette*, and *Romanova* cases make clear that for transformativeness of the secondary use to tilt the first factor in the direction of fair use, the new use needs to have "a purpose and character that is sufficiently distinct from the original." Especially if the new use is a commercial one, it needs to be justified as separate from the original.
- Even though the transformativeness that emerged from the 1994 *Campbell* case may have lost some of its preeminence, that case's call for holistic analysis remains critically important for the principles by which legal assessments proceed.
- Rather than the four factors being seen in isolation from each other and assessed in a straightforward additive way, cross-factor assessment may become the rule, with focus especially on the relation of the first and fourth factors.[22]
- Fair use remains critically important because without it, the entire copyright system would atrophy. The five decades since it was made statutory have witnessed more and more technologies for producing a broadening array of expressive works, but they have also seen greater public access to, and deploying of, tools that enable the people to take matters in their own hands in a desire for a more inclusive culture.
- Archivists are still left without much that specifically speaks to our holdings, our users, or our mission. Still, fair use is an equitable rule of reason, making it too valuable a resource for us not to depend on it as we pursue our mission. Even if we have to live with the "bad news" that there's no case law specifically regarding archival fair use, the fact remains that the text of the law, the four factors, and much of what the courts have said should serve as a professional standard for how we respectfully steward the creators' expressive works in our archives and how we share those works with the public we serve.

- When it comes to actual cases against archives and archivists, there are next to none, and that's obviously a good thing.[23] That lack of cases may result from care, caution, or maybe even too much caution in archives management, though that would be difficult to document. On the other hand, the dearth of infringement claims against archives may be explained by the fact that the "market" for copyright litigation is dominated by works and alleged infringements relating to commercial works and activities where enough money is at stake to make a compelling claim, as well as to underwrite legal fees.

From these perspectives, one clear takeaway for archivists is to avoid engaging in commercial activity that might touch on the exclusive rights found in § 106 and to exercise great caution when using works having noticeable copyright market value. Of course, the *Bond v. Blum* case shows that there's no telling when someone might step forward and claim "infringement" for reasons unrelated to the purpose and legal foundation of copyright. Nevertheless, we should not let the theoretical possibility of a suit for almost anything we hold and anything we might do keep us from pursuing our mission.

Finally, it is important to remember that the very fluid character of fair use cases is as much a "feature" as it is a "bug." That is, from its creation, fair use was intended to create flexibility when an otherwise strict reading of copyright's exclusive rights would preclude activities important to a democratic and educated society. On the other hand, no one really knows whether any given action is fair use until it has been tested. As much as we might like to see sharper lines to guide us, archivists need to scrutinize very carefully any legislative proposals to amend § 107, especially since it, much more than § 108, can support a broad range of archival activities.[24] For better or worse, § 107's fair use remains the most commodious home we have in US Title 17.

6 Copyright's Strange Relatives

You might think that with US copyright law weighing in at over 330 pages, it would be all you need to know to handle intellectual property issues that arise in your archives. Essentially, it should be, except for the fact that copyright has a number of "strange relatives" who, like a mix of long-lost and unfavorite relatives, sometimes show up uninvited to your holiday dinner.

And, as with those relatives whom you barely know, you don't want to just slam the door in their faces, especially not at holiday time. You do, however, want to remember enough about them to know where to fit them in among your better-known guests so your party does not come undone.

Copyright, the primary form of intellectual property that archivists regularly confront, has near and distant kinfolk as well. That's why it's important to know some basics about these "strange relatives," lest you inadvertently become sidetracked by rules that belong to other rights regimes. Though these other neighboring rights are outside of copyright per se, as an information professional you still must understand and respect them.

This chapter will identify several of the most relevant of the neighboring rights you may encounter as an archivist. These include patents, trademarks, trade secrets, privacy, publicity, and "moral rights." These will be briefly introduced to guide you in seeing where they might overlap or conflict with copyright. The goal is to help keep them from ruining your copyright party while making sure you don't intrude upon them out of ignorance.

6.1 Patents

Patents have had a common parentage with copyright since medieval times. In the United States it is through their foundation in the same authorization from the Constitution, Article I, Section 8, which reads: "To promote the progress of science and useful arts, by securing for limited times to authors and inventors the exclusive right to their respective writings and discoveries." This grant of authority to Congress was for the creation of two distinct types of limited monopolies. The shared purpose was to support the cultural, intellectual, commercial, and industrial development of the newly independent and geographically isolated United States. Whereas copyrights were implicated by the references to "science," "authors," and "writings," patents were invoked by references to "useful arts," "inventors," and "discoveries." On this foundation, the first Congress moved to utilize the Constitution's authorization by enacting the United States' first patent and copyright laws in Spring 1790, within less than two months of each other.

As with copyright, the patent law has undergone a handful of major revisions and a number of modest changes through periodic amendments. However, the Constitution's initial distinction between legal protection of writings and of inventions has remained in place even as both copyright and patents have expanded their scope well beyond what was imagined in the early republic. Nevertheless, both were designed to balance the grant of monopoly rights with the expectation that the resultant inventions and discoveries or the resultant "writings" would be made available to the public at large to encourage further innovation and learning.

Patent law's support for the creation of useful devices has facilitated archival practice in many ways, but it does not present many challenges for the archivist's management of documentary materials. Indeed, the dividing line between copyrightable works and patents is made clear at the outset of today's copyright law. After listing the current broad array of works eligible for copyright, § 102 establishes the ineligibility of ideas, procedures, processes, systems, methods of operation, concepts, principles, and discoveries. In other words, it notes the very focus of patents—devices, machinery, compounded materials, etc. As for patent law, it has come to include three types of inventions or improvements on existing inventions. *Utility patents* are used for processes, machines, manufacturing, or composition of matter.

Design patents cover the ornamental design of a useful object. *Plant patents* cover new varieties of living plants.

The fundamental nature of a patent is to exclude all but the patent holder or their assigns from using the invention. Unlike copyright's exclusive rights being automatic upon the initial fixation of an eligible work, patent's exclusive rights exist only after a lengthy process of formal registration with the US Patent and Trademark Office (USPTO). To achieve enforceability, the inventor must first describe in detail the process of its creation and disclose its methodology to the public through their application to the patent office. USPTO's examination determines whether the invention meets the standards of novelty and non-obviousness. If approved, the patent registration can be enforced for a term of 20 years from the date of the initial filing except for design patents, which have a term of 15 years. Once that term ends, the disclosed process is available for anyone to re-create and to market as an identical product, commonly seen in how generic drugs routinely become a lower-cost option for health care.

Given the specific focus on the nature of works eligible for patent, it would seem that patentable works would be clear of the copyright challenges that arise with archival materials. After all, the copyright law provides a list of works ineligible for copyright (§ 102 (b)), and patent law mandates public disclosure of the processes for the invention. However, by this point in the book, it should come as no surprise that all is not rationally consistent when it comes to copyright law. For example, there can be overlap in at least two areas—designs and software can be covered by either, but generally patents would apply to different aspects of each. Regardless, it would seem highly unlikely that digitization of most archival materials would pose questions of patent infringement. Furthermore, given the more reasonable 20-year term of a patent and the fact that the patent's owner can be discovered by a search of the USPTO's convenient online registry, patents would seem unlikely to create as much of a problem for us as the orphan works so common in our archives.[1]

Design patents, however, may present an exception, and historically the courts have struggled with the relation of design patents to copyright.[2] Applying for a patent of an ornamental design requires submission to the patent office of a drawing. The result is something that clearly qualifies as a copyrightable pictorial or graphic work (§ 102 (5)). For example, the drawing

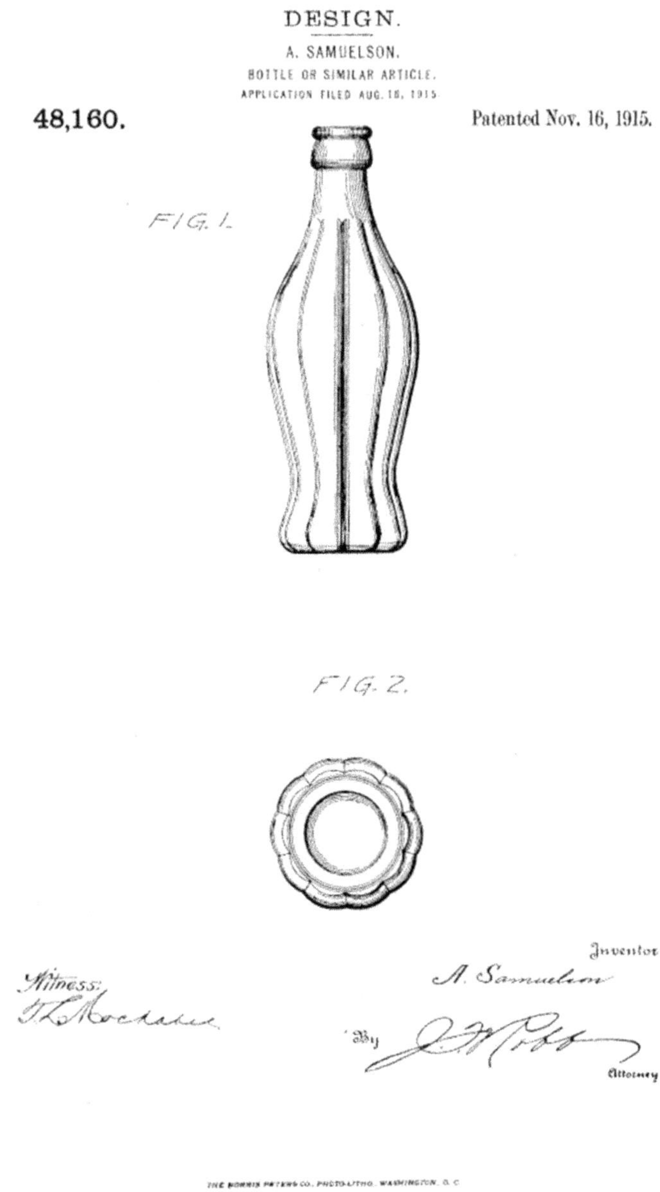

Figure 6.1 Example of design patent. A. Samuelson, Bottle or Similar Article, Design Patent 48,160, filed August 18, 1915, and issued November 16, 1915, accessed July 20, 2025, https://patents.google.com/patent/USD48160S/en. This patent can also be found by entering in "D048160" into USPTO Patent Public Search Basic "Quick lookup" prompt found at https://ppubs.uspto.gov/pubwebapp/static/pages/ppubsbasic.html

used in a 1915 application for a patent in a "bottle or similar article" would not only have provided a basis for a design patent but also would have been eligible for copyright. In theory, the creator could have then held both a design patent, albeit for its then-current term of 14 years, and a drawing registered for copyright for at least the then-current renewable term of 28 years, thus providing some protection beyond the patent's term. However, until the 1990s, the US Copyright Office refused to accept a registration for a design that had been simultaneously submitted for a patent.[3]

This example illustrates the complications involved in relying on simple rules, such as that items covered by patents are by definition out of scope for copyright or that the expiration of a patent would mean that the work is also free of copyright. In all likelihood, the specific image of the drawing submitted for a design patent in 1915 probably does not present a *copyright* problem if used non-commercially and not in a way that might implicate another of copyright's distant relatives—trademark.[4]

6.2 Trademarks

In 1870, as American commerce grew following the Civil War, Congress amended several parts of the Copyright Act. This included giving copyright protection to marks and symbols of items in commerce. However, those provisions were declared unconstitutional in 1879 by the Supreme Court, which reasoned that creation of federal protection of marks and symbols of trade was inconsistent with the Constitution's "Copyright Clause" (Article I, Section 8, Clause 8). It ruled that a trademark law could only be enacted under authority of the Commerce Clause (Article I, Section 8, Clause 3), and Congress passed a compliant trademark act in 1881. Currently, trademark is governed by the Lanham Act, amended several times since its 1946 enactment.

In US federal law, trademark is a grant of exclusive use of a word, phrase, or logo to identify a product or service offered in commerce. Its purpose is to protect consumers from confusion about the source and quality of goods and services. Trademarks function to identify a seller's goods and distinguish them from others in the marketplace; to establish the source of products and services; to provide consumers an indicator of the standard of quality among various products from the same source; and to serve as advertising for their

Figure 6.2 Cancelled "WOOLCO" trademark 72149989 or 86805574, once owned by F. W. Woolworth

source. Because trademarks provide a ready identifier of product or service, they can become important to the public identity of a business and an asset to be used as items of commerce in themselves. In addition to applying to symbols, words, images, and sounds, trademarks can also extend exclusive rights to "trade dress" to cover the distinctiveness of packaging and visual appearance of a product. For the sake of this overview, I will use the term "trademark" or "mark" to cover all three areas: product, service, or dress.

Federal trademark protection is available for goods and services offered for interstate commerce and is enforceable only after formal approval of the registration by the USPTO. Once approved, the mark can bear the symbol ®, and the right continues for 10 years after registration. It must be renewed before expiration. Trademark protection is also possible under common law and many state laws. That is a useful option for businesses and organizations not involved in interstate commerce and those wishing trademark protection without the significantly higher costs of establishing a federally registered mark. Where state laws provide for trademark protection, registration is also required, and such marks can bear the identifiers of ™ (trademark) and ℠ (service mark). They generally must be renewed before their term expires. Whether federal or state, even if registrations are renewed, the general rule is "use it or lose it." That is, a trademark needs to remain in continued use, or it could be subject to abandonment. Likewise, if a trademark owner does not pursue others who appear to infringe on their trademark, the owner can be deemed to have abandoned the mark.

As with patents, trademarks provide a legal basis for excluding anyone other than the mark's owner or their licensee from its use. Infringement of a mark can occur when someone commercially uses the mark or a mark of substantial similarity in a way that would likely cause confusion among consumers. Trademark violations are a matter of civil law, and the trademark holder is solely responsible for bringing a suit.

Trademarks, however, can fit within the copyright law's scope of subject matter when it is a pictorial, graphical, or musical work (§102(a)). However, as a practical matter, thanks to copyright's exceptions for fair use and some library and archives functions, archivists can generally avoid trademark liability as long as they steer clear of using someone else's mark in a commercial way that would compete with products of the mark's owner. It is highly unlikely that an archives might create and offer for sale a smartphone that would compete with Samsung or Apple, but it is not that unlikely that some of those company's logos and marks might appear on documents an archives might exhibit or post online in a way consistent with fair use. However, when creating a logo for your own archives or historical society, you might be inspired by a design element from another history museum or library. That could be problematic because archives, libraries, museums, and other non-profit organizations can hold trademarks, and your new design could create consumer confusion because the term "commercial" and "in commerce" can apply even if the organization is "doing business" outside the scope of a for-profit business.

Trademark status does not necessarily preclude the application of copyright law if the trademark or trade dress incorporates literary, graphical, sculptural, or other works that are eligible for copyright as subject matter listed in § 102(a) and being used in a way consistent with copyright. This principle is clearly illustrated in the previously mentioned case of the artist sued by Mattel for photographing Barbie dolls in strange poses. There, Mattel accused Forsythe of infringing trademark and trade dress as well as infringing copyright. A California District Court ruled that Forsythe's use infringed neither trademark nor copyright but was clearly a fair use as a parody and commentary. On appeal, the Ninth Circuit Court conducted a similar analysis and affirmed the lower court ruling. In regard to trademark and trade dress, it found that Forsythe's non-commercial use made it highly unlikely that he would have either created any confusion by members of the public or diluted Mattel's brand in Barbie. Regarding copyright, Forsythe's use was a non-commercial one for a parody to comment on commercialism and objectification of women. Furthermore, when considering the award of attorney fees and court costs, the Circuit Court sternly reprimanded Mattel for having invoked trademark law for something they were clearly in a position to know did not apply, and it assessed penalties (see Chapter 4, Box 4.11).[5]

6.3 Trade Secrets

As unlikely as it is that archivists will have to deal with the exclusive rights of patents and trademarks, there is one other commercial right that is even more unlikely—trade secrets. By their very definition, trade secrets would seem to be the real unicorns of the intellectual property family. However, the topic arises occasionally when talking about copyright and archives. Trade secrets are strategic information of critical value to a business's operations, generally something that has been carefully managed to maintain its confidentiality and which has value by the fact that it is not known generally. This can include technical and non-technical data, formulas, programs, methodologies, financial information, and customer lists that have business value that would be eviscerated if disclosed beyond a limited group.[6] In recent years and especially in technology areas, such as artificial intelligence, trade secrets increasingly are being relied on as a tool to protect processes and business methods that otherwise might be patented.

Whether the confidentiality is breached by an individual with authorized access to the information or by an unauthorized person gaining access through improper means, the knowing misappropriation of the information is a violation of the law of a specific state.[7] In the absence of a specific state law, it could still be acted on as a tort in common law as an unfair competition. Penalties include injunctions and payment of damages for actual loss and "unjust enrichment." Such a misappropriation could also be a criminal violation of the Federal Economic Espionage Act of 1996 (Public Law 104–294). In some cases it's possible for a trade secret to be discovered lawfully through independent development or reverse engineering.

Archivists commonly have responsibility for confidential and restricted information, but it seems unlikely for an archivist to have charge of actual current trade secrets. If you are, then presumably you would have been informed through your employment contract or other agreements that referred to a specific trade secrets act of your state or territory. However, as far as copyright is concerned, if the content of a trade secret loses its secret status, then the usual exclusive rights, limitations, and exceptions of copyright law could apply unless the creating organization establishes access restrictions similar to what it might apply to other sensitive information already managed by the archives.

6.4 Privacy Rights

Respect for the right of privacy in one's person is fundamental to society and important for ethical management of archival collections. The SAA Code of Ethics emphasizes that,

> *Archivists recognize that privacy is an inherent fundamental right and sanctioned by law. They establish procedures and policies to protect the interests of the donors, individuals, groups, and organizations whose public and private lives and activities are documented in archival holdings.*[8]

Thus, respecting privacy is basic to being a professional archivist, but to ensure that copyright is not stretched to protect privacy, as was asserted in the *Salinger v. Random House* case, it is important to understand the scope of privacy and how breaches of privacy are handled by laws separate from copyright.

Federal laws deal with privacy in only a few specific areas, such as education and health care. Other areas of privacy, such as personal employment or consumer information, may be governed by laws that vary from state to state. Beyond the aspects of privacy addressed by a specific statute, any other privacy wrongs would be adjudicated through common law at the state level. Although it is difficult to generalize, privacy has been classically understood as the right to be left alone.[9] More specifically, it is a right to be free from unwarranted exposure and the resultant emotional harm. Privacy can be violated by one or more of "four prongs":

1. Intrusion on a person's seclusion or personal affairs, as might occur with invasion of personal space where the person has the reasonable expectation of privacy. "Space" includes not only physical space, but also places in which one might store personal information, such as a diary or personal calendar. Emotional distress may arise even if nothing was discovered or disclosed in the course of the intrusion.
2. Public disclosure of private facts that would be highly offensive to a reasonable person and of no legitimate public concern.
3. Being publicly placed in a false light, whether the "facts" disclosed are true or not. A privacy violation occurs by the presentation of those "facts" in a way to create a false light that would be highly offensive to a reasonable person.
4. Appropriation, without permission, of one's name or likeness, especially when used for commercial purposes.

To be actionable, a violation of privacy must be offensive and objectionable to persons of reasonable sensitivity. The seriousness of a violation is influenced by whether the "taking" occurred in a public place. For instance, a person doing something embarrassing in a public place where cameras are commonly present would not have so strong a claim as if the behavior were in their own home. Because privacy rights are not absolute but are in tension with the First Amendment, the violations of privacy may be balanced with a public right to know, especially when dealing with public figures.

In addition, privacy is a right belonging to an individual person. Thus it endures only so long as that person is alive.[10] In most cases, by common law as well as by state statute, privacy does not endure beyond death, although some states, such as Illinois, have developed posthumous protection for the fourth prong—commercial appropriation (see section 6.5). Although personal privacy ends at death, it has long been recognized in common and state law that the privacy of living survivors can be invaded by the emotional distress caused by revelation of sensitive facts about the deceased soon after death.[11]

Regardless, because a significant focus of privacy relates to factual matters which are excluded from copyright by §102 (b), copyright law is a poor instrument for privacy protection. Unfortunately, the lines between copyright and privacy are often confused by owners, users, and archivists. This can happen if copyright is invoked to preclude use of something perceived as private. Legal scholar Wendy J. Gordon has noted: ". . . no copyright cause of action would lie for uncomfortable facts gleaned from even the most private diary. In addition, a host of differences between copyright law and privacy rights would make it difficult to know how to shape a privacy claim in copyright law."[12] However, as I have stressed elsewhere, an important reason to learn about copyright is to enable you to understand where it applies and where other domains, such as privacy, apply so you can keep these two areas separate when dealing with archival collections, donors, and users. Focusing on the above basic principles ("prongs") of privacy and referring to the § 106 exclusive rights of copyright should help in making such distinctions.

6.5 Publicity Rights

According to J. Thomas McCarthy's authoritative treatise, *The Rights of Publicity and Privacy*, the right of publicity is "the inherent right of every human being to control the commercial value of his or her identity."[13] Generally speaking, then, the right of publicity is the right of an individual to control the commercial value of his/her name, image, voice, or persona and to prevent others from appropriating that name, image, voice, or persona, especially for financial gain. As with copyright, overly ambitious enforcement of publicity rights can impede public affairs.[14] Like trademark, it is commercial activity that is central to a finding of infringement, but unlike federal trademark, registration is not required for publicity rights.

Generalization about publicity rights is very difficult, not just because there is no federal law on publicity rights, but also because these rights have emerged from the rather strange trio of the appropriation aspect of privacy law; the legal "tort" of unfair competition; and/or common (judge-made) law regarding property.[15] Although publicity rights are linked to the personal privacy of anyone, litigation and jurisprudence has been less about an individual's inalienable right to their personhood and more about protecting mostly those with market value in their personality (think Elvis or Marilyn Monroe).

Nevertheless, the right has evolved into a type of intellectual property right. Despite the celebrity focus of the case law, it is the rise of social media, and especially the ability of artificial intelligence to create digital replicas or "deep fakes," that has resulted in recent calls for broadening these rights beyond just celebrities.[16] McCarthy, in fact, is emphatic that non-celebrities have the same right as celebrities against infringement of the commercial value in their person. A recent study by the US Copyright Office did note that the digital replica problem fell outside of copyright, but the office still called for legislative action, including at the federal level (see Chapter 10, Section 10.2).

Currently, adjudication of publicity rights cases is largely through state courts. That is particularly frustrating because the two dozen or so state publicity laws vary widely. Fundamental differences exist relating to duration; protected subject matter; defenses available against unauthorized uses; and residence of the person making an infringement claim. Furthermore, in those places where the right of publicity, unlike privacy, is transferrable and able to survive death, the length of duration varies greatly from state to state (e.g., 10 years in Tennessee, 50 in Illinois and California, 100 in Indiana).[17]

Despite publicity rights' long durations, violation of the right is also subject to some limits that vary state by state. For instance, factual representations for news reporting or education are generally allowable, but commercial uses, especially advertising, tend not to be permitted. In Illinois, "commercial" also includes fundraising. Generally speaking, it is the law of the domicile of the person at the time of death that will govern how the right of publicity will be applied, but in some states, such as Indiana, all that is required is that the offending act (e.g., selling t-shirts with photographs of a celebrity) has occurred in Indiana.[18]

As a practical matter, questions about publicity rights may arise for archivists whose collections contain materials relating to public figures with a commercial value in their name, image, likeness, voice, etc. Of course, public relations photographs and other materials relating to celebrities can occur anywhere in your archives, so be careful. The risk of a publicity right violation might seem minimal, but not if your archives commercializes items, e.g., reproducing images of celebrities, athletes, or other living individuals on products to be sold in a gift shop or distributed as bonuses for fundraising events. However, non-commercial uses that would align with a strong fair use justification, including news reporting, course papers, scholarly articles, etc., should fit within the limitations within many publicity laws.[19] Still, it is wise to check with counsel before engaging in commercial activities, even for fundraising purposes.

As a final caution, you should remember that many of the works that have publicity-rights value may also be copyrighted works. After all, Marilyn Monroe's publicity rights may no longer be enforceable in all jurisdictions or circumstances, but the photos of her taken in 1955 by a local photographer or a member of the crowd during her visit to tiny Bement, Illinois to judge a beard-growing contest would quite possibly have been a copyright-eligible work that is still covered by § 106's exclusive rights.

6.6 Moral Rights

US copyright law differs from copyright laws in much of the rest of the world because of a fundamental conceptual difference. US law focuses on granting exclusive rights that provide an economic benefit to a person in order to generate works that will benefit society at large. Many other countries apply a natural law approach that considers the creation of a new work as the embodiment of a creator's personality. Because their works are thereby seen as inseparable from their personality, the author/creator has what are called "moral rights," distinct from the pragmatic and economic rights in US copyright law.[20] Although the exact application of "moral rights" may vary from country to country, they are largely unenforceable in the United States, except for one highly specific area to be noted below.

This section will provide a general overview of moral rights because understanding them will help you decide whether or not you need to dig deeper and read further sources. The overview is also intended to help you better understand how to navigate rights so as to avoid imposing even more demands on how we manage copyrighted works.

The idea and principles of "moral rights" can be traced back centuries, but they were developed legislatively in France and Germany in the eighteenth and nineteenth centuries. They are currently a prevailing legal concept in many European nations as well as among several other nations that were colonized by European countries. Because moral rights focus on the personality and personal genius of the work's creator, these rights cannot, in theory, be extinguished by the mere economic exchange on which copyright hinges. The word "moral" should be understood less as a matter of ethics than as implying the spiritual basis of an author's creation, and thus is tied to the notion of artistic integrity. Nevertheless, a careful review of the purpose and scope of moral rights should resonate with archival ethics that respect the creators of the documents we curate; even if US copyright law does mandate such rights.

To appreciate how different a moral rights regime is from US copyright law, we need to look at how large the scope of moral rights can be. While "moral rights" countries may not implement all of the following or implement them in the same way, they can theoretically include quite an expansive menu that US archivists would not consider as part of copyright. They can include rights of:

1. Integrity (creator's right to prevent distortion or mutilation of their work).
2. Attribution (*droit de paternité*), or the right to claim attribution as the author, the right to be free from being falsely named as author, and the right to remain anonymous.[21]
3. Exposure (*droit de divulgation*), or the creator's right to control if and under what circumstances their work will be released to the public.
4. The right to withdraw (*droit de repentir*) a work from circulation.
5. Resale and royalty right (*droit de suite*), the right to share the proceeds of future sales, e.g., for works of art.

These rights remain with the author/creator even after they have released economic interest in the work. In many cases the rights may be inalienable and remain in perpetuity.

As US copyright law evolved over its first 185 years, it remained isolated from moral rights and other international developments, including the 1886 Berne Convention for Literary and Artistic Works.[22] The United States started moving toward compliance with Berne in the mid-1970s when our copyright was made automatic on creation of a work. It wasn't until later, however, that the United States finally entered Berne, following the 1988 passage of the Berne Convention Implementation Act (BCIA). In doing so, we accepted the relatively narrow scope of moral rights found in the first paragraph of Article 6bis of the Berne treaty.

Fortunately, Berne's rather minimalist articulation of moral rights[23] did not incorporate many provisions that would require significant changes to our laws. However, one year after the United States joined Berne, Congress passed the Visual Artists Rights Act (VARA). It placed moral rights into US copyright law for one highly specific area but limited them to the rather minimal array of rights listed in Berne Article 6bis. Discussed above in relation to § 106A, VARA conferred moral or artistic rights of attribution and integrity on creators of narrowly defined works of visual art that exist in a single copy or in up to 100 successively numbered copies individually signed by the creator (see Chapter 4 and Box 4.6). The rights would only belong to the author and not extend beyond their lifetime, and only apply to works created on or after the act's effective date, December 1, 1990.

Legal scholar Peter Jaszi has argued that moral rights are not in the marketplace, but are inalienable, and thus their application would impede the free commerce in intellectual and artistic production that has long been supported by Anglo-American copyright. He also noted that moral rights can provide a charter for censorship.[24] Thus, we should be on the alert for legislative attempts to expand their entry into US law beyond the current point for copyright as well as for First Amendment reasons.[25]

To appreciate the complications that could arise from more extensive "moral rights," consider the dispute over two different productions of playwright Samuel Beckett's *Endgame*. For a production by the American Repertory Theater in Cambridge, Massachusetts (1984–5), Beckett was unsuccessful in barring that production's planned use of music by Philip Glass as well as the setting of the play in an abandoned subway station with the detritus of modern civilization. By contrast, he was able to force a famous French director to abandon his plan to use music and pink lighting as part of a production of the same play at the Comédie Française in Paris.[26] In both cases, Beckett was basing his claim on moral rights, but only succeeded outside the United States.

6.7 Rights in Traditional Cultural Property

Consider this scenario. A few decades ago, the widower of a faculty anthropologist visited your archives to drop off several boxes of his long deceased wife's files that he discovered in the attic while preparing to move across the country. The archives staff at the time completed a summary arrangement and description of the files. You recently decided to reprocess the collection to solve chronic problems when accessing it for reference service and to expand access.

A novice staff member did the reprocessing and noted that, in addition to important files on the early development of the Department of Anthropology, the files also included material from the professor's graduate student days, when she was living among a Native American tribe in the US Southwest.[27] These materials included field notes on tribal practices, drawings, photographic prints and negatives, and other items documenting their culture, daily life, and related archeological sites.

Excited about the Native American material, the staff member wants you to approve scanning and use of the materials to create an online exhibit to accompany the newly expanded finding aid and to promote use of the collection. You hesitate to approve because of current sensitivities about cultural anthropological items obtained many decades ago. Seeking guidance, you start by following your vague memory of news stories you had read about a law Congress passed years ago that called for museums and universities to return Native American items to the indigenous communities from which they were taken. On searching the web you see that the National Park Service has a website on the law that corresponds to your memory—the Native American Graves Protection and Repatriation Act (NAGPRA). There, you learn that the law's main focus is on protection and return of Native American human remains, funerary objects, sacred objects, and objects of cultural patrimony and does not seem to relate to the bulk of this anthropologist's collection, although there have been recent calls for expanding the scope of NAGPRA to include documents.[28]

These and other web sources and guidelines relating to NAGPRA have persuaded you that its policy and recommendations are not helpful for resolving your unease about the proposed digitization or web exhibit. Instead, they have made you realize there could be rights in the materials that might be infringed if copies were made and distributed via the web. This book has probably taught you more than you ever wanted to know about copyright, but is that knowledge sufficient to make an informed decision on whether to do the exhibit or what should be included or excluded from it?

The answer is "no." That's because US copyright law is an inadequate guide for the responsible management of traditional cultural property from indigenous communities. Materials such as photographs and field notes on daily life, customs, ceremonies, etc., call for special treatment that current national and international standards address only insufficiently.

Because US copyright law falls short of what's needed in your approach to cultural rights in traditional knowledge and cultural expressions, this section will emphasize highlights of the guidance provided by the First Archivist Circle's *Protocols for Native American Archival Materials*.[29] Before exploring the relationship of copyright to traditional cultural materials, you should become aware of some working definitions of key terms as well as key conceptual and practical differences between copyright and traditional knowledge/ traditional cultural expressions.

6.7.1 Terminology and Definitions

Acknowledging that there are conceptual distinctions among those working in this field, the following are working definitions sufficient to help you understand the issue of Native American materials in the context of US copyright.

Cultural property "means property which, on religious or secular grounds, is specifically designated by each State as being of importance for archaeology, prehistory, history, literature, art or science."[30]

Indigenous knowledge "is a systematic way of thinking applied to phenomena across biological, physical, cultural, and spiritual systems. It includes insights based on evidence acquired through direct and long-term experiences and extensive and multigenerational observations, lessons, and skills. It has developed over millennia and is still developing in a living process, including knowledge acquired today and in the future, and it is passed on from generation to generation."[31]

Intangible cultural heritage means "the practices, representations, expressions, knowledge, skills—as well as the instruments, objects, artefacts and cultural spaces associated therewith—that communities, groups and, in some cases, individuals recognize as part of their cultural heritage. This intangible cultural heritage, transmitted from generation to generation, is constantly recreated by communities and groups in response to their environment, their interaction with nature and their history, and provides them with a sense of identity and continuity, thus promoting respect for cultural diversity and human creativity."[32]

Traditional cultural expressions (TCEs) are "tangible and intangible forms in which traditional knowledge and cultures are expressed, communicated or manifested. Examples include traditional music, performances, narratives, names and symbols, designs, and architectural forms."[33]

Traditional knowledge "includes the intellectual and intangible cultural heritage, practices and knowledge systems of traditional communities, including indigenous and local communities (traditional knowledge in a general sense or *lato sensu*). In other words, traditional knowledge in a general sense embraces the content of knowledge itself as well as traditional cultural expressions, including distinctive signs and symbols associated with traditional knowledge."[34]

6.7.2 Comparing Fundamentals of Traditional Knowledge and Copyright

Table 6.1 illustrates core conceptual and functional differences between traditional cultural property rights and those of U.S. copyright.

Table 6.1 Conceptual and Functional Differences Between Traditional Cultural Property Rights and Those of US Copyright

Traditional Knowledge Key Characteristics (UNESCO and WIPO)	**Copyright Key Characteristics (Title 17 U.S. Code)**
Traditional knowledge (TK), traditional cultural expressions (TCEs), cultural practices, skills, etc. that communities, groups, and individuals recognize as part of their heritage	Original works of authorship by individuals or "corporate persons" including literary, musical, dramatic, choreographic, pictorial, graphic, architectural works, and motion pictures and sound recordings.
May be in unfixed expression or in physical objects	Expressions fixed in a tangible medium
Collectively owned	Exclusive rights belong to an individual or corporate creator
Transmitted from generation to generation and constantly re-created by communities and groups in response to their environment	Exclusive rights endure for only a limited time, and eventually the work goes into the public domain
Cultural knowledge and items of patrimony may be inalienable	Ownership in whole or in part is transferable by written instrument
Can include culturally/spiritually sensitive materials & privileged knowledge	Exclusive rights only cover the work's expression, not facts, processes, or object in which the work is fixed
Making decisions on exceptions for access to TK and TCEs belongs within the community	By law, exclusive rights are qualified and subject to limitations and exceptions (e.g., fair use, library and archives activities, and exhaustion on occasion of first sale)

6.7.3 *Copyright Is Unhelpful*

It's no coincidence that the above definitions come from three different international bodies. In the midst of a market-centered and networked digital environment, the protection of traditional cultural heritage has become a global concern over the past three decades. It reflects the continued power differential between the "modern" world and that of the formerly colonized populations sometimes known as the Global North and the Global South.

Whether in North America or elsewhere, multiple issues arise from the diversity of indigenous communities, even within a country's own borders, as well as from the differences among their cultural traditions. Unfortunately, misappropriation by non-native societies is especially frequent. Moreover, there is often a significant mismatch in the typical solutions offered by international norm-setting bodies that prioritize intellectual property regimes based on the legal concepts of the former colonizing nations without regard to the concepts of the indigenous communities themselves. There may be no more concise description of the nature of the problem than the title of a 2011 study about the challenges faced by West African indigenous makers of traditional fabric patterns—*The Copyright Thing Doesn't Work Here: Adinkra and Kente Cloth and Intellectual Property in Ghana*.[35]

Thus, it's no surprise that US copyright law is also of little help in protecting traditional Native American cultural materials because it does not address core issues of: community ownership and management of rights; community interest in protecting religious and sensitive information from public disclosure; and protection of unfixed oral tradition and intangible property. In addition, the expiration of copyright's term, as well as exceptions (§ 107, § 108, § 109), can override indigenous community interests in continuous protection of culturally sensitive knowledge and expression over successive generations. As one expert put it:

> *One problem with copyright from an Indigenous perspective is that it expires and protects authors and publishers but not the interests of those whose culture is described or depicted. Indeed, Western copyright laws are based on principles which are diametrically opposite to Indigenous legal approaches to knowledge. Virtually every Indigenous society has traditions and laws regarding specialized knowledge, yet these practices are not recognized by Western law.*[36]

6.7.4 Help from Beyond Copyright

The *Protocols for Native American Archival Materials* is an aspirational statement of best practices for the culturally responsive care of Native American/Native Hawaiian archival material held by non-tribal organizations. It challenges us to think about archival responsibilities in relation to Native American/Native Hawaiian materials, and it can also be an introduction to considering parallel issues with traditional societies outside of the United

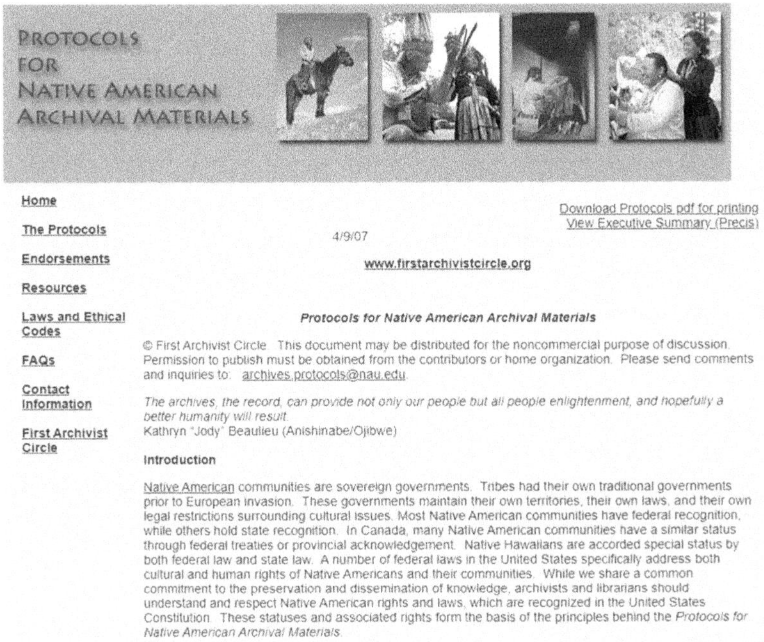

Figure 6.3 Protocols for Native American Archival Materials homepage, First Archivist Circle, accessed August 3, 2025, https://www2.nau.edu/libnap-p/protocols.html

States. A respectful reading of *Protocols* will require us to set to the side much of what we understand as the basis for copyright law. In particular, it requires us to refrain from assuming the universality of what we understand about ownership, exceptions, and the temporal limitations as found in Anglo-American copyright law.

As noted earlier in this chapter, indigenous cultural materials are the products of values and perspectives in tension with those of the world that gave birth to copyright and intellectual property. That's why it is important to look beyond what the US copyright law provides. Indeed, the *Protocols* state that: "Libraries and archives must recognize that Native American communities have primary rights for all culturally sensitive materials that are culturally affiliated with them. These rights apply to issues of collection, preservation, access, and use of or restrictions to these materials."[37]

Consistent with the inherent global focus of the concepts of indigenous knowledge, the *Protocols* deal with many matters beyond this book's efforts to make US copyright law intelligible to archivists. Especially following the SAA's 2018 endorsement of the *Protocols* as an external standard, they should be the go-to resource for any of you whose archival collections include indigenous materials.[38] They provide guiding principles for archival work relating to acquisition, repatriation or return of items, preservation, rethinking description, and user service facilities. In all areas, the overriding principles are respect for differences, acknowledgment of the continuing negative effects of colonization, and the importance of consultation and collaboration for finding a way forward.

My book cannot be a guide to all that needs to be considered to deal properly with traditional cultural materials for which your archives is responsible. However, our main focus, copyright, can serve as a first step for understanding how the existential differences of traditional knowledge and culture can affect the entire spectrum of archival functions. As stated in the *Protocols*:

> *Existing copyright legislation does not address issues of significance to Native American communities such as: community ownership of works and management of rights; community interests in public disclosure of religious or sensitive information; protection of older or ancient works (e.g., rock art); the antiquity and accumulative nature of traditional knowledge; and the protection of oral traditions, songs, and other culturally sensitive intangible property.*[39]

Above all, just because copyright law might allow or preclude you from doing something with conventional collections, you cannot assume that it gives you license to do, or not do, the same with indigenous archival materials. The alternative is to seek guidance from the specific native communities related to the materials.

The *Protocols*, however, do provide a sound start. They include a useful listing of the kinds of archival materials needing special treatment because they contain culturally sensitive knowledge. This may arise with images of ceremonies and sacred places, with sound and video recordings of songs, music, oral histories, as well as with maps, and archaeological data. The listing alone can open the eyes of an archival worker still unfamiliar with Native American cultural materials. They may help you to think about an anthropologist's research files in terms of user access issues that would be unlikely in the papers of a biologist or political scientist. The *Protocols* provide an adept explanation of the impact of the traditional ways of knowing on the role and meaning of documents, while also serving as a reminder of the history of the removal of traditional cultural expressions from their creators. Understanding this can be a foundation for ways of thinking about curatorship beyond what would come from detailed technical standards.

More specifically, from the standpoint of what can be made available to the public at large or to individual users in the reading room, the *Protocols'* advice on accessibility is especially important:

1. Recognize that previous conditions relating to open or restricted use may have been established without or contrary to community knowledge or assent.
2. Consult actively with authorized community representatives to arrive at agreement on access and use policies, or even repatriation/return, if that is deemed best.
3. Exercise extreme care in providing materials in digital form, particularly online, and in ways that allow separation of items from their cultural context.
4. Respect community requests to restrict access to materials containing ceremonial or religious knowledge.
5. Even more than with conventional/Western works, do not seek commercial publication, permission, or use fees, and in rare instances where fees may be paid, ensure that the source community receives the benefit.

The above recommendations are only a distillation of the guidance found throughout the *Protocols*, not a comprehensive listing.[40] This summary is intended only to introduce the need for a distinctive mode of thinking when approaching traditional cultural materials from the quite different perspective of Anglo-American copyright law. There is no substitute for your own close and considered reading of this important document.

Clearly, then, traditional knowledge systems are philosophically different from Western systems, in which individual ownership dominates and copyright proliferates. Thus, community ownership of traditional cultural knowledge—"texts," stories, and artifacts—can be in tension with copyright's dependence on notions of property, transfer of ownership, and exclusive rights. We cannot change the fact that the presence of indigenous materials in non-indigenous archives is an artifact of colonial and post-colonial hegemony, but we can work to get beyond that power differential by professionally and proactively collaborating to arrive at best practices for today's world.

To return to the hypothetical scenario that introduced this section, it should be clear that in light of all of the above, following only the rules of US copyright law would be disrespectful of the cultural property rights of the Native Americans whom the now deceased anthropologist had studied and documented decades ago. Luckily for our hypothetical archivists, the *Protocols* have alerted the supervisor that the novice staff member's proposal to digitize and place online the images and field notes from the anthropologist's research and time with the tribe may need to be reassessed. A more experienced staff member, preferably someone who has familiarized themselves with current thinking on Native American archival materials, should also review the collection in its entirety to assess and determine the presence of other items of potential cultural sensitivity. The archivist should also seek out a specialist on Native American studies within the parent institution for advice and direction on where to go externally for professional help. The goal should be to locate and begin a collaboration with the relevant community(ies) the anthropologist had worked so hard to document when she was a graduate student.

To provide a quick overview of the multiple facets of all these relatives of copyright, the following tables look at each of these separate legal domains in regard to the nature of rights, ownership, purpose, origination, infringement, and overlap with copyright.

Table 6.2 Copyright's Relatives: Patents

Legal Basis for Right	Object/Right Involved	Presumed Owners	Purpose and Impact	How Originates / How Ends	How Infringed	Overlap with Copyright
Constitution Article I, Section 8 *Federal law* (title 35 of the United States Code)	Exclusive right over methods for making an invention. 1) Utility patent (process, machine, manufactured article, composition of a material); 2) Design patent (physical appearance of produced item); 3) Plant varieties bred asexually. All inventions must be novel and nonobvious to receive a patent.	The inventor or creator of the process, machine, article, material, plant, or design.	Incentive for development of new devices, drugs, plants, and designs by providing exclusive rights for a limited time. Enable the availability of the methodology of the invention for free public use once the patent expires (e.g., generic drugs).	Submit to USPTO a detailed description of process to be patented. "Pending" until USPTO completes review and grants or denies. Utility and plant patents last 20 years after 1st effective filing date. Design patents expire 15 years after submission. Lose patent if do not pay maintenance fees.	Make, use, or sell the invention without permission of the patent rightsholder. Civil liability only.	Design patents for manufactured articles may also be eligible for copyright. Fair use for research of product or process.

Table 6.3 Copyright's Relatives: Trademarks

Legal Basis for Right	Object/Right Involved	Presumed Owners	Purpose and Impact	How Originates / How Ends	How Infringed	Overlap with Copyright
Federal: Lanham Act Title 15, Chapter 22, Subchapters I-IV. *Common Law* rights through state courts.	Word, phrase, or logo to identify the source of goods or services. Includes "trade dress" (design and shape of product packaging).	*Federal*: Person/-business which registered the mark with USPTO. *Common law:* Business owners who created and sustained continuous use of the mark.	Protect consumers from confusion by providing an indication of the source of a product or service. Practical effect is to support the building of an identity for owner of the mark. In some cases it can become more than a mere signifier but an item of commerce in itself.	*Federal*: registration for mark used in interstate commerce on goods/ services. Expires 10 years after registration, but can be renewed. *State/ Common law*: Use mark in commerce, and vigilantly police others' use of mark. Registration varies by state. In both, trademark can be lost if stop using it or abandon it by failing to pursue others who use the mark or identifier.	Use of the mark, or of a mark of substantial similarity, in commerce in relation to the same general range of products/ services as the mark's owner and in a way likely to confuse consumers.	The textual, graphical, or audio identifier could also be a work subject to copyright. Copyright's fair use exceptions can be applied to use of a trademark. Key: avoid use of a trademark in ways that could cause confusion among consumers or that involves commercial activity.

Table 6.4 Copyright's Relatives: Trade Secrets

Legal Basis for Right	Object/Right Involved	Presumed Owners	Purpose and Impact	How Originates / How Ends	How Infringed	Overlap with Copyright
Present in most states laws based on Uniform Law Commission's *Uniform Trade Secrets Act*. Previously dependent on common law and adjudication of torts.	Business information that's subject to reasonable efforts to preserve confidentiality and which has value because not generally known in the trade.	Business and other corporate entities that have strategic value in lists of customers, modes of operation, product formulas, etc.	Protect the competitive position of a business or other entity in the marketplace.	Information with economic value not generally known or readily discoverable & subject to reasonable efforts to protect from disclosure. Ends when security is breached and information becomes available to public or competitors.	Acquiring the information by improper means or through breach of confidence. Finding infringement requires demonstration that defendant used improper means to obtain it. Generally only a matter of state civil law.	In theory, the information could qualify for copyright protection based on subject matter, scope & authorship (§102). In practice copyright unlikely to arise unless confidentiality is breached.

Table 6.5 Copyright's Relatives: Privacy Rights

Legal Basis for Right	Object/Right Involved	Presumed Owners	Purpose and Impact	How Originates / How Ends	How Infringed	Overlap with Copyright
Common Law, US Constitution (implied right), *Federal statutory* law: FERPA, HIPPA.	One's "right to be let alone."	Living natural persons/ living human beings.	Freedom from unwarranted exposure and resultant emotional harm.	Privacy right ends at death of the natural person, but disclosure of "private" facts about the deceased have been found to violate the privacy of surviving relatives.	1) Intrusion on a person's seclusion. 2) Public disclosure of private facts (matters that would be offensive to a person of reasonable sensibility). 3) Being publicly placed in a false light. 4) Appropriation of one's name or likeness.	Sometimes invoked in copyright disputes, but privacy rights relate to facts, not works. Copyright endures for life of the author + 70 years, but privacy ends at death. Privacy can be compromised by public availability of copyright works that otherwise might be eligible for fair use.

Table 6.6 Copyrights Relatives: Publicity Rights

Legal Basis for Right	Object/Right Involved	Presumed Owners	Purpose and Impact	How Originates/ How Ends	How Infringed	Overlap with Copyright
State Law: Extension of privacy right's "appropriation prong." Many states establish it as an explicit right, but can be addressed in laws of unfair competition and by common law.	Exclusive property right to the commercial use of one's name, image, voice, or other identifying features.	Individual persons.	Protect the identity and the property interests that individuals have in their name, image, and likeness.	Publicity right may continue after death for varying number of years from state to state (from 10 to 100 years).	Commercial use of name, image, voice, or other identifying features of a person without authorization.	Whether still in copyright or in the public domain, works in archival collections may include images or objects that could violate publicity rights if used in a commercial fashion.

Table 6.7 Copyright's Relatives: Moral Rights

Legal Basis for Right	Object/Right Involved	Presumed Owners	Purpose and Impact	How Originates/ How Ends	How Infringed	Overlap with Copyright
Berne Convention, Article 6*bis*	Non-economic but personal artistic rights in creative works.	Original author/ creator of the work; not transfer-able.	Right to claim authorship, withdraw a work, and object to alteration or distortion of work.	Originate on creation of a work. Inalienable and perpetual in many countries, but in other countries ends at death of creator.	Failure to provide attribution of work; falsely claim authorship of work; distorting, modifying work, or other derogatory action which would be prejudicial to author's honor/ reputation.	Not enforceable under US federal copyright, except for narrow category of works of visual art. See Chapter 4's discussion of § 106A.

Table 6.8 Copyright's Relatives: Cultural Property Rights

Legal Basis for Right	Object/Right Involved	Presumed Owners	Purpose and Impact	How Originates/ How Ends	How Infringed	Overlap with Copyright
Largely absent from US statutory provisions, but can be matter of professional ethics and standards, e.g., *Protocols for Native American Archival Materials*.	Culturally sensitive materials, in any documentary form, and related to practices, expressions, knowledge, skills that communities recognize as part of their cultural heritage.	Collectively owned by the community(ies) of origin.	Contribute to the identity of the community and preservation of its cultural heritage.	On creation and continuing through community's re-creation by transmission from generation to generation.	Used in ways contrary to the values and protocols of the community of origin.	In theory, opposite of copyright's objectives of public access; transferability, ownership; and eventual expiration of rights. Uses allowed by copyright may violate cultural property rights.

7 Taming the Copyright Beast

Administering Archives for Copyright

Congratulations! You've made it through the copyright maze! You now have a sense of how to think about the law's web of exclusive rights, duration, exceptions, and loopholes, and even how it may or may not relate to other types of property rights. However, you've been seen at your desk lately scratching your head while trying to figure out how to use this arcane knowledge in daily archival work—the job you trained for and are lucky enough to do every day.

Where do you start? An experienced driver would never think of pulling an owner's manual out of the glove compartment while in the middle of a congested expressway, to figure out how the "infotainment" system works. So, it's not realistic for you to be pulling up Title 17 or reviewing public domain charts or fair use checklists when you meet with prospective donors, answer reference questions, or scan documents for preservation or use. Responsibly following copyright law while managing everything else that the archival mission requires is just too demanding to be either constantly checking the US code or improvising in the middle of daily archives work.

To help you absorb copyright matters into your daily archival practice, this chapter will provide the foundation for incorporating copyright management into ongoing archival work. It will provide an overview of which aspects of copyright law relate to the major functional domains of archival work; identify the most important areas needing policy documents; and outline essential elements of those policies.

As noted at the outset of this book, no two archives are the same. There are many differences among archival materials, resources, administrative settings, and user communities of the repositories typically holding the archival materials that have been the focus of this book's guidance on copyright. Considering these divergences, a full set of policies and procedures for administration of copyright is beyond what can be presented in one chapter. Rather, effective archives management of copyright ultimately depends on sound institution-specific policies that knowledgeable staff can apply consistently but flexibly. Thus, the focus here will be on identifying the core areas where policies will be needed and the key elements to put those policies into use.

Before proceeding, we need to acknowledge a relevant observation from archivist Aprille Mckay: "Copyright law is sadly out of step and fails to protect our mission of responsibly acquiring, caring for, and providing access to digital documents of cultural significance. Though it is possible that Congress will act to amend the law . . . the reality is that we must figure out how to cope with our unsatisfactory legal framework."[1] Meanwhile, our collections, user communities, technology, and professional best practices continue to evolve. Because both the law and its judicial interpretation evolve in ways that may either hinder or occasionally assist our work, our policies and our procedures and forms require regular review and revision.

7.1 Distinct Domains of Archival Practice: General Policy Needs

As a foundation for this book's analysis of copyright for archivists, Chapter 1 provided an overview of seven functional domains at the center of archives work: authorization, authentication, appraisal, arrangement, description, preservation, and use. To varying degrees, copyright policy issues can arise in most, if not all, of these domains:

Authorization (the founding mandate and the administrative reporting line of the archives):

- For an organizational or institutional archives, is there a general statement as to what extent the organization/institution claims copyright ownership in works created by the institution's employees? Is your institution one where certain professionals work independently enough that they are not subject to work-made-for-hire rules?[2]
- For a "manuscript repository" or general historical collection, what is its institutional authority to collect and make materials available?

- How much latitude does the archives have to set its own policy?
- Does the archivist have the authority to grant copyright permissions for works authored by institutional employees?

Authentication (practices to ensure that records are what they purport to be):

- Maintaining or documenting the chain of custody of records.
- Establishing who are the original owner and successive owners of material being transferred within the institution or acquired from external parties.
- Documenting a formal written transfer of copyright when there is a physical transfer.

Appraisal (selection and transfer of materials to be part of the archives):

- Assessing whether copyright ownership in the material can be established clearly.
- Determining whether the source person, unit, or organization is willing and legally able to transfer copyright with the materials.[3]
- Acquiring collections with a Deed of Gift that clarifies ownership rights.

Arrangement and *Description* (sometimes grouped together as "processing"):

- Maintaining *respect des fonds*, document provenance, and maintaining the original order to provide future archivists with the means to track copyright ownership and assess possible works-made-for-hire conditions.
- Applying detailed descriptive practices to provide an evidentiary trail when separating documents based on physical formats.[4]

Preservation (protecting and ensuring the survival and future viability of archives):

- Taking full advantage of the preservation exceptions in the copyright statute's clear legal path to make copies for preservation.
- Carefully following the relatively modest threshold of qualifying requirements in § 108—copying only works for which an unused replacement cannot be obtained at a fair price and ensuring that preservation copies carry a notice of copyright.
- Limiting the number of preservation copies to the amount needed to ensure secure backups and complying with the § 108(b) and

(c) prohibitions on making the digital copies available beyond the premises of the library or archives.

Access and Use (whether use is by the archives staff or people beyond the staff) employ policies that:

- Reflect the distinct implications of varying formats that fall within the scope of copyright.
- Acknowledge the full scope of exclusive rights (copying, distribution, adaptation, performance, and public display).
- Make full use of the exceptions built into the law (§ § 107, 108, 109, 110).
- Develop policies, procedures, and forms that reflect risk-mitigation factors discussed in Chapter 8.
- Create and utilize user registration agreements, user copying and scanning regulations, citation and use guidelines, and FAQs on copyright basics.

7.2 Primary Role of Policies

7.2.1 Establishing Policies

Put three archivists in a room, ask to see their copyright policies, and it's unlikely you will find a single version to adopt above all others. Instead, you may find some of the phrases recurring, but you will also find many variations in how the policies are written and even some divergence in their underlying principles. That's because institutional placement, collections held, and user community shape specific organizational policies and procedures, and that is consistent with this book's emphasis on the primary role of archives to serve the public.

So, it's no surprise that this book can't give you all-purpose specific language for policies to navigate the copyright maze. There are, however, objectives and principles for policies that should remain constant in the face of inevitable compromises between strict control, user friendliness, staff resources, institutional oversight, and the need to be compatible with allied units handling cultural heritage collections.

The daily administration of copyright can be simplified by creating policies that are developed carefully, applied routinely, and reviewed and updated periodically. These policies can also play a key role in managing risk by bolstering your defense when complaints arise. As statements of your archival goals, such policies can help you develop specific procedures and forms to aid in your daily operations. Remember—thoughtful policies can help bridge the gap between a copyright that is inconsiderate of archives and your institutional and societal mission.

Where to start? Unless you have the luxury to create a full suite of policies before ever opening your doors for business, the first step is to survey what copyright-related policies already exist. Do you have deed of gift templates? User registration forms? Search room rules? Your survey may reveal an array of gaps, some of which may need immediate attention by replacing inadequate existing language. Later, you can address changes as needed to deal with new issues that emerge with evolving collections, user needs, and laws.

7.2.2 Elements Needed in Major Policy Areas

7.2.2.1 Policy Elements re Ownership of Copyright

As should be obvious from the historic and legal foundations of copyright, its essence is ownership of a work—an ownership that is transferable and lasts a very long time. Thus, archival institutions should work to have copyright ownership transferred whenever physical or digital materials are transferred. Best practice calls for the preparation of a formal, written deed rather than a deposit agreement, whether oral or written.[5] Obtaining ownership will provide the clearest legal path possible for the archives to make copies for preservation and use, make material available to users, post material online, and respond to permission requests when users move to publication or other public dissemination. An archetypical deed of gift will:

- Be in writing and be cosigned.
- Identify the donor, the intended legal recipient (the donee), the materials being donated, and the rights being transferred.
- Make clear the materials are being donated for public, educational, and general research use but acknowledge, at a summary level, any areas needing limited-term access restrictions.
- Grant permission for the archives to reformat materials for preservation purposes.

- Provide authority for the archives to separate materials deemed to not be of enduring value and provide an indication of whether they are to be returned to donor, discarded, or other disposition.
- Call for the transfer of not only rights of copyright, but also any rights of privacy, publicity, or other intellectual property rights that the donor may own in the material.
- Stipulate that future additions to the collection will be covered by the same terms as the current deed.
- Attest that, to the best of the donor's knowledge, they own the materials and the rights to which the deed refers.

Typically, a deed will include an attachment inventorying the materials being donated, but because a deed should be prepared and concluded prior to or on receipt of the physical materials, the attachment may need to be limited to a summary description noting the volume, general subject scope of the materials, documentary forms in the acquisition, and any other salient characters of the collection. In all cases, beyond signatures of the donor(s) and the archivist/curator, the deed should be transmitted to and signed by the authorizing officer of the parent institution of the archives. Once fully executed, all signatories should receive a signed original, although using emailed PDFs that are signed physically or electronically is an alternative if all parties agree.

Working with a prospective donor on a deed of gift requires time and substantial interpersonal and listening skills. No doubt your standard deed template may not fit some circumstances, and some donors may want to take exception to one or more clauses. If a prospective donor looks at a draft deed and immediately believes that they need to consult their attorney, the archivist should support that wish even if it could lead to proposals for amendments that complicate the negotiation. Some flexibility is appropriate, but the more changes made from your standard deed, the less useful it will be as a policy template. Overall, both you and your donors will be well-served by providing them with the Society of American Archivists' "A Guide to Deeds of Gift" (https://www2.archivists.org/publications/brochures/deeds-of-gift). It is a sensitively written narrative summary of the elements of a deed, and it explains to donors why each of the elements is needed to accomplish their goals and the needs of the archives. It is also available as a brochure that can be purchased in quantities for archivists to have on hand to send to all prospective donors as part of the archivist's initial conversation with them.

Another issue that sometimes arises: a prospective donor may suggest that, instead of completing a deed of gift, they can just add a provision to their will to donate the collection or the intellectual property rights following their death. This is inadvisable because a will can be changed at any time. Even if the will is not changed, there's always the possibility that the estate could be challenged or otherwise need to go through probate.

There is an alternative way to address a donor's concern or interest in continuing to exploit their copyright, as may arise if they are an active writer, artist, musician, or other creator. In that case, the deed should be written to transfer copyright at the time the deed is signed, but should also include a provision for the donee to license back to the donor specific rights for their lifetime (see Box 7.1). In a few rare cases, the prospective donor may want such licensed-back rights and the income therefrom not just for their lifetime, but also for that of their heirs. This can complicate both the original acquisition and the ongoing management of the collection for many years. However, if special circumstances make it necessary to accommodate this interest, the duration should not extend for more than one generation beyond the donor's lifetime. Furthermore, if used, the continued validity of such an extended license should require that each of the named successor beneficiaries keep the archives and its parent institution informed of their current address.

Box 7.1 Alternate Clause in Deed for Donor to Continue to Exploit Their Copyright

A sample clause to both transfer copyright and to license back rights to the donor might be: "To facilitate the research use of the Materials, the Donor hereby gives and assigns to the Donee those rights of copyright which the Donor may have in the Materials as well as any rights of privacy and publicity in the materials which the Donor may hold. The [*insert name of the archives*] is hereby authorized to administer any copyright permissions related to the Materials. In return, Donee hereby grants to the Donor during their lifetime the right to use the Materials for any purpose, including publication. Donor and Donee shall, to the extent possible, inform each other of any major publications."

Deeds and related work with donors can be time-consuming, but it is largely a matter of the relationship-building that is central to many other aspects of archives as living institutions. Once carefully completed, a deed is a "gift" to both the donor and to the archives as well as to its future staff and users. Nevertheless, deeds may not always be ironclad guarantees. Sometimes, a donor, especially a family member of a deceased original creator, may think they own all the rights they agreed to transfer in the deed. They may be unaware of a prior transfer or assignment of rights or unaware of a works-made-for-hire clause in the deceased creator's employment contract. No deed can do more than say that the donor is transferring rights they "may have" in the materials. If you are later approached by someone or an institution/organization that believes either the donor or creator did not own some of the rights in question, having a well-written deed will provide a solid base to demonstrate good faith so that you can work collegially to negotiate an arrangement that meets both parties' needs.

There are a few other ownership-related questions to explore and document that do not need to become formal policies themselves:

- Who at your institution is the officer or unit to be named as the legal recipient (donee) of gifts?
- How extensive of a role does the institution give to the archivist to research permission requests from users and to proffer a best estimate as to the copyright status of donated works being requested for publication or dissemination?
- Who or what institutional office can provide the archivist with authoritative advice on complex copyright permission requests? Once that is known, you should develop a relationship with them to help them understand the murky world of archival copyright.
- Who at the institution is the officer or unit for officially granting copyright permissions requested by archives researchers now wishing to quote from or reproduce documents, the copyright of which is owned by the institution?
- If you are the archivist for the official records of an *external* institution or organization, how broadly or narrowly does the *external* body interpret works-made-for-hire ownership in works made by their employees, whether mundane or highly creative?
- What will be the archives and its parent institution's policy on the copyright ownership of materials held on deposit, whether of

currently active or defunct organizations? If an active organization wishes to retain copyright ownership in materials on deposit, who in that organization is responsible for timely response to permission requests?

7.2.2.2 Policy Elements for Copying and User Services

Most established archives will already have policies, procedures, and forms for services provided to users and related rules for the search room. These may suffice as templates that can, with modest amendment, be adapted to address copyright concerns. That would be the preferred approach. If not, then new stand-alone policies or forms to deal solely with copyright issues could be prepared, although limiting the number of forms that confront users has its advantages. Regardless of approach, core copyright elements for policies related to user services and copying include:

- Clarity on whether your staff is responsible for making all copies for users or whether you allow both self-service copying and staff completing copy orders. If all copying must be done by staff, you have greater control for both physical protection of items and adherence to rules to keep copying within the bounds of fair use or library/archives exceptions (§ § 107 or 108). A policy of staff-only copying may not be possible in archives with fewer staff. Barring users from cellphone photographs of documents may not be viable for either enforcement or public relations reasons.
- When staff do the copying, § 108 requires that: copies not be made for direct or indirect commercial advantage; the copy becomes the property of the user; copying is done for isolated and unrelated reproduction or distribution; and copies must carry whatever copyright notice appeared on the original, or at least a statement of "this work may be protected by copyright." Of course, § 108(h) does not permit making copies for users of "a musical work, a pictorial, graphic or sculptural work, or a motion picture or other audiovisual work other than an audiovisual work dealing with news." For those, a fair use assessment would need to be made.
- If self-service copying is allowed, whether by photocopy machines, overhead book camera, flatbed document/photo scanners, or a visitor's personal camera, tablet, or mobile phone, such copies should be only for private study and personal use. Consistent with

recommendations of the Copyright Office, there should be readily visible copyright warning notices on or near any reproduction equipment or places where users would be allowed to take pictures.[6] Copyright warning advisories about use of self-service reproducing equipment, whether personal or owned by the archives, also should be incorporated as advisories in the user registration form.

Other advisories less specific than what the copyright law requires might include:

- Notices of charges for staff-made scans or digital images, as well as turnaround times or potential limits on the number of items that can be digitized without creating backlogs for other orders.
- Notice of guidelines the archives follows on amount of time that staff can spend researching the copyright status and ownership of works.
- Order forms should call attention to the fact that certain types of works (musical, pictorial, graphical, sculptural, and audiovisual works) are precluded by § 108 (i) from the library/archives exceptions for making copies for users. For those, the form or the staff should ask users to provide information about the nature of their intended use, especially if they have plans beyond private study. The staff can then use that information to assess how well the planned use might fit with a fair use justification. This could also take the form of asking the requester to indicate if they have contacted or will be contacting the copyright owner for public use of the work being requested.

7.2.2.3 Researcher Requests for Copyright Permissions: Policy Elements

A challenging policy matter arises from the likelihood that someone who has previously done research in your archives, or received copies through a remote order, will be required by their publisher to obtain written copyright permission from wherever the researcher obtained the works they now wish to quote or otherwise use in their own work. Even if a researcher's use might seem to qualify as fair use, their publishers or other intermediaries almost invariably require authors to obtain written permissions.[7]

They seem to be haunted by the first cases that involved fair use claims—that involving the Gerald Ford memoir (*Harper & Row v. Nation Enterprises*) and the J. D. Salinger biography (*Salinger v. Random House*), even though those decisions are now 35 to 40 years old. Each decision noted that the unpublished nature of a work weighs against a finding of fair use. Subsequent cases and law have noted that, by itself, the unpublished nature of a work does not preclude a fair use finding so long as the other fair use factors were considered. Nevertheless, publishers or their counsel still want the clarity of signed permissions. Unsurprisingly, they do not want to rely on going to court to make a fair use defense. As a result, researchers wanting to use archival materials in their books, articles, or documentaries are directed to secure formal permission from where they obtained the items.

An archives' response to a researcher's permission request is best done on a case-by-case basis. When it's clear that the archives owns or manages the copyright in a work that is the subject of a permission request, the archives should be responsible for acting on the request. Granting such permission should be relatively straightforward. However, as is often the case, the diverse authorship in most archival holdings means that many permission requests will involve works in which the archives neither owns nor manages the copyright.

In these cases, it is not a great fit for archives to simply post a policy, or issue boilerplate replies, saying that the archives does not respond to permission requests and instead point the users to fair use guidelines. If the works involved are archetypical library items—published books, journals, and similar items it might not be an unreasonable policy because such works once had an active market and still carry basic identifying information about the author and copyright holder.

However, that's not the case with archetypical archival content, where the majority of our holdings are unpublished works lacking readily identifiable owners. These are considered to be copyright orphans. A policy that leaves the researcher on their own, with no more than a pointer to fair use, will not only frustrate them, but would be contrary to the archival mission that has been at the center of this book's concern. Moreover, archivists have a responsibility to take a more engaged approach because we, not the requester, have the tools and information to address the problem.

Because our cultural heritage institutions have acquired, processed, and preserved collections for their enduring value to the institution and society, it is incumbent on us to do what we can to facilitate the direct use of materials by those in our search rooms or those off-site who are using digitally supplied materials. Our responsibility should not end with that initial interaction. Fulfilling the archives' mission requires us to recognize and facilitate the "indirect use" that comes when our researchers employ their findings to create new works that reach the public and benefit society at large. This is consistent with the constitutional purpose of copyright. Furthermore, it's only through what a researcher creates based on our holdings that archives can achieve the "impact factor" that makes administrators take notice at budget and strategic planning times.

Of course, providing such service can be challenging. Orphan works make up a large portion of archival holdings, and it may often be impossible to find much about the original owner or subsequent owners to give the requester what they need to provide the permission their publisher is seeking. More often than not, the archives may be unable to do more than help the user to demonstrate that there has been a good faith but unsuccessful effort to locate the owner. If the researcher is fortunate enough to have a flexible publisher, having the archives state that the item appears to be an orphan work might be enough to satisfy the publisher, along with a statement that the archives has no objection to the use.

All too often, publishers or other intermediaries may not understand or accept the reality of orphan works. In these cases, the researcher is not in a position to indemnify or assume liability should a copyright owner file a complaint. Then, the researcher may need to find a way to adapt their work around the publisher's demands.[8] Regardless, even with limited resources available, the archives' policy should state a willingness to research and report on the basic facts about the works for which permission is sought.

A few administrative controls are needed, however. Minimally, they might include clear time limits, and that no search should be initiated unless the user has provided specific citations to the works in question. The information the archives can offer might be limited to the identity of the author, their position or capacity at the time they authored the work, and the last address if known. That's the sort of information that should be discoverable in the collections themselves or in the archives' administrative files. In personal experience with archival collections containing large amounts of unpublished works of "everyday" organizational or personal business, I've found that the result of many searches is often that the work is indeed an orphan.

That leaves the researcher with only two options—to not use the work or to rely on fair use. The fact that neither the researcher nor the archives staff can find a rights holder effectively is a "negative finding" but one that still has some utility. It supports a conclusion that the work is indeed orphaned, and a copyright claimant cannot be located. For a systematic and professionally informed way to conduct a search to determine orphan status for a work or collection, see Box 7.2 for a "high level" paraphrase of the SAA's "best practices."[9] All of these facts about not being able to locate a rights holder should bolster the fourth factor of a fair use defense.

Do your archives staff or administrative superiors balk at your dedicating resources to entertaining permission requests? They need to recognize that merely telling the researcher to do their own searching will generate the researcher's logical response of submitting a new reference request seeking facts that can be found only in your archives. That, of course, simply redirects the work back to you and your staff. In other words, from a pragmatic standpoint, having an upfront policy for providing a defined minimum amount of research relevant to a permission request will not only save time and resources but also control use of your resources in a predictable fashion while staying faithful to an essential part of reference service. The good will that this approach can engender is an additional benefit.

Make sure your policy on responding to permission requests has some guardrails concerning the amount of time the staff can spend on any given request, whether it is as little as 30 minutes per work/author sought or more if there are extenuating circumstances. It should also state the limited kind of information that can typically be found and what may be beyond reach. In addition, before the staff can start on a request, the policy should require the researcher to provide a clear and accurate citation to where in the archives they found the item they now want to use.

When granting the permission, or even just stating the archives does not own the rights but has no objection to its use, the response should indicate the citation and credit lines the researcher must use when an item appears in a publication or other work. Examples of formats for citations and credit lines have been developed by the Rights Statements Consortium, available at http://rightsstatements.org. In addition, your policy should also require that any results from your permission research should be documented and retained internally with the administrative "control file" for the relevant collection, both for record purposes and to aid when there are future permission requests involving the same work or same author.

Box 7.2 Orphan Works Search, Key Points

Orphan Works: Materials presumably still in copyright but where the rights owner cannot be identified or cannot be located.

Avoid vague idea of a "diligent search" and decide on a "minimal," "extended," or "extraordinary" search according to circumstances of authorship, nature, and age of the work.

Create a summary record/inventory of your completion of the following phases of your search to substantiate a good-faith effort:

Identify the creator or rights holder

Can the creator be identified from the works themselves?

If not, do the works or related contextual materials enable an identification?

Might the creator's rights have been transferred by a formal agreement or a will?

Might the materials have been created as works-made-for-hire?

Locate copyright holder

What address information might be in the works themselves or in the archives administrative files?

Calibrate the extent of searching according to the commerciality of the works, uniqueness of creator's name. Consider whether the author might be tracked down by following leads in occupational or professional directories related to whatever position they held when the now orphan work was created.

Use the Watch File database (https://norman.hrc.utexas.edu/watch//) to locate a literary agent or rule out the presence of one.

If an obituary can be located, be creative with your use of common internet search engines to locate heirs or others who might know of next of kin or literary agents.

If the creator may have written books, contact the publisher to determine what rights they hold. Similarly, follow leads with other sources for which the author may have created works for public distribution, e.g., magazines, photography and recording studios, etc.

A further policy issue to consider is whether you as the archivist wish to limit certain types of works or certain types of use where permission might not be granted, e.g., conversion of a work into an exploitative commercial product. Caution here is essential because such limits could come close to censorship. There is also a policy decision to be made about whether a permission fee should be charged. Fees may be defensible for certain types of uses, e.g., commercial or exploitative reproductions of works, *but only if* you are the copyright holder. However, there is a trend in the archives profession to not assess any permission fees at all for use of works from the archives.[10] Such fees can generate ill will. Moreover, unless the archives is sure it holds the copyright in the works being used, charging fees based on the nature of the use can undermine your claims of fair use and could even provide cause to be cited for contributory infringement.

7.2.2.4 Policy Elements for Digitization Projects

Over the past 30-plus years, the advent of networked graphical browsers and the increasing availability of digitization hardware and standards for digital imaging have caused many archives to launch or be encouraged to initiate projects to digitize their collections or put substantial portions online. As should be obvious from the preceding chapters, creating digital images of existing works conflicts with a copyright owner's § 106 exclusive right of reproducing copies. Placing those copies online also conflicts with the § 106 exclusive right of distribution. Moreover, placing items online increases the likelihood that any of your uses without authorization will be discovered. These concerns are important but should not be an automatic barrier to considering what and how to digitize. Instead, they should inform you how to think about planning digitization projects, even if you do not plan to put the material online beyond the premises of your repository, as allowed by § 108(d) and § 108(e). This book cannot provide a comprehensive guide to digitization or its technical and copyright requirements,[11] but from an administrative perspective, the following questions can provide a solid basis for policies to guide digitization:

- Will, or when would, the copyright status of a work be a make-or-break factor in selecting a work for digitization?
- How will the copyright status of items be assessed? At the level of individual works? Individual authors? By clusters or groups (genre, age, record series, importance, known demand), etc?[12]

- In assessing copyright status, what tools will you use to determine the status of a work(s) as orphan, public domain, or work-made-for-hire?[13]
- What limits might you, or can you, apply to downstream use of digitized archival content?
- How will you provide a takedown notice to be associated with digitized content posted online?

This last question points to a very essential risk management step and policy consideration when planning online projects. As noted in Chapter 8 on Risk Management, placing a takedown notice that is easily discoverable by anyone viewing your online content is important both as a means of allowing copyright owners the opportunity to assert their interests and a way to provide you with a means to respond promptly to reduce further liability. This can possibly help to arrive at an early, amicable resolution; see Box 7.3.[14]

A takedown policy will only be useful if you have put into place very clear procedures so that, regardless of whether the request comes as a phone call, email, or cease-and-desist letter, and regardless of who receives it, the matter is immediately referred to the archivist. Prompt action by the archivist should

Box 7.3 Sample Takedown Notice

As a cultural heritage and educational institution the [*name of your repository and name of your parent institution*] archives/historical society digitizes archival materials and makes them accessible online to support education and research. Where possible, we provide attribution to authors and rights holders, but because of the nature of historical archives, it is often not possible to determine the copyright owner.

If you are the author/creator or holder of copyright in works we have placed online without attribution or with any other error, please contact us at [*your repository's email address*] so we may correct our records and address your concern.

If you are the copyright holder for material we placed online without your permission, or which may exceed exceptions in US copyright law, and you wish to request it be removed from the internet, please contact us at [*your repository's email address*] so we may provide you with instructions to complete a formal takedown request.

include temporarily disabling online access to the item(s) in question. A courtesy letter should also be written promptly to acknowledge the request. The letter should acknowledge receipt of the request and note that the work has been temporarily disabled while investigating the request. It should also ask for basic follow-up information and commit to working toward a mutually acceptable resolution. Once everyone catches their breath, the complaint should be investigated carefully. Often, given the predominance of orphan works in archives, having someone step forward with a complaint should be seen as an asset that enables you to learn more about the collection.

7.3 Staff Training

By now, it should be apparent that archives staff need to be conversant with the basics of copyright and particularly the special aspects of copyright related to archival materials. No one wants yet another training mandate, but a key copyright administration task is to make sure that all staff have an awareness of copyright, its pervasive presence in archives, and its strictures on what they and users can do with the material.

Asking all permanent staff to read a full text on copyright or asking all part-time or transient staff (e.g., students) to read one article on copyright, is probably a non-starter. Instead, why not give staff latitude as to what they would like to review from a short list of the publications or websites you find most useful. Are there articles or web tutorials they can look at?[15] Are there books they can refer to quickly? In fact, it might even be productive to ask them to brainstorm about whether there are less academic ways to build copyright awareness and knowledge. You could try creating a basic outline on copyright, then let them select their own readings. Periodic discussion groups can also help. They might learn more on their own and from their peers than from a mandated reading list.

One handy device to engender interactive conversations is to call their attention to the latest copyright case that has arisen in the press, such as the 2023 case involving chord progressions used by pop musician Ed Sheeran or what the monkey selfie case from 2015 to 2017 teaches us about copyright and artificial intelligence. There never seems to be a shortage of these. Even when the particulars of the many cases that get media attention seem to have little relation to archives, there's a lot to learn from looking at the issues that the legal profession manages to cook up. In other words, look for ways for the staff to have fun with what they know about copyright. In the spirit of International Edible Book Day, have the staff organize humorous, respectful, or bitingly critical ways to celebrate one or more of these curiously created quasi-holidays: Public Domain Day, World Fair Use Day, World Book and Copyright Day, World IP Day, or National Archives Day. As some of my examples in this book show, sometimes copyright can be good for more than a few laughs.

8 "Yes You Can!" Risk Management for Copyright in Archives

The plot of this melodrama so far might seem discouraging for archivists who want to make sure we stay within a law that fails to speak to us. Despite occasional references to unpublished materials in the long history of copyright, neither legislation nor court decisions have paid much attention to the unpublished materials or the functions that are central to the archival mission. Instead, the preceding chapters reflect an inexorable expansion of monopoly rights in response to nearly every advance in information technology. Does that mean we must live by these restrictions and face liabilities if we happen to make a mistake in our zeal to make information available? Are the two options below our only choices?

1 We do all we can to follow the law precisely. That would leave us in contortions trying to address the law's many nooks and crannies, but still leave us at risk of making a mistake or misunderstanding the complex law and thereby unintentionally infringing on someone's copyright.

—or—

2 We give the archival mission priority and do things we know, or should have good reason to know, are contrary to the law, and we just cross our fingers in the hope that we are not called to account, with the possibility that our actions later become a cautionary tale in archives case law history.

Not only does the second option create the chance of negative and costly consequences, but it also would be a disavowal of a professional's basic responsibility to respect the rights inherent in the legacy entrusted to us. Lest you think, however, that the first option of following the law carefully is the safest choice with the least liabilities, it carries with it the major liability of failing in our professional mission to manage the knowledge of the past for the benefit of the present and future.

Luckily, there is a way to find better options, and that should be the priority for any archivist's work with copyright. We need to think holistically. In fact, the key to survival, if not success, is to be found at the intersection of three types of knowledge that are all within our reach: cognizance of the law, deep familiarity with the collections we hold, and professional intelligence. These knowledge domains will help you find the needed balance between trying to avoid the negative consequences of either violating the law or neglecting our mission. They can help you balance liabilities against rewards so that you can accept and manage risk when working with copyright in archives. That's what's known as risk management.

The term "risk management" has most commonly been used by the insurance industry, often with an emphasis on preventing incidents that would require financial compensation via insurance. For a number of decades, the term has also had wide currency in the business management world, especially as part of strategic planning.

Perhaps the first serious examination in the library literature to apply risk management to legal challenges faced by librarians and educators came in 2006 when Thomas Lipinski made a broad survey of copyright liability. However, he generally steered clear of the role of risk management in digitizing orphan works.[1] Issues relating to the risks involved in orphan works were not considered by library literature in depth until a series of 2011–13 articles reporting on the experience of a number of North Carolina digitization projects.[2] Together, these writings laid a foundation for the research library community to embrace risk management in support of orphan works digitization at a time when prospects for Congress to solve the orphan works problem were dimming.

In 2016, the Harvard Library released an extensive survey of the statutory and case law of potential relevance for reducing risk in library orphan works projects.[3] The survey included some references to archives and special collections, but its greatest in-depth analysis related to published works with a known author, rather than the unpublished works that predominate in archives. That result is not uncommon in library literature analyses of risk management where the particular problems of archival orphan works tend to be overshadowed by ways to deal with published orphaned works.

A review of American archival literature itself shows that archivists preceded librarians in embracing risk management as a way to address difficult decisions relating to information resources. By the early to mid-1990s, risk management for archives began to appear frequently in discussions of practical appraisal decisions on the growing mass of modern records and the looming challenges of electronic records systems.[4] By 2005, risk management was identified as a general term in SAA's *Glossary of Archival & Records Terminology* to describe ways to solve decisions relating to threats, losses, and recovery.[5] In short order, archivists seized upon risk management as a way to proceed with large-scale digitization projects, including for collection-wide or multi-collection archival projects involving numerous unpublished works by diverse authors. Particularly influential was the first expansive discussion of the usefulness of risk management for archival digitization that appeared in Hirtle, Hudson, and Kenyon's 2009 *Copyright and Cultural Institutions*. It remains a valuable and highly accessible map of risk assessment for published and unpublished works. In a more narrative fashion, Heather Briston's "Managing Copyright in Archives: Risk Management" provides a thoughtful review essay.[6]

Thus, it seems well established that risk management is a mode of thinking for archivists to make informed decisions. In fact, it may be the only systematic way archivists have to determine how great a role we should give copyright in managing the preservation and use of our textual, graphical, and audiovisual holdings. The limited scope of archives-specific copyright exceptions and a general shortage of fair use cases relating to archival materials means that risk management strategies are essential, whether we are working with multi-author projects or making decisions on an individual work of a single, high-profile author.

"In archives as in life, zero risk is quite unrealistic."[7] However, deciding to accept risk must be more than merely labeling a project's *modus operandi* as "risk management." That's not management, but indeed it *is* risky behavior. There must be a process to examine the many unknowns. Unfortunately, neither the breadth and complexity of copyright nor the inherent uniqueness of archival collections lend themselves to a mechanical process that provides universally applicable decision trees, sequential checklists, and formulas.

Instead, the idea of copyright risk management for archivists is better understood as a way to think about the landscape of risk. It should be the process of gathering as much information as possible to reduce the unknowns. Once that's done, you can make sounder decisions in the contextual and aggregate manner that have been the hallmark of modern archives practice.

Risk management, then, is best seen as a strategy that incorporates multiple specific tactics, any one of which may not be sufficient to eliminate risk, but which, when deployed in a structured way, can support archivists engaging in activities that might otherwise seem to create risk of legal harm.[8]

To start working in this holistic, environmental way, we first need to explore some basic components and processes for you to apply as you make your own journey doing actual archives work in the face of copyright.

8.1 Definitions

The SAA *Dictionary of Archives Terminology* defines risk management as "the systematic control of damages or losses to archival records and institutions, including the assessment of threats, mitigation and prevention, and response and recovery efforts."[9] What are the underlying assumptions of this terminology? A serviceable sense of the term might come from common sense, life experience, or even a quick look at the most basic dictionary, but a more authoritative place to start might be with standards-setting bodies, such as the International Organization for Standardization (ISO). However, their definition of risk is a bit sparse: "the effect of uncertainty on objectives." For our purposes, the International Electrotechnical Commission (IEC) has a more useful definition of risk as "the combination of the probability of occurrence of harm and the severity of that harm."[10]

Note that these and the common dictionary definitions all link risk with the likelihood of negative outcomes of an action. In the context of this book's goal of helping archivists to work in a world constrained by copyright, remember that although any action can have negative consequences, a balanced consideration means that an action can also have neutral or good consequences. In other words, not all actions are equally risky, nor are all risk consequences equally negative.

Furthermore, in considering how we think about copyright risks in archival activities, we should note that the ISO guidelines provide a useful typology of the consequences of risks as either certain or uncertain and either positive or negative. To that typology, we should add that the consequences of risks may be either significant or trivial. Because the most basic copyright problem archivists face is that of orphan works, we should also add a further qualifier—some actions regarding copyrighted works will be more discoverable than others. Overall, the risks and negative consequences will vary depending on the controls or safeguards we apply to decrease the amplitude of the risk as well as how we respond when someone steps forward to voice a concern.

8.2 Risk Analysis and Risk Assessment

To effectively apply risk management to a collection or multi-collection digitization project, start by recognizing that risk management is a process involving activities unfolding over separate phases, including analysis of what and where the risks are, assessing their potential severity, and then reviewing what steps can be taken to mitigate the risks involved. While there is a logical sequence to these steps, they also can overlap and be iterative.

Will your project involve just one rights holder? Or might it involve digitization and online presentation of an entire collection containing many authors/rights holders? The extent of analysis to determine the relative risks of either collection will vary. Thus, effective risk analysis and risk assessment cannot start until the intellectual and documentary scope of the potential project has been described in a formal written document. It needs to answer a number of questions to enable you to assess risks:

1. Has the project proposal been vetted with relevant archival and subject matter specialists?
2. Have you consulted information technology specialists regarding what types of controls can be placed on particular documents or the entire body of digitized content?
3. Have you consulted legal counsel, institutional risk management staff, and the administrators to whom you report?
4. Might the material involved present risks beyond copyright, e.g., sensitive personal information or traditional cultural knowledge?

The essential work of analyzing and assessing the materials for the project cannot be done effectively unless you have established the overall context into which the many separate copyrighted works will fit. That context is critically important so that all parties can understand the overall archival logic for including any single work in the project that you want to present as a collective whole. The matter of the "whole" might later become strategically important for mounting a fair use defense.

8.2.1 General Considerations for Doing Risk Analysis

It's so easy to go down a rabbit hole if you attempt a comprehensive analysis of works being considered for digitization and eventual online availability. To avoid that, you should start with a collection- or aggregate-level assessment along the lines recommended by OCLC Research's *Well-intentioned Practice for Putting Digitized Collections of Unpublished Materials Online.*[11] Aggregate review can proceed in two phases. First, start with a "high-level" survey of the material to obtain a general sense of the contents and array of authors represented in the materials. This can be followed by a more detailed, hands-on examination of a limited number of samples selected on the basis of findings or questions that arise in the preliminary survey impressions. When working at the collection level, make sure you understand the original purpose for which the records were created and gathered into the particular filing units. Being able to understand and articulate the contextual relationships among works found within collections and being able to determine the purpose and character of their creation will be especially useful in making a credible fair use defense—a pivotal risk mitigation activity.

Determining the purpose and character of the works may lead to finding information on the commerciality of the works and authors within the collection(s). That information will be invaluable to assessing whether you might succeed on the first-factor fair use defense. Even if your survey identifies authors whose works had commercial value, it still may be possible to include them in your project if the purpose and character of your use does not compete with a work's original purpose and character. This will be especially true if your use is not for direct or indirect commercial benefit. In other words, the less your new use of the works in creating an online digital research source would compete with the original purpose of the works, the more that fair use might be significant in mitigating risk. It's also an essential step to minimize the serious risk of the criminal penalties outlined in § 506 (see Chapter 4, section 4.5 and Box 4.12).

By surveying the original purpose and character of the works under consideration, you may also discover risks beyond copyright, e.g., publicity, privacy, or cultural property rights. That's where my Inventory of Risk Assessment Attributes (Table 8.1), presented and explained in section 8.4.1, may be a helpful tool. The inventory incorporates a rating scale to create data that will help guide your decisions.

These surveying steps should provide preliminary answers about attributes that affect risk and may even help you to identify specific risk mitigation steps. With these answers as your guide, you can decide whether to proceed with digitizing all works or to exclude certain categories of works or certain authors from the project.

If all of this seems too general or amorphous, that's because the content of archives and the kinds of uses we want to make of that content are focused on collection-level control. Their meaning is based less on their individuality than on their contextual relation to several other individuals and documents. Copyright law, on the other hand, is inherently focused narrowly on specific works by specific authors.

There's a remedy to the law's rigid logic and focus on infractions related to individual works. That is to use the combination of our understanding of the law, basic common sense, and our professional knowledge of how archival materials were created. It is the original evidential connections of document to document, series to series, and collection to collection that establish their meaning and, in copyright terms, their purpose and character. It is exactly the collective meaning and connections among the works being digitized that, if explained in the original project design, may later contribute to a fair use defense, thus reducing risk in the project. This is because the ultimate value of a digitization project to archives users depends on the fact that individual documents are presented within the collection as an aggregate—not as isolated works. A project designed to provide individual works within the context of how they originally occurred in a collection can establish their character as something transformative. That can help the "character" part of the first fair use factor to weigh favorably, especially if the project's purpose is focused on an audience of students or scholars.

8.2.2 Surveying and Sampling for Risk Analysis and Assessment

Once the project scope has been firmly established and you have approval to proceed, you should do a general survey of the materials to gather facts about the nature of the materials and begin to gain a sense of the risks and consequences involved with them. "Survey," rather than "inventory," is the operative word. The work should proceed at the group or aggregate level rather than at the item level regardless of whether the collection consists of analog or digital material. You are surveying to get a sense of the number of authors, the possible presence of authors known to actively exploit their works commercially, the general age of the materials, and possible privacy, publicity, or cultural property issues, etc.

Some of this can be done by examining a finding aid, if it is detailed enough, but it will likely require some actual examination of materials within the collection to develop broad estimates. In some cases, the survey may lead you to do a deeper examination and analysis of strategically selected portions. This further research is especially important to give you confidence about knowing whether and how much of the material includes works with prominent authors of notable commercial value, or whether the content touches on rights beyond copyright. Although the content of the collection is the primary focus, it should be done against the backdrop of the project's relation to the educational and research purpose of your archives, knowledge of the law, and the goals and principles of the profession.

A variation developed in the United Kingdom focuses risk management on narrowing things down to certain authors who should be approached for copyright clearance. This approach to risk management can be found in the multi-institutional project to develop a digital library for the Wellcome Library's "Codebreakers: Makers of Modern Genetics."[12] The Codebreakers project involved collections from a number of institutions, resulting in an overlap of authors, some of them quite prominent. Therefore, the project first sought to identify those copyright holders from whom they would pursue permissions. To do this, the collaborating repositories classified the authors into medium or high risk based on prominence, past assertion of rights, etc. Their risk criteria were, of course, attuned to the specific collections and scientific fields being documented. The way they distinguished between medium and high risk is particularly interesting. It can be seen, fully quoted, in Box 8.1.[13]

Box 8.1 "Wellcome Library's Risk Criteria"

Medium Risk—When all of these three factors apply the material is classed as medium risk and should be added to the long list,

- The author/creator has (or had) a high public profile.
- The author/creator is alive or is known to have a literary estate (as recorded in the Writers Artists and Their Copyright Holders database https://norman.hrc.utexas.edu/watch/).
- The material appears to have been published/broadcast and/or prepared for commercial gain, rather than to advance academic knowledge or in a not-for profit environment.

High Risk—If any one of the following applies the material is classed as high risk and should be added to the long list,

- The author/creator is a well-known literary figure, broadcaster, or artist.
- The author/creator/literary estate/publisher is known to actively defend their copyright.
- The relationship between the holding institution and the author/creator/publisher is awkward.
- There is a large proportion of material from an author/creator which appears to be in copyright, i.e., more than 20 percent in a box.

To support a general survey or subsequent selective sampling, this chapter's concluding section (8.4) and its related Appendix 2 include a specific process, with supporting charts and criteria, to make assessments at the individual record series or collection level. In effect, it should provide you with your own case study and generate numerical ratings for making recommendations on material being considered for digitization.

Your next step should be to supplement the initial findings with selective research and analysis of either a random or strategically selected sample of physical or digital documents. Together with the initial survey, the deeper look at one or more samples should reveal enough "facts" about the works and rights holders to help you perceive different types of risks, their likelihood, and their seriousness so that the risks themselves can be evaluated. From those findings, it should also be possible to identify which risk mitigation practices can be applied.

Once this analysis has been completed, your final assessment should be based on how the gathered information interacts with your tolerance for risk. Questions for you to consider include:

1 Will the action you take result in undesirable consequences?

2 What types of negative consequences might arise?

3 How great is the risk of negative consequences?

4 How amenable might those risks be to the mitigation factors discussed below?

For example, the result might be that the risk will be no more than a letter of complaint followed by negotiations with the aggrieved party to remove the offending item from the web. Or your first notice of the complaint might be a letter saying a suit has been filed in federal court. The former may be more likely in the case of works authored by a member of the general public. The latter may be more likely when the author has had a career of creating works with commercial value, especially a celebrity author. In between, a less prominent but still commercially active author might have an agent or attorney send you or the institution's senior administrator a cease and desist letter. There is also the possibility that someone who is conversant enough with the law could file a takedown request on their own or prepare a claim for the Copyright Claims Board (see, Chapter 4's discussion of 17 U.S.C. Chapter 15).

Regardless of how you hear of a complaint, it is important for risk mitigation that you respond promptly to the first whisper of concern. If done well, your general survey and follow-up sampling should have alerted you in advance of the possible instances of authors/creators with greater incentives or means to initiate formal legal action. Knowing that will strengthen your overall risk management strategy, but this is more readily done at a micro-level that is not practical for larger projects. That's why your risk assessment survey and your sampling need to differentiate between the materials that most likely were never in commerce and works that were created for a market. The more you know about the collection, the better you will be able to determine whether and how deeply to sample for a closer look.

You should also remember that risks involved in projects for online or public release of content are not limited to those found in copyright's § 106 list of exclusive rights. For instance, the 1987 *Salinger v. Random House* case shows that it was Salinger's strong desire for privacy that drove much of his copyright suit. Thus, you should take advantage of your general and selective surveys to identify instances where there are privacy, publicity, cultural rights, or other sensitivities that could be infringed and lead someone to lodge a formal complaint on grounds other than copyright. Such complaints could lead to questions about your archives' professionalism.

An important additional part of your risk assessment should be to consider the type and potential severity of being called to account for having transgressed someone's rights. Receiving any complaint, even if it's just a troubled email or phone call, can be not only demoralizing, but also demanding of time required for consultation and response. It also has the potential to create personal or professional embarrassment that detracts from the rest of your archival operations. Thus, part of your analysis should include a consideration of your archives' administrative preparedness to meet these challenges.

Regarding your collection surveys, you should remember that some aspects of the law can function as buffers or safe harbors that might mitigate the risks of more significant penalties (see section 8.3.3). For example, as noted in parts 4.4 and 4.5 of Chapter 4, there are threshold requirements for an aggrieved rights holder. For instance, the rights holder must first register their work before pursuing formal legal action if they are to obtain the more lucrative damages and attorney fees. Thus, your survey should attempt to give you a general sense of the extent that the materials contain works by individuals most likely to want to launch an expensive suit. Will they be likely to quickly register their work and pay whatever extra fees there are for expedited service? Authors who created works for a commercial or public market might be prepared to do that. The costs and procedures for litigation, however, are considerable enough that not every person unhappy about their works appearing online via your project is going to be prepared to go the route of legal action in federal court. Knowing or at least having a general sense of this will help you assess the potential magnitude of negative outcomes.

Lest this discussion leave the impression that it is purely a matter of looking for all the bad things that theoretically could happen, remember that the core idea of risk management is to understand not just the potential negative consequences, but also the counterbalancing good outcomes. Yes, a number of copyright risks may result from our everyday archives work, but that overlooks the good that can flow when our actions are dictated less on strict adherence to the law's exclusive rights and more on our distinctive materials, users, and mission. Sometimes, it's deliberatively choosing to "color outside the lines" that enables us to support research and connect society with its heritage.

8.3 Risk Reduction and Risk Mitigation

Having systematically examined collections in summary fashion to identify potential risks, it's time to move from a zero-risk approach to one that accepts a variety of risks when working to support your institution, community, collections, and profession. This phase of risk management requires tempering your awareness of provisions in the law with the knowledge of best professional practices. Taken together, they can reduce risks or provide buffers against potential negative outcomes and make it easier to make decisions on which risks to accept. Success will lie in being able to tap into different knowledge domains, the most helpful of which are:

1. Knowledge about your collections, especially relating to the provenance of each and what sort of author rights may or may not have been transferred with the material.
2. Knowledge of the inherent interconnectedness of the archival material you hold, especially in regard to how the evidential value and usefulness of any given document can be connected to others within the repository.
3. Knowledge of professional standards and best practices for selection, arrangement, description, preservation, and user services, as well as how to communicate those standards and goals to institutional specialists in legal, risk management, and information technology offices, whose assistance will be needed in conducting a digital project.

Equally important will be strong skills in communicating your copyright concerns, your archival mission, and your goals to staff and to institutional superiors.

Your knowledge of the collections and best professional practices for all the domains of archival work may be your "superpower." It's highly unlikely that any copyright owner will have as full a picture of your collections as you have, especially concerning the contents and circumstances of the creation of the works. In fact, this knowledge should be understood as a risk mitigation asset by itself, provided you know when and where to apply it.

Remember, we don't have to be exhaustive and understand every last detail of the copyright status of material in the scope of our project. As archivists, we should follow our instinct and look at the aggregate level. We have the experience and ability to understand that the meaning of a collection, or of any particular document in a collection, is inseparable from the meaning of the other documents in that collection and the archives as a whole. This enables you to juxtapose the atomizing nature of copyright and individual authors rights with the social and intellectual value of archives. Importantly, this knowledge contributes significantly to key elements in risk mitigation—being able to argue the first factor in a fair use defense.

8.3.1 External Guides and Best Practices for Risk Mitigation

Beyond the above areas of general and archival knowledge, it will be important to become familiar with a number of tools and guides that can shape practices to navigate and reduce risk. Especially useful are:

1. A fair use checklist to provide you with a general picture of how well the four fair use factors might apply to the kind of use you are considering. Kenneth Crews' checklist is the most familiar. Available in Appendix 1 and at https://copyright.columbia.edu/basics/fair-use/fair-use-checklist.html.
2. Some tools can help you to determine whether a work is a type that is actually covered by copyright. For an overview of the array of issues, consult the Copyright Office's *Circular 22: How to Investigate the Copyright Status of a Work*, https://www.copyright.gov/circs/circ22.pdf; or the University of Texas's "Copyright Crash Course." Available at https://guides.lib.utexas.edu/copyright/whoowns.
3. To consider whether the term of copyright of an eligible work has expired, consult Cornell University Library's *Copyright Services: Copyright Term and the Public Domain.* Available at https://guides.library.cornell.edu/copyright/publicdomain.[14]

4 For guidance on how to conduct searches for copyright owners of orphan works, and how exhaustively to search, see the Society of American Archivists' *Orphan Works: Statement of Best Practices*. Available at https://www2.archivists.org/sites/all/files/OrphanWorks-June2009.pdf.

5 If your survey of the collection discovers a large number of documents created by one individual author, or the presence of even a few works from renowned authors/creators, use the Writers Artists and Their Copyright Holders website—"the WATCH file"—to determine whether there is a literary or other agent who can be approached for permission for works still in copyright. The WATCH website also includes Firms Out of Business (FOB), which covers printing and publishing firms, magazines, literary agencies, etc., no longer in existence. The WATCH and FOB databases are most useful for notable authors and related publishers and agents. Thus, not finding a database entry for the author or publisher you are seeking is not definitive evidence that there is no copyright claimant who could be found through one of the common web search engines, but checking these sites will assist to your being able to show a good faith effort. Available at https://norman.hrc.utexas.edu/watch/.

6 To frame your thinking about larger digital projects where tracking down the copyright owners may be impossible, read OCLC's *Well-intentioned Practice for Putting Digitized Collections of Unpublished Materials Online* (W-iP) mentioned above (see section 8.2.1). To understand best professional practices for its use, read the SAA Intellectual Property Working Group statement endorsing the W-iP document. Available at https://www2.archivists.org/groups/intellectual-property-working-group/well-intentioned-practice-for-putting-digitized-collections-of-unpublished-materials.

7 For standards for writing clear statements of what you know, understand, or do not know about the rights in works you are putting online, see https://rightsstatements.org/en/.

8 For archives-focused guidance on how to describe the rights of materials you post online, see the SAA's *Guide to Implementing Rights Statements from RightsStatements.org*. Available at https://www2.archivists.org/sites/all/files/RightsStatements_IPWG%20Guidance.pdf.

9 Looking at what your professional peers are doing may or may not be helpful. Library and legal professionals have developed the Association of Research Libraries (ARL) *Code of Best Practices in Fair Use for Academic and Research Libraries*. Available at https://www.arl.org/wp-content/uploads/2014/01/code-of-best-practices-fair-use.pdf. This document argues that a consensus understanding among the community of research libraries can provide a foundation for a broad use of fair use to support large-scale digitization projects. It proposes a particular and rather expansive interpretation of fair use based on what it describes as the "community of practice" among like institutions. Considering that archivists are otherwise left with hardly any court precedents relating to copyright in archival works, the concept of consensus-based community standards is attractive. The *Code*, however, was developed without rights holder involvement. That, and the fact that some more recent (2022–5) court decisions have scaled back the fair use defense, make me hesitant to put too much weight on the *Code* as a primary tool for risk mitigation, compared to the more faceted items cited in numbers 1–8 above, as well as the steps in the lists that follow in section 8.3.2. Moreover, as both this chapter and the Harvard Library's *Digitizing Orphan Works* study make clear, there are several risk mitigation tactics beyond fair use.

8.3.2 Internal and Institutional Policies Contributing to Risk Mitigation

The above external guidelines, checklists, and statements of principle will be helpful for thinking about how to strike a balance between copyright's monopoly and the archival mandate to make material available. Insofar as they can lead to general ways to approach taking risks, it will be equally important to have them reflected in practices, internal policies, and procedure documents developed by your archives. The details of some of the documents are addressed in Chapter 7, but they are summarized here as critical components of risk mitigation:

1 Development of an overall copyright policy identifying broad categories of works in which the archives owns, or seeks to own, copyright, and those where it does not. It should also call for use of copyright notices, user registration forms, and policies for the search room and websites, and for responding to permission requests.

2 Posting of copyright notices at the place where copy orders are accepted, and notices on any copying equipment in public areas, and notices where visitors may use their own copying equipment. These will support your use of § 108 exceptions and reduce the likelihood of being cited for contributory infringement.

3 User registration forms incorporating a notice that the user has the responsibility for adhering to copyright law when going beyond private study. The user should be required to accept these terms as a condition of being granted access to archival materials.

4 Written policy on the extent of copying/scanning that the staff will do for local and remote users, along with a notice of the schedule of fees to cover the service costs for the reproduction and delivering of copies (but not permission or use fees).

5 Written standards for the text of citations and captions to accompany any copies supplied as well as for captions embedded in watermarks or in descriptive metadata in digital files.

6 Template text identifying copyright ownership, when known, of works placed online. (See item 6 in the External Guides, section 8.3.1.)

7 Template language for copyright disclaimers for all online content when the archives is unsure of the ownership or has not been able to seek or to locate the owner. These should be written in a way to encourage inquiries from anyone with concerns or knowledge about the owner.

8 To encourage early notification of copyright, privacy, or cultural property concerns, there should be template language for a takedown policy to be included with any online posting of archival content, and procedures to facilitate rapid response of the archives.

9 Creating and following practices dealing with takedown requests, as discussed in Chapter 7, may contribute to the reduction in damages and liability for attorney fees that may be assessed (see section 8.3.3.2, items 4, 5, and 6, relating to §§ 411, 412, 504, and 505). It is important that you have brief written procedures and supporting text for any staff member to use in responding whenever a viewer or visitor requests a takedown or raises other concerns about a potential infringement.[15]

10 An active communication policy regarding digitization is essential for operational transparency. When conducting large-scale digitization projects aimed at placing content online, the more basic the publicity

archives can provide about the project, the better. Especially important will be ensuring that it is easy for the public to find the names of the works and authors that are being placed online. This is not just because of the importance of facilitating research use of the materials, which can contribute to the first factor of fair use weighing in your favor. It is also because the wide availability of information about what and whose works are being put online contributes to a "laches" defense if litigation arises relating to orphan works projects.

In simple terms, "laches" is an equity doctrine used to limit judgments in favor of plaintiffs who have "slept on their rights to the detriment of the defendant." David Hansen has noted that laches "limits the ability of plaintiffs to bring old or stale actions, and its purpose is different and its application more flexible than the Copyright Act's statute of limitation."[16]

In addition to policies and procedures emphasizing early and frequent publicity for digitization projects, your finding aids should make names of authors easily discoverable via common internet search engines. Ideally, early and continued transparency about the authors of content placed online should encourage potentially aggrieved parties to contact the archives so that you have an opportunity to resolve a dispute before formal legal action is started. Such transparency is not a guarantee against litigation, of course, but it can position you for an early takedown of material, thus avoiding liability for continuing infringement. It could help create an argument for equity in reduction of damages if the copyright holder has been negligent in filing a suit beyond the time when they knew or reasonably could have known of the infringement.

11 Prepare for future storms. Even the most careful planning and close attention to the law's rules and safe harbors cannot eliminate all risk of a complaint or legal action being initiated. Nor can you always be sure that you have applied the law correctly. You need to be prepared for things to go wrong. Therefore, develop relationships with your institution's legal counsel staff. If you're in a small institution without an actual general counsel office, work to develop relations with those senior administrative staff who contract with private counsel when the institution needs legal services. Unfortunately, not all attorneys will be familiar with copyright issues that arise with cultural heritage materials, and very few will understand copyright in relation to the unique circumstances of archives.

Nevertheless, an excellent forward-looking approach is to use OCLC Research's "Well-Intentioned Practices" document to start a discussion with the legal staff when you are in the planning stages of a project, or even if you have just moved to a new job at an archives that has already placed copyrighted material online. If you have not had a chance to develop relations with the legal staff in advance, contact them as soon as you receive notice that someone may be going to pursue formal action for the archives having infringed their rights. Whether you think you have a good defense or not, and especially if you believe you have made a mistake, your chances of success are likely to be very slim without the involvement of professionals formally trained and licensed in the law.

Because there is so little case law involving copyright in archives, especially for orphan works, you may need to educate your legal team in the ways modern archives are composed of material rarely created for commercial markets, as well as the rather developed literature on issues such as fair use and library/archives exceptions. Regardless, those trained in the law are likely to know much better than you about defenses beyond those in the copyright law, and they might have an understanding of rules of evidence and civil litigation. You should encourage them to review the Harvard Library report, *Digitizing Orphan Works: Legal Strategies to Reduce Risks for Open Access to Copyrighted Orphan Works*, noted above.

8.3.3 *Mitigation Factors Found in the Law's Exceptions and "Safe Harbors"*

As Chapters 4 and 5 reflect, copyright law is complex, but it does contain rewards for those who look carefully for aspects that may provide buffers or working room, as well ways to mitigate negative outcomes for what we do as archivists. Becoming familiar with those sections and subsections should be a foundation of your overall risk management strategy because this knowledge will be important when seeking assistance from legal counsel.

8.3.3.1 Exclusions and Exemptions in Copyright Law

The following is intended as a table-of-contents guide to the relevant parts of the law that create exceptions or possible "safe harbors" that could reduce your risk. For a fuller explication of the provisions, refer to the greater detail in each of the relevant items in Chapters 4 and 5. As always, read the full text of the copyright statute on these items before taking action or talking to counsel about them. Not all of these mitigating exceptions, buffers, relief valves, or safe harbors operate in the same way or at the same time. Some overlap, and some may be unambiguous enough to preclude the need to seek further risk mitigation, so be careful and deliberative. Remember that thinking you are certain about an answer to any copyright question is a warning sign that you may have overlooked something.

1. § 102(a) and (b) make clear that copyright does not apply to all kinds of works found in your archives, nor does copyright protect facts or ideas found within works.
2. § 107's fair use provisions offer a defense against infringement for certain types of use, especially research, education, commentary, and news reporting. Of course, as Chapter 5 emphasizes, fair use is only definitively established after a court decides on the relative weight among the four fair use factors. Nevertheless, having reasonable grounds for fair use based on an analysis guided by checklists or other tools can contribute to reduced liability, as noted in the references to § 504(c)(2).
3. § 108(e) allows qualifying libraries and archives to make a copy of an entire work and supply it to a user if a copy cannot be obtained at a fair price—a set of conditions that effectively describes unpublished works. Caution is needed because § 108(e) does not cover the making of multiple copies. Also, § 108(i) precludes the use of this exception for certain kinds of works, such as graphical, audiovisual, and musical works (see Chapter 4 at 4.1.8).
4. § 108(h) allows for preservation copying and distribution of *published* works in the last 20 years of their copyright terms, under conditions described in § 108(h) itself (see Chapter 4 at 4.1.8).
5. § 109 allows an archives or library to display a copyrighted work in a public place.
6. § 110 (1) allows the performance or display of a work for educational purposes in face-to-face settings, as might happen with curricular instruction sessions in the archives.

8.3.3.2 Escape Valves and Safe Harbors in the Law

Beyond the formal exclusions and exceptions and limitations found in Chapter 1 of the copyright law, other parts of the law contain elements that could function as buffers, escape valves, or safe harbors to mitigate the extent of negative consequences. The following is only a "high level" summary, so please review the actual text of the law and the summary of related portions of Chapter 4.

The provisions for ownership of copyright in §201 through §205 may not be a way to avoid risk, but they can be a way to manage its negative consequences. Being aware of these sections can prepare you for strategic responses when approached by someone believing you have violated their property right. To make a copyright claim, an aggrieved person must be the actual owner of the rights in the work, not just a relative of the owner or a prior owner of the physical object in which the copyright exists.[17] The following are the questions to consider posing in as diplomatically a way as possible:

1. If they are the original author or creator of the work, might they have previously transferred their ownership?
2. Was their creation of the work actually done under conditions that would have made it a work for hire?
3. If they are the descendent of a deceased author, were the copyrights transferred to them by will or operation of law, and if so, are there other heirs who may have given you permission to make the use you did?

Especially important as a matter of risk mitigation is that you use the first contact with the aggrieved party as an opportunity to have a conversation rather than a confrontation. The more you allow their concern to become the foundation of a future relationship rather than of an adversarial encounter, the more likely you are to mitigate untoward consequences.

4. Do not risk claiming ownership of something for which you or your institution have no basis for such assertion. Do not engage in activities that are the exclusive rights of the copyright holder or attempt to prevent others from making use of the work. Do not place the copyright symbol (©) along with your name on a digital copy of the work or provide formal grants of permission to publish. Not only do such actions undermine the ability to demonstrate non-commercial fair use, but they

also may constitute a form of "copyfraud." According to § 506(c), (d), and (e), such activity could even expose you to criminal penalties.[18]

5 Because a copyright term will eventually end, §301 to §305 can provide some working room for older works. The text of these sections can be hard to follow, so take advantage of the Cornell *Copyright Services: Copyright Term and the Public Domain* chart noted above. Remember, always double-check your facts. It's possible that a seemingly unpublished original photographic print found in the papers of a local photographer, known to be deceased more than 70 years ago, may have been published unbeknownst to you in a book or magazine some decades after the image was first taken. That means it could still be under copyright.

6 If a claimant has approached the archives and asserted that you have infringed, take their challenge seriously. Even if you have doubts, your goal should be to make sure you understand their concerns, which may not always be ones covered by copyright law. Your goal should be to lay the basis for settling the matter without going to court. Gather all the information you can from them and try to determine if they have registered their copyright in the work according to provisions of § 408 and § 409. Remind them that registration is required before any civil infringement action can begin (§ 411), and direct them to where the Copyright Office posts rules, fees, and response times for registration.

7 Meanwhile, keep in mind that, according to § 412, no award for statutory damages and attorney fees (i.e., § 504 and § 505) can be made for infringement in an unpublished work before the date of registration. That's a significant safe harbor because it shelters you from the significant cost of being taken to federal court. However, § 412 is only a partial safe harbor since archives could also be held responsible for actual damages (§ 504(b)). Also, the infringement could still result in being subject to impoundment and destruction of infringing articles. It could also result in the destruction of the means by which the infringing items were made (§ 503(b)). Overall, the requirements of § 412, when connected with the way damages and penalties are described in § 504 and § 505, can have the effect that the lower commercial value of the orphan works typical in many archives might deter copyright owners from going to court, unless they happen to be owners of commercially valuable works. Regardless, the § 411(a) and § 412 provisions requiring registration can give you time. So, act quickly to take down offending items as soon as you or your staff learn about a complaint. With skill, the archivist should use that time to build a relationship with a claimant and thereby mitigate the more negative consequences.[19]

8 § 504(c) (2) provides a significant but not comprehensive safe harbor that can mitigate some risk. It states that the court "shall" refrain from imposing statutory damages on those infringers who were employees of nonprofit educational institutions, libraries, or archives if they had reasonable grounds for thinking that their use was a fair use. Unfortunately, it concludes the sentence with a reference to "infringed by reproducing copies." The lack of case law on this qualifying phrase leaves ambiguity as to whether this safe harbor provides clear protection in the case of infringing by distribution (e.g., by web posting).[20]

9 § 511(a) and (b) are explicit that the Constitution's 11th amendment grant of sovereign immunity to States does not apply to copyright penalties. Nevertheless, a handful of cases since the 1990s have left open the possibility that a limited category of state government entities, such as state universities, may have partial immunity from damages in copyright suits. The immunity would only be from monetary damages, not injunctions or impoundment, and would probably not extend to immunity of employees of the institution. If you are in a state institution and wish to factor sovereign immunity into your risk mitigation strategy, you should first check with your institution to determine whether your state has waived immunity and whether your institution's legal counsel or governing board supports asserting a sovereign immunity defense.[21]

10 Caution! If part of your risk management strategy relies on the assumption that the particular nature of your holdings is such that works you put online may have never been in commerce, it may be risky to rely only on the safe harbors that preclude federal suits. That's because a federal court case is not the only recourse for an aggrieved copyright owner. Without having to hire an attorney or pay court costs, the owner could instead go to the Copyright Claims Board, and it can award damages up to $30,000. That amount may be less of a financial concern, but a CCB ruling is a risk that can be mitigated. When the law creating the CCB was enacted, it included a provision allowing libraries and archives to opt out of the CCB process (see § 1506(aa) (1) and (2)).

> To opt out or not is a decision you and your institution should make according to your institution's own circumstances and risk calculus.

This survey shows there are a variety of factors in the law that can mitigate risk or guide your response once a risk has materialized. In addition, risk can be reduced by managing the level of access you provide to materials. While guarding against compromising your mission to serve users, your overall knowledge of your collections may help you identify those where access should be granted only with a higher level of staff mediation, for example with unprocessed accessions or collections with only bare-bones finding aids. However, blanket rules should be avoided. Instead, effective copyright risk management for archives requires considerable attention to the content of the archives' collections together with the many ways that copyright or other rights might be accidentally infringed. Keeping all of this in mind is a tall order for programs with limited staff and resources, but avoiding copyright risks should probably receive as much attention as protecting against fires, floods, and theft. Managing any of these areas starts with preventive steps built on knowledge of the threats. One need not have a graduate degree in chemistry or engineering to understand environmental threats to archival material. Similarly, one does not need a law degree to understand the logic in copyright law and to be aware of simple steps to reduce liability.

8.4 Decision Time: Practical Steps to Taking Risks

Now that we have reviewed the range of risks that copyright presents to archivists and have reviewed some ways to mitigate those risks, it's time to see how all the facts can be brought together to guide decisions in archival administration. Sections 8.3.1, 8.3.2, and 8.3.3 have surveyed strategic and practical risks and ways to mitigate risks. The next key step should be to identify your own tolerance of risk, knowing that substantial sums of money may be at stake if you are wrong.

So, how ready are you to take archival actions that could involve expensive copyright consequences? Are you concerned that the complexity of your own collections and user communities make it difficult to provide a quick, single answer on the many issues where copyright law intersects with your professional work? As with much of copyright, "it depends" may be an archivist's most common answer. The materials we hold are so far from being monolithic that just relying on a general guess as to our risk tolerance may not have much value for operations.

Nevertheless, neither the complexity of our collections nor the complexity of copyright law can be an excuse to shortchange the work of risk assessment. You either go ahead with projects and activities while ignoring rights that exist in the works or you let fear of being taken to court for infringing make you very restrictive in what you do. Neither choice is professionally responsible. The former fails to respect the owners' rights in the materials we steward; the latter fails our mission to preserve the record of the past for present and future benefit. Instead, we must find options between these two extremes so we can prepare to take actions that acknowledge the varying levels of risks in our collections. We must embrace the risks that are amenable to mitigation.

8.4.1 Identifying Specific Risks

When the archival action is to copy and place online a single work or several works from a single author, it is reasonable and logical to complete a detailed risk assessment involving research into the author's circumstances and the past life of the work. Unfortunately, this kind of narrowly focused research is not scalable for larger collections with many different works from multiple authors who are frequently unknown or untraceable. So, what to do if we want to use current networked digital technology to promote access and discovery? A useful approach is to follow the guidance of OCLC's *Well-intentioned Practice for Putting Digitized Collections of Unpublished Materials Online*, which encourages making decisions in the aggregate way that has been a hallmark of much of modern archival theory and practice. It advises making decisions on copyright at the collection level or sometimes at the level of multiple collections when doing well-defined thematic projects. That approach requires us to abandon risk assessment at the individual work level or often even at the individual author level.

The following three tables (8.1, 8.2, and 8.3) are tools to narrow down the discovery of where and how great the risks are and how to make decisions. They provide a sequence of steps that help you to: (1) identify and quantify those attributes of a collection that create greater or lesser risk; (2) establish a risk level and a course of action with the collection or collections; and (3) measure how confident you should be in your risk assessment and decision.

They are especially designed to support work at the collection level but theoretically could be used when considering a multi-collection project. The tables were created as a teaching tool for a workshop in which archivists worked through a case-study exercise involving a hypothetical *administrative mandate* to digitize the *entirety* of a handful of analog collections that had been processed several years earlier. To facilitate informed decisions on whether to, or how much to, digitize of the sample collections, the case study called for archivists to do a broad-brush survey/assessment of several attributes of each of the sample collections and select from decision options. If just reading this description and looking at the blank forms in these three tables seems too abstract, look at Appendix 2 for examples of how the forms might be filled out for two sample collections.

There are a number of attributes of archival materials that influence how knowable or how great a particular copyright or other curatorial risk might be (see Table 8.1). In the workshop exercise, the archivist–students were provided summary scope and content notes for five or six collections. They ranged from administrative correspondence and case files to photographs and published promotional materials. They were largely analog materials but with some digital surrogates.

In over ten years of use in workshop settings, the archivist–students found this assessment scale helpful. Their greatest frustration was that the only thing they had as a basis for their fact-based review were the paragraph-length scope and content notes. Fortunately, for your own projects, you can do what they were not able to do—start with the complete finding aid for collections in your archives, and then take advantage of being able to examine the actual collections being considered for digitization. In looking at a few sample boxes or selected digital file directories of electronic files, you can use the Attribute Inventory (Table 8.1) as an investigative tool to help you assess what might make a digitization project either less or more of a risk. That should then help you arrive at an aggregate-level decision.

The numbers proposed for rating each of the variables are not intended to provide absolute truths. This is not an exact science, and variance is to be expected. In fact, it is likely that when you ask three or more of your staff to apply these ratings for any given collection, you will probably get three different responses. Instead, the rating scale is primarily to direct your thinking about which attributes of collections may involve liabilities related to copyright or other rights. The goal of the Attribute Inventory is to

Table 8.1 Risk Attribute Inventory

Attribute	Scoring Factors	Risk Score
Age	Date of Creation 0 = created ≥120 years ago 1 = created 70 > 120 years ago 2 = created 30 > 70 years ago 3 = created < 30 years ago	
Heterogeneity	Multiplicity of authors 1 = 1 to 3 authors present 2 = 4 to 20 authors present 3 = 21 to 99 authors present 4 = 100 to 200 authors present 10 = uncounted or unsampled number of authors present	
Anonymity/renown	0 = No evidence that authors had an economic interest in works 1 = Presence of prominent individuals in collection, but not known to have exercised an economic interest in their works 2 = Presence of authors known to have sought to benefit or actually benefited economically from their creative works 5 = Readily identifiable rights management/ permissions for some authors in collection (high risk unless obtain permission)	
Cultural sensitivity	Subject content or function of records related to items of known cultural sensitivity, especially traditional cultural expressions, race/ethnicity, political identity 0 = None 1 = Limited amount present 2 = Medium amount present 3 = Considerable amount present	
Personal Privacy	Subject content or function of records related to items of personal privacy, such as educational, employment, health, sexual preference, personal finances 0 = None 1 = Limited amount present 2 = Medium amount present 3 = Considerable amount present	

Attribute	Scoring Factors	Risk Score
Ownership/ authorship	Preponderance of works authored by the archives'"parent" institution 0 = **entirely** created as works-made-for-hire by employees of the parent institution **or** the copyright was transferred by deed or license 1 = **predominantly** created as works-made-for-hire by employees of institution, **or** the copyright was transferred by deed or license 2 to 3 = mixture of "parent"-owned works-made-for-hire and externally created materials (e.g., incoming correspondence) 4 = majority of material created by external persons	
Size/Extent of Collection	0 = ≤1.0 cubic/linear foot 1 = 1.0 to 10 cubic/linear feet 2 = 10 to 40 cubic/linear feet 3 = 40 to 100 cubic/linear feet 4 = 100 + cubic/linear feet	
Creative nature of content	Factual vs. fictional or creative (expressive) nature of material 0 = Non-expressive factual material, especially statistics and lists 1 = Narrative administrative reports, correspondence, documentary photos, etc. 2 = Mix of administrative materials and creative materials 3 = Largely composed of moderately creative materials 4 = Composed of highly creative material intended for external circulation	
	Attribute TOTAL:	

obtain a general idea of how extensive those liabilities might be. Its greatest contribution, then, is as a tool to bridge the gap between the impossibility of researching the rights status of each work or author and going ahead with an online digital project with no more than a belief that the lack of lawsuits against archives is a sufficient risk management strategy.

When using the Attribute Inventory, you may wish to add some other risk-related attributes for assessment, or you may want to modify the numerical values used for the variables being assessed. To aid in your customization, Microsoft Word versions of Tables 8.1, 8.2, and 8.3 are available under a Creative Commons CC BY-NC-SA license and can be obtained directly from the author.

8.4.2 *Deciding on a Course of Action*

The Attribute Inventory and its ratings are just a preparatory step toward actually taking action on a digitization project. Table 8.2 asks you to select a course of action among eight different options, ranging from proceeding with full digitization (and presumably web presentation) to abandoning the project entirely.

Table 8.2 Risk Level and Action Decision

Decision on Course of Action	Risk Level
Proceed with digitization of the collection.	1
Proceed with caution.	2
Proceed on basis of a single collection-wide argument after obtaining review and concurrence of institutional risk management of this approach.	3
Conduct a systematic sampling of collection to locate sensitive materials or high-risk copyright items, then proceed with caution on expectation of viability of fair use defense and expectation of institutional support, as above.	4
Proceed with selective or complete digitization but only after making a good-faith effort to locate the rights holders for persons who are known or believed to have exploited their works for economic benefit, and excluding works of those where you cannot locate or secure permission of rights holders, or where it is not feasible to complete a good-faith effort.	6
Proceed with complete digitization but with digital access limited to only onsite users.	7
Abandon project.	8
Risk Level Rating	

At any stage in using the Attribute Inventory or the Decision on a Course of Action tables, it's always appropriate to pause and do a bit more research or sampling. You may want to consider variations on the decision options in order to examine what was otherwise insufficiently clear from the finding aids. Also, note that for Table 8.2's decision options "1" through "8," the choices are not binary. They offer scenarios for developing a strategy for selective digitization or for creating varying levels of internal-only vs. external access to digitized content. Again, as with much of archival practice, there is rarely a single valid answer to the decision question. However, rather than just settling for ambiguity, the Risk Attribute Inventory should have provided you with an evidence-based approach to arrive at a reasonable range of flexible decision options.

Any decision based only on Table 8.1 is only as good as the information you already have regarding your collection. Table 8.3 on the other hand, provides a further way to determine how confident you can be in your calculations regarding risk level, on a scale from a high of six down to zero "stars."

Table 8.3 Level of Confidence in Risk Assessment

Confidence Level	Extent of intellectual and physical control of the collection
★★★★★★	Very well arranged and described in detail, providing a high level of confidence in ratings assigned to above attributes
★★★★★	Generally well arranged, material generally foldered by name of correspondent or with an index mechanism that identifies authors and dates/date range of documents
★★★★	Finding aids have provided an effective means to complete the Attribute Inventory
★★★	Names of majority of authors in the collection do not appear in the finding aid or indexing system
★★	Poorly described with material listed only at the box level.
★	Described only at the series level
0	Unprocessed

By comparing your results from Table 8.1 with the "star ratings" in Table 8.3, you can determine whether you should go ahead with your plans for digitization and online accessibility. For example, a collection with what seems to be an acceptable attribute rating but a two-star or lower confidence score would not be a good candidate for an online project. More hands-on research in the collection, or even re-processing, should be done to determine whether to amend or confirm your decision.

The scores developed from Tables 8.1, 8.2, and 8.3 are, of course, subjective. Still, you may find them useful in providing a systematic way to make complicated decisions. They are not magical. They just apply the use of the common-sense notion that the greater the number of information inputs into a decision, the higher the possibility of a good decision.

These risk assessment and decision guidelines may be most useful when planning digital projects for wide public audiences, but they may be too cumbersome and unnecessary when there are only a few works or a few authors involved in your proposed project. Still, they can provide a degree of confidence even for smaller projects.

No book, of course, can identify all the risks or all the ways to reduce and respond to risks. My hope is that this chapter will help you move from a paralysis caused by fear of the law to confidence that you can still achieve your mission as an archivist. It's all part of accepting the responsibility that comes with stewarding materials in your archives that contain the creative products of many writers, artists, and creators.

9 "Pay No Attention to the Man behind the Curtain" The "Realpolitik" of Today's Copyright Law

US copyright law is a creature of an economic system. It is not a child of a moral system arising from the natural rights of creators and users. As archivists, it's important for us to be aware of the political and social forces at work in how copyright's various components have developed and operate. Perhaps no one presents the crux of its problem more concisely than Emily Dickinson in her poem "Publication."[1]

> Publication—is the auction
> Of the Mind of Man,
> Poverty be justifying
> For so foul a thing.
>
> Possibly,—but we would rather
> From our Garret go
> White unto the White Creator,
> Than invest our snow.
>
> Thought belong to Him who gave it—
> Then to him who bear
> Its corporeal illustration. Sell
> The Royal Air
> In the parcel. Be the merchant
> Of the Heavenly Grace,
> But reduce no human spirit
> To disgrace of price!

Dickinson celebrates the notion that creative works may be too personal to belong in the marketplace. Her seeming preference for unpublished work certainly aligns with those of us who believe that the greatest value archivists deliver is the care we provide to exactly those documents that have never appeared in print and were never subjected to commerce.

I've quoted her poem here for a number of reasons. First, it calls attention to how an individual's creativity becomes embodied in works of authorship. Second, it projects the image of an author's creativity as emerging from solitary work in humble conditions. Third, it clearly perceives publication (exclusive right § 106 (3)—in copyright-speak, "distribution") as an act of commerce—not of creativity.

Helping the impoverished artist make a living is often cited by the copyright industry as a major benefit it brings to the world. However, foremost to Dickinson is the tension between the spiritual nature of personal creativity and the worldly domain of published distribution. This speaks to the dependence of the commercial intermediaries on the creativity of others. Without the quite unspiritual regime of copyright, that distribution cannot happen.

For Dickinson, the engine of creativity is not the potential of commerce, but the spiritual inspiration from which the works emerge, and that's what makes the copyright industries free riders on the creativity of others. In other words, rather than US copyright being a handmaiden of a moral system for protecting individual expression, copyright's monopoly ownership is the cornerstone for an economic system. Thus it should be examined in the context of the political and social forces leading to its development and operation.

For archivists to fully understand why copyright continues to be such a stumbling block for archival work, we must go beyond the chronicles of its legislative enactments and its judicial interpretation, including some parts of this book. Instead, we need to acknowledge that copyright, like so much of law, is the product of political and economic forces beyond our control.

Dickinson's poem was written in the middle of the Civil War but never published during her lifetime. Still, it is a particularly apt way for archivists to start thinking about why copyright is what it is and why changing it is so difficult. She sets the scene for the copyright industry's favorite image of the lonely, attic-dwelling artist at center stage in their appeals to expand monopoly rights and impose longer copyright terms. Dickinson, however, elevates creative work above price. This helps us look behind the curtain and see that those ostensibly advocating for the rights of authors and creators may be more interested in governmental protection of their own role as commercial intermediaries than in the authors themselves or the essence of the authors' creative works.[2]

In fact, Mark Rose's 1993 exploration of the "invention of copyright" noted that, following the 1710 Statute of Anne, copyright morphed from an instrument of censorship to the foundation for a cultural industry based on the work of others. It was the emergence in the Enlightenment of the modern notions of "author" and "work" that became the linchpins of a copyright legal theory that has become today's workhorse for the copyright industry's appeal for expansive and constricting rights. According to Rose, "copyright is not a transcendent moral idea, but a specifically modern formation."[3] The British publishing industry could have progressed on the narrow, naked power of the term-limited printing monopoly provided by the 1710 statute. However, it was the abstractions of "author" and "work" that emerged from the settlement of copyright legal disputes later in the century that led to the romantic vision of the author as a transcendent creative being that has become important to today's publishing and entertainment industries. That's how they justify their business model of profiting from the creative works of others.

For well more than a century, the history of copyright has been the subject of books and myriad articles, but few go much beyond rehashing enactments, legal battles, all while celebrating the constant mechanical and technical innovations that have regularly disrupted business models for commerce in works that fall within copyright's scope.[4] Sociologist Laura Ford's 2021 *Intellectual Property Law of Nations*, however, provides a historically informed and intensive look at the development of intellectual property as a concept that became empowered by, and embodied in, law. She shows how the legal and religious basis of today's intellectual property law traces its roots from Imperial Rome through early Christian Europe, common law, and the Reformation to arrive at the current symbiotic relationship of IP law and the modern nation-state. Hers is one of the most in-depth and convincing cases for understanding the inseparability of state power from the existence of property and copyright. Moreover, Ford's work makes it difficult to argue that Western copyright law is socially neutral and somehow devoid of the imprint of state power. Although she somewhat optimistically concludes that both IP and the nation-state enable innovation for community welfare, she does so with a clear warning: IP policy must be managed to "protect ourselves against a dehumanizing logic of ever expanding economic growth."[5]

But ever-expanding growth of intellectual property is exactly what has happened, especially since 1980 when computer software was formally admitted into copyright law. As communications scholar Anne Wells Branscomb noted, copyright's focus switched from being about creative works to needing to be about the new world in which information could be duplicated, stored, and communicated via new technologies. Now, copyrighted material was no longer locked in formats, such as print, that prevented duplication. Now, copyrighted material began to be seen not as works of human creativity, but more as commercial assets whose value required policymakers to create new legal protections.[6]

Meanwhile, in the mid-1990s, the burgeoning internet and its potential for widespread dissemination of content, whether educational or entertainment, was met with industrial efforts to expand legal controls to protect existing copyright investments. In response, scholars in widely varying fields began to demonstrate that neither the existing law nor the proposed changes could be seen as inherently neutral and divorced from existing power structures. For instance, through a series of journal articles and a 1998 monograph, anthropologist and legal scholar Rosemary Coombe presented a postmodern analysis that emphasized how the government-enabled intellectual property regimes created protection for works that reinforced existing power structures while often depending on cultural appropriation.[7] Although much of her attention is focused on the consumer and commercial world, especially trademarks, her observations on copyright are revealing. She argued that the romantic notion of the author as an individual creator is actually a legal fiction that has provided the ideological support for the institution of copyright. It is this fiction, in her view, that reinforces commercial market forces over the rights of the creator.[8]

Lest any of you think I'm inherently anti-business or anti-capitalist by calling attention to intellectual property laws as state-sponsored monopolies to benefit already well-situated private enterprises, you only need to look in the direction of the Digital Millennium Copyright Act (DMCA) of 1998. The primacy given to copyright insiders in the Act's drafting and passage has left archivists, like other consumers, with a complex legal straitjacket that impedes our mission when we must deal with digital records or try to apply digitization and network technology to achieve our archival goals.

When the Internet came into the public consciousness in the early 1990s, early adopters and consumers were enthusiastic about the technology as a tool for expanded communication and wide public availability of informational, educational, and cultural works. On the other hand, the existing media, entertainment, and information industries saw its potential as a new distribution mechanism to reach greatly expanded audiences, but they especially worried about its vulnerability to widespread unauthorized copying and distribution.

The creation of laws to support the "Information Superhighway" was advertised as a way to protect or restore the United States' global economic position. Thus, managing this new information infrastructure became a public policy matter to negotiate in treaties and to implement in domestic legislation. The resultant DMCA law transformed copyright. Instead of an instrument to provide legal protection of incentives for creators to make new works to benefit the public good, copyright became an intellectual property regime designed to secure controls so commercial intermediaries could wield power over the technology used to transmit works in the digital environment.

For a thorough deconstruction of the process that led to the drafting and passage of the DMCA, one need only look at legal scholar Jessica Litman's highly readable 2001 *Digital Copyright*. She shows that the Act was the copyright industry's ultimate response to the threats and opportunities posed by networked digital technologies as the Internet came into public consciousness in the 1990s.[9] She "connects the dots" between the major copyright industry leaders, especially in the entertainment industry, and the governmental policymakers who shaped a law that expanded copyright to control not just content, but also the means of accessing content to be able to read, view, or listen to creative works. Litman's account also shows how, in the initial policy development stages, consumers, and cultural and educational stakeholders were left out of the discussions, and in the eventual legislative stages, they were overwhelmed by more powerful lobbyists.

The result was a law that simultaneously enabled a digital market for the copyright industry, but also legalized digital locks and criminalized any unauthorized access by consumers. It was sold to Congress by claiming that these extra-copyright measures were needed to address the US trade imbalance and to reinforce the United States' role as a leading global purveyor of entertainment. William Patry, as a copyright lawyer and former copyright counsel at Google, observed, "Thanks to the DMCA, the copyright market has now come to resemble the planned Soviet economies of the early twentieth century, but with the market planning is [sic] done by corporations exercising government-created monopoly power."[10]

The 1998 legislative successes of the DMCA and that year's Sonny Bono Copyright Term Extension Act (CTEA) were then reinforced by a number of court cases in the early 2000s, including the infamous 2001 *A&M Records, Inc. v. Napster, Inc.* In this case, a Circuit Court ruled that Napster's peer-to-peer internet music indexing service constituted contributory copyright infringement. That quickly led to Napster's demise. A 2005 ruling by the Supreme Court in *MGM Studios, Inc. v. Grokster, Ltd.* had a similar effect for Grokster's video file sharing service.

Those efforts, however, failed to stop peer-to-peer music file sharing, so the Recording Industry Association of America (RIAA) launched a campaign, between 2003 and 2008, that attempted to sue over 30,000 individual consumers.[11] Meanwhile, the Supreme Court's *Eldred v. Ashcroft* ruling in 2003 upheld the constitutionality of Congress's addition of 20 years to copyright term. These events led to biting criticism of the music and movie industries, such as that by Patry[12] and Litman.[13] Their commentaries clearly aligned with the analysis provided a generation earlier by Critical Legal Studies (CLS) scholars who identified the key role played by industrial entities in manipulating the levers of legislative and judicial institutions to maintain their own elite status.[14]

By the early 2010s, opposition began to appear against new, overreaching legislative proposals coming from the copyright industry. Now, there arose widespread public resistance, rather than just complaints from the legal, library, and communication scholars who had predominated in the 1990s fight against the push for new exclusive rights. In early 2012, protests included some popular internet sites "going black" for one day in response to the proposed Protect IP Act (PIPA) and the Stop Online Piracy Act (SOPA). There were also global public demonstrations against an international treaty called the Anti-Counterfeiting Trade Agreement (ACTA), which had been drafted in closed sessions and that would have supported aggressive cross-border enforcement of IP rights. Public participation in these events led a trio of communication and digital scholarship academics to proclaim that Critical Legal Studies had now given rise to what they dubbed "Critical Legal Activism."[15] The trio of Ekstrand, Famiglietti, and Nicole celebrated public activism's role in the demise of the two proposed US bills and the demise of ACTA, for which the United States had been an active negotiator.

Over the next decade, legal scholars and a broad range of social scientists continued to investigate what were now seen as the politically non-neutral basics of copyright law. Particularly insightful was Jessica Litman's 2018 "What We Don't See When We See Copyright as Property."[16] She noted that although property law courses are a foundation of the curriculum in law schools, the actual nature of property has significant but overlooked implications for copyright. She argued that the role of copyright as a property right has serious consequences for the dispossession of authors and creators. She drew a telling parallel between copyright law's effect on authors and the dispossession of Native Americans that resulted from the late nineteenth-century Dawes Act. While that act did grant Native Americans a legal right to own land as private property, its long-term effect was subdivision, alienation, and lack of access to lands that had previously been held in common before the United States had forcibly seized them. Similarly, copyright's grant of ownership to authors of their works did provide them with an initial tool to bargain for compensation, but that came at great expense. Once ownership is transferred to a commercial intermediary, often at a reduced value, the authors have no bargaining power and become irrelevant. She notes, "When the law transforms something that was not formerly property into a property right, the accompanying alienability will cause control to flow to those with the most bargaining power."[17]

The effect is that despite the large amount of money in the copyright system, only small amounts benefit the creators. The disparity has only increased, thanks to copyright law amendments that have expanded the scope of copyright and extended its term despite the common theme in calls for amendments to help individual impoverished creators and their malnourished children. It is the industrial owners, whose very business models depend on holding others' alienated property, who have "enough political power to insist on watering down reform proposals until they will be of little actual use to creators, and … [they exercise] that power to revise legislative and treaty proposals in their favour."[18]

The orphan works that predominate in archives will always be of diminished interest to such commercial intermediaries precisely because they are works with no identifiable owners in a position to transfer valuable rights. Likewise, those same policymaking intermediaries, whose only interest in reform extends to whatever leads to commercial exploitation, will have little interest in helping beleaguered archivists try to obtain legal reform in order to make orphan works available through digitization.[19] Overall, the nature of property and its alienability has only become more egregious since Emily Dickinson's complaint about forfeiting creative work for "the disgrace of price." What has grown instead is the disparity of that price for any author interested in laying bare their soul before the public.

In fact, as is aptly shown by Glynn S. Lunney's "Copyright and the 1%," most benefits from recent changes to copyright law go to the intermediaries plus a few superstar creators, not to the "starving artists" of copyright myth.[20] His article notes, "No one ever argues for copyright on the grounds that superstar artists and authors need more money," but increasing the earnings of superstars is exactly what is happening at the same time that the added incentive actually reduces their production of new works.[21]

Lunney shows this via mathematical distribution graphs that plot demand and sales for gaming industry works, ranked from most popular to least popular. His finding: the top one percent of games accounted for nearly half the players; the top 10 percent accounted for 90 percent of players. He found the substantially same market distribution for use of the Spotify music service.[22] In other words, only the superstar creators are benefiting from copyright's increasingly long terms and penalties, not other creators and performers.

Archivists are the collateral damage in this legal fiction. Neither superstars nor starving artists, we are responsible for large volumes of historically valuable but otherwise "mundane" content that falls outside of anyone's idea of a market demand. In other words, Lunney's statistical analysis reinforces why we need a copyright law that carves out a *pro forma* exception for uses of all of those archival works that were swept into copyright's net by the 1976 revision of the law's adoption of the idea that copyright should be automatic on the initial creation of a work.

Meanwhile, the 2020 murder of George Floyd resulted in a wave of social science and humanities scholars turning their sights on other rarely questioned social and political norms, including intellectual property law. Among the most enlightening research examinations in this regard is Robert F. Brauneis's 2024 "Copyright, Music, and Race: The Case of Mirror Cover Recordings."[23] He observes that US copyright law may have never explicitly invoked race, but that "copyright doctrines that are facially race-neutral were formulated in a racially charged context in which it was clear that the doctrines were going to disparately impact African American composers, musicians, and vocalists."[24] To demonstrate this, he describes the complicated history of music copyright and provides a thoroughly documented account of a court case that concluded it was legal for a major (white) record label to issue a "mirror" or "cover" recording of a performance previously issued on an independent, Black-owned label.

That precedent-setting case was *Supreme Records v. Decca Records* 90 F. Supp. 904 (S.D. Cal. 1950). It provided a foundation for over a decade of the widespread practice of prominent white artists issuing their own "covers" of rhythm and blues performances from recordings made by Black performers. In this case, Supreme Records issued a recording with an arrangement and performance by Black artists of *A Little Bird Told Me*. It was a hit that rose quickly on the R&B charts, only to be almost immediately surpassed by Decca's sales of its own version for the mainstream market, in which white artists copied the music and interpretative performance elements from Supreme's recording.

Why did Decca think it could get away with this? Because the 1909 copyright act left musical arrangements and performances unprotected unless they had been documented in written notation and either published with notice or registered with the Copyright Office as an unpublished work. Without that step, the distinctive characteristics contributed by the musical performers on the Supreme disk were free to be copied by any others. The technical challenge of the long exclusion of sound-recordings from the scope of copyright was only compounded by a structural barrier. "Often catapulted to success from a neighborhood street corner, . . . black musicians seldom had access to good advice about record contracts, royalty payments, marketing, promotion, or career development."[25] Even if it might be argued that technology is neutral, general social and economic conditions could be a defining influence on the ability of an individual artist to benefit from the copyright system.

So, what was left for the judge to decide? The very subjective notion of "creativity." In his decision, Judge Leon Yankwich wrote,

> *The effect of the plaintiff's recording is thin, mechanical, lacking inspiration, containing just the usual accompaniments and the usual intonations which one would find in any common recording. The impression one receives from*

the Decca recording is entirely different. It is rich, against a musically colorful background. It sounds full, meaty, polished. The difference derives from the different quality of the voices of the artists, the more precise, complex and better organized orchestral background, the fuller harmonization of the responses, the clearer intonation and expression, and the more musical entrances in the Decca record.[26]

In other words, in his opinion, what the Supreme recording incorporated into the performance did "nothing to the essence of musical creation." As a result, Supreme Records lost the $400,000 damage award it sought and soon went out of business.

More importantly, the case meant that white performers and their record labels were free to expropriate the wealth of music and arrangements of Black artists to create "cover" recordings that sold to the rapidly expanding post-Second World War market. Now, the large record labels could sell thousands of "cover" recordings without payment or attribution to the arrangers and performers while the original composers were paid no more than what was required by the statutory licensing system—two cents per disk sold. By 1953, the sales of "white covers" of R&B recordings reached $15 million.[27] Thus, the circumstances of the *A Little Bird Told Me* case laid a basis for the post-Second World War popular music market while demonstrating how this supposedly racially neutral law, written and revised to protect particular business interests in evolving markets, worked to the detriment of the many individual creators who were unable to "work the system" and obtain adequate remuneration.

Copyright law, like the state powers that enforce it, has not been neutral in its political and social effect. Society's acceptance of exclusive rights reinforces market-based institutions, which privilege the very individuals and businesses that hold the levers of public policy. Although there may not be much that archivists or other members of the general public can do about the power structure of the society in which we work, it's arguable that we should not ignore how this reality can hinder our responsibility to serve all populations, including marginalized ones, in our daily archival practice.[28]

Yes, we have a responsibility to comply with the law, but we must remember that using any of copyright's standard repertoire of principles as benchmarks for archival actions has distinct downsides for archivists. We may be seen not only as furthering a terribly complicated legal regime, but also as enabling the disadvantaging of members of society who may have very little power.

Legally or politically, we may not be positioned to resolve the law's injustice, but we should balance attention to the law with the fact that archival materials contain the stories and voices of so many who are absent in the published record. That requires us to take advantage of the meager allowances in the law that support the active use of archives and reuse by the public.

10 Time to Start Thinking about Artificial Intelligence?

In the few seconds it took me to write the words "Artificial Intelligence," whatever I was thinking of writing on this topic has probably already changed. Yet we archivists, whose job it is to preserve the past for use by the future, must begin now to contemplate how this ill-defined and metastasizing technology will affect our work for decades to come. Computer science and technology experimentation are evolving so quickly that today's observations may be obsolete as soon as they are printed, if not before. More importantly the politics and media attention, as well as the public's rather amorphous understanding of AI, have all combined to require that we face the foundational question—Just what is AI?

It often seems that no two people can agree on what the definition of artificial intelligence is. Instead, it appears that the media, who shape public perception, and the politicians who want to rush to write laws governing its use, are content to invoke "artificial intelligence" as a magical spell to draw attention to themselves.[1] Is AI a super-computer? Is it a massive cloud of content? Is it a coming financial bubble? An autonomous robot that will either take us to a higher plane of existence or bring about the end of life on the planet?

The lack of specificity, of course, hasn't stopped the proliferation of issues and lawsuits where intellectual property rights and artificial intelligence might intersect. On the one side, there are authors, musicians, and publishers rushing to court to claim infringement by AI agents. On the other side, there are efforts by technology moguls to pressure the government to ensure that new laws and policies protect their industry's interests. Meanwhile, the media's insatiable appetite for larger audiences has created a steady diet of sensationalist news stories on the wonders or horrors of the AI world.

There seems to be a sort of moral panic among individual authors, publishers, musicians, and entertainment enterprises, all of whom may be launching copyright infringement suits against AI companies that have copied books, news stories, songs, etc., into AI training datasets. Combine that with the many columns and stories by or about individual artists concerned with how the technology can generate new works that could be market substitutes for their own creations, and the panic itself seems to be growing alongside of warnings from some technologists that there's a "non-zero" chance that AI will lead to human extinction. Compare that to what looks like the beginnings of a cozy collaboration between technology moguls and politicians, who are seeing AI as a new frontier that must be conquered and controlled to ensure US international economic and political dominance.

The problem is that, currently, the text, graphical, and audiovisual source material for one type of artificial intelligence, generative AI with its Large Language Models (LLM), includes conventional copyrighted works. Insofar as the outputs of such systems may carry some of the hallmarks of copyrighted works, then copyright law and policy unavoidably will be at the center of contention if new exclusive rights are proposed.

No doubt, archives, archivists, and archives users may use and benefit from some AI tools for their own work, but archives, as always, seem to be on the periphery of the major issues now in dispute. Given past history, there's little reason to think that our needs and interests arising from copyright's lock on archives content will play much of a role in the present epic conflict. To make things murkier, some commentators have even argued that copyright law itself may be inappropriate when considering how AI might be regulated or framed for society's benefit.

So, why this chapter? Anyone concerned about how the eventual sorting out of AI and copyright might affect archives will appreciate a vantage point from which to gain perspective on what some are calling a New World Order.

10.1 "AI": An Idea in Search of Definition

For all the media flurry, public discussion, and political fulminations on that "thing" called AI or artificial intelligence, the exact meaning or even a general sense of what people are talking about is rarely offered. Instead, it's cloaked in imprecision. Thus, before considering how AI might relate to law or archival risk management or administrative policy and practices, we need to know exactly what we are talking about.

Ask the specific question, however—"What is AI?"—and the result will often be either a deafening silence or a dozen different answers. It is, of course, possible to have a brief conversation about what might be described as an advanced computational tool with the ability to generate outputs that go beyond what the tool used as inputs. However, we still need greater precision if we want to act intelligently and responsibly when deciding which societal rules and norms should exist about the propriety of inputs and outputs, and whose rights might be involved.

Considering that, technically, we are talking about a computational tool, it is only logical to start with how the leading computer science textbook uses technical language to explain the AI. It describes the field as "the study of agents that receive percepts from the environment and perform actions. Each such agent implements a function that maps percept sequences to actions. . . . "[2]

More pertinent are the musings of James Boyle, of Duke University Law School. As a long-time advocate for the societal need for a less restrictive copyright, he has recently turned to how artificial intelligence systems and their products raise questions about the very nature of legal and human personhood. In his 2024 book *The Line: AI and the Future of Personhood*, he draws a distinction "between the artificial intelligence system that translates your email into French or recognizes the faces of your children in iPhoto, and a machine that exhibits, or can surpass, all aspects of human thought." His research has caused him to "refer to the first as artificial intelligence, lower case, and the latter as AI or Artificial Intelligence."[3]

It's the latter that drew his interest because of how AI may challenge our notions of legal and human personhood. Boyle's terminology can definitely help in confronting the social and legal challenges posed by AI, but archivists need something more practical as we think about the contours between US copyright law and present or future archival content.

Looking to Congress for clarity normally may seem like a waste of time, but occasionally it can do something in a bipartisan fashion that gives a grounding for public understanding. The National Artificial Intelligence

Initiative Act of 2020 (NAIIA) provides a definition that may help the current discussion:

> *(3) ARTIFICIAL INTELLIGENCE.—The term "artificial intelligence" means a machine-based system that can, for a given set of human-defined objectives, make predictions, recommendations or decisions influencing real or virtual environments. Artificial intelligence systems use machine and human-based inputs to—*
>
> *(A) perceive real and virtual environments;*
>
> *(B) abstract such perceptions into models through analysis in an automated manner; and*
>
> *(C) use model inference to formulate options for information or action.*[4]

In early 2023, the US Copyright Office launched an "AI Initiative" that has resulted in some useful studies about AI and copyright (see below). As part of that project, the Office issued a "Notice of Inquiry" (NOI) in August 2023 for public comment on artificial intelligence relating to a range of twenty-eight technical, legal, and factual questions.[5] The NOI provided background about the Office's engagement with AI issues, and fortunately for our purpose, included a "glossary" of eight terms. The most relevant for us is "Artificial Intelligence (AI): A general classification of automated systems designed to perform tasks typically associated with human intelligence or cognitive functions." As their source, the Office cited the 2018 John S. McCain National Defense Authorization Act that defined "artificial intelligence" as including systems "developed in computer software, physical hardware, or other context that solves tasks requiring human-like perception, cognition, planning, learning, communication, or physical action."[6]

Each of these three definitions (2018 defense authorization act, 2020 NAIIA, and the Copyright Office's 2023 NOI) maintains the focus on AI as a process, system, or method of operation. If you had not fallen asleep when reading earlier parts of this book, your ears might have perked up at the words "process, system, or method of operation," and you would have exclaimed, "that isn't copyright, so I can quit reading right here!" And you'd be right. As my Chapter 4 (section 4.1.3) and Chapter 6 (section 6.1) explain, those characteristics of AI are actually items excluded from copyright by the plain language of § 102(b). They certainly seem more relevant to patent law, and they are not descriptive of the physical or digital objects retained by archives. Thus, the Copyright Office's NOI made a significant step forward for having fruitful discussions of the relationship of copyright to what goes into, is manipulated by, and generated from such a system, process, or method of operation.

10.2 Copyright Office Guidance and Studies

As part of its "AI Initiative," the Copyright Office also published policy guidance in mid-March 2023 on whether works created by AI could be registered, i.e., be eligible for copyright.[7] Their review of the law and court cases dating back to the nineteenth century led them to emphasize that, for something to be treated as a copyrighted work, it needed to be authored by a human. In other words, if an AI system "determines the expressive elements of its output," the resultant work would not be eligible for copyright, but if a human were to select or arrange AI-generated items in a sufficiently creative way, then the human's work might be eligible for their own contributions.

After receiving a large number of comments in response to the August 2023 NOI, the Office released its first report in July 2024. It focused on the capacity of AI systems to produce digital replicas such as "a video, image, or audio recording that has been digitally created or manipulated to realistically but falsely depict an individual." Its concern was with so-called "deep fakes," by which an AI-generated image or audio–video work would impersonate someone to spread disinformation or embarrass a person. Based on their analysis, the Office concluded that digital replicas did not pose a copyright issue, but based on the NOI feedback, the Office concluded that there was an urgent need for federal protection for all individuals during their lifetimes from unauthorized distribution of digital replicas.[8] Thus, it seems that the first congressional legislative moves toward regulating AI dealt with this one facet of the issue. In May 2025, the "Tools to Address Known Exploitation by Immobilizing Technological Deepfakes on Websites and Networks Act" (the TAKE IT DOWN Act) was enacted. Further legislation is likely, including at the state level, dealing with other types of digital replicas, e.g., relating to politicians, celebrities, musical performances, etc.

The second report on AI from the Copyright Office is more closely connected to the exclusive rights of copyright as discussed in Chapter 4, section 4.1.6. Appearing in January 2025, it examined whether products generated by AI are copyrightable, a question that was raised in approximately one-half of the over 10,000 comments responding to the NOI. Most agreed that "material generated wholly by AI is not copyrightable." No wonder that this second report stated: "The case has not been made for additional copyright or *sui generis* [unique/on its own] protection for AI-generated content." The report did recognize that a case-by-case examination might confer copyrightability if it found that "a human has been able to determine the expressive elements" contained in the output. However, prompts alone "are unlikely to satisfy those requirements."[9]

The Copyright Office's third report was released in a "pre-publication version" in May 2025.[10] It focused on the use of copyrightable works as "training material" used in a generative AI system. Not only did it deal with questions at the center of much of the litigation against AI companies, but its content may have been the triggering reason for the summary dismissal of the head of the US Copyright Office that month.[11] It is also perhaps the most pertinent to our concerns as archivists.

In brief, the third report focused on copyright implications of ingesting and machine-processing of existing copyrighted works—the cause of the lawsuits and all the tears being shed by fiction and non-fiction authors, publishers, news media, musicians, and movie producers who fear generative AI threatens their existence.[12] The Copyright Office's report on copyright and generative AI training is worth considering if for no other reason than that it parses out one large aspect of the intersection, or maybe the collision, of AI and copyright.

In discussing the technical processes involved in generative AI's collection and processing of works to create a basis for deployment, the report focuses particularly on points at which exclusive rights of copyright might be implicated. "Creating and deploying a generative AI system using copyright-protected material involves multiple acts that, absent a license or other defense, may infringe one or more rights," states the report. The infringed rights would include reproduction, distribution, public performance, public display works, and preparation of derivative works.[13] The report emphasizes that avoiding prima facie infringement is only possible with formal permission of the copyright owner (i.e., a license) or a defense based on an exception in the law. Acknowledging the overwhelming challenge of seeking permission for all the works that AI systems are hoovering up, the bulk of the report focused on fair use as the most probable way forward.[14]

A bonus for archivists wanting to better understand the inner workings of fair use case law: nearly one-half of the report includes detailed footnotes explaining how courts have determined whether a particular use was or was not "fair." The Office's third report concluded with this classic illustration of the spectrum of decision making regarding what may be or may not be a fair use:

> *When a model is deployed for purposes such as analysis or research—the types of uses that are critical to international competitiveness—the outputs are unlikely to substitute for expressive works used in training. But making commercial use of vast troves of copyrighted works to produce expressive content that competes with them in existing markets, especially where this is accomplished through illegal access, goes beyond established fair use boundaries.*[15]

From an archivist's perspective, it's frustrating that the analysis comes so close to touching upon the kind of copyrighted material that might be found in archives—unpublished works. But it did not get there. Instead, unpublished works are addressed only in an oblique, and ultimately unfriendly, way with the repetition of the overused statement that originated in the 1985 Supreme Court ruling in *Harper & Row Publishers, Inc. v. Nation Enterprises*—that the unpublished nature of a work weighs against fair use. The Office's third report unfortunately never acknowledges the possibility that collections of unpublished works might be among the works to be ingested and incorporated into a generative AI training data set.

Perhaps we shouldn't be surprised that archives were ignored. After all, what the Copyright Office was attempting to address were concerns of the economic value and the exploitation of works intended for the marketplace, something that is the opposite of what archives are about. That, however, leaves archivists needing an ancient Greek oracle adept at reading entrails to figure out what all this means for our mostly unpublished holdings.

The report's analysis does, however, provide some encouragement, independent of AI considerations, for archives wanting to conduct digital projects. The report's discussion of fair use's fourth factor—the effect on the market—is encouraging for us. It states, "Where licensing markets are available to meet AI training needs, unlicensed uses will be disfavored under the fourth factor. *But if barriers to licensing prove insurmountable for parties' uses of some types of works, there will be no functioning market to harm and the fourth factor may favor fair use.*"[16]

10.3 AI Closing Considerations

The Copyright Office's studies may not have provided direction for how we should think about the relation of AI to archival materials, but by connecting the public hype about artificial intelligence to copyright issues, the reports can help us understand the copyright issues amidst a complex and rapidly shifting policy battlefield.

Of course, generative AI is not the only form of artificial intelligence, but it is the one that recently has captured public attention the most. Maybe that's because, aside from its important copyright implications, it raises unique existential questions. If AI can reproduce much of what we believe makes us human, then what does AI's future hold for humanity itself? As seen in the responses to the Copyright Office's notices of inquiries and the current interest by a wide swath of politicians, Generative AI clearly presents some significant intellectual property dilemmas. It's hard to read the various stakeholder comments in the Copyright Office reports without being reminded of the terms William Patry used nearly two decades ago about the post-DMCA "copyright wars." The current discussion has all the earmarks of what he dubbed "moral panics," along with more than a few of the "folk devils" he described as central to the battle between the copyright industry and users adapting new technology to the use of copyrighted works.[17]

On reading some of the comments submitted to the Copyright Office's NOI, one wonders whether applying the fair use doctrine to support generative AI's ingesting really will cause "the contribution to American culture of the professional creator class . . . [to] all but cease" within a generation because of the actions of "financially cannibalistic takers of the AI community."[18] Meanwhile, comments from the generative AI moguls illustrate their own panic. They warn that unless they can proceed on their current path of wholesale copying and modifying copyrighted works to create their LLM, the models will be weaker and less effective. They claim that such an AI "in turn will imperil the United States' current role as the home for AI innovation, opening the door for other countries . . . to become the preferred destination for AI development."[19]

Unfortunately, the best the Copyright Office's third study has to offer is a hike through the fog-enshrouded briar patch of fair use. That seems to promise even less clarity and utility for the new terrain of advanced digital systems than it did back in 1841, when Justice Story created the foundation for fair use in the *Folsom v. Marsh* case in 1841. As Chapter 5 has shown, that path could leave all the key parties dissatisfied, except for, perhaps, litigating lawyers.

Now you're probably thinking that copyright law is not the right tool for dealing with the intersection of AI and the production and use of creative content for the advancement of knowledge. You are not alone. That's the conclusion of Carys Craig, a scholar of US and Canadian law on the faculty of York University's Osgoode Hall Law School. In a 2024 symposium paper, "The AI-Copyright Trap," she argued that "copyright law is neither apposite nor equipped to govern the development of AI. Insisting that it should do so, and imagining that it is somehow up to the task, could be a course-setting and costly mistake."[20] She contends that artists, authors, and other creative professionals concerned about the unauthorized use of their works by generative AI will find copyright law to be a "false friend" if they seek to use it to protect their interests in cultural production.

Rather, any law or regulation that might be developed to reinforce authorial rights will merely "reinscrib[e] the logic of exclusivity, private property, and cultural control over information and cultural expression."[21] She writes,

> *The publishers, the recording industry representatives, and the copyright collectives are lining up, cap in hand, to paint a picture of the worthy, struggling artists they purport to serve and on behalf of whom they demand compensation. In theory, the more that users pay for the use of creators' works, the more these intermediaries will pay creators for them—but we have spent decades expanding copyright while creators get poorer.*[22]

Instead Craig would focus the question of AI policy not on regulation or protection of a rights-holder's exclusive property, but on "the public's interest and protection of the public domain from private appropriation and corporate control . . . [and] ensuring that the training materials necessary for the development of ethical and responsible AI systems are *open and available for all to use*."[23] Craig's analysis is trenchant, and her recommendation to focus on regulation based on inclusivity and the public domain is quite appealing. Unfortunately, as even she acknowledges, there is a strong historical precedent of copyright intermediaries managing to gain control of new technologies for their own benefit.

Nevertheless, her careful parsing of the rhetoric in the current AI/copyright war leads me to foolishly risk a prediction about AI and copyright. Regardless of the great uncertainty of how generative AI and copyright policy may develop, it is highly likely that the copyright intermediaries and the AI industry will rush to Congress for a solution that ends up as unsatisfactory as the way the 1996 WIPO Treaty and the 1998 US Digital Millennium Copyright Act "solved" the digital technology problem brought on by the internet. Should we really believe government and the industry can find a Solomon-like solution regarding AI on behalf of society at large?

In light of the large and complex policy problems and the weighty players involved, those of us who are concerned with the intersection of archives and copyright might just need to sit on the sidelines and be creative in how we adapt our archival needs to whatever aspects of the law might be hammered out for others' benefit. Might that mean relying more on the fourth factor of fair use for digital projects when authors cannot be identified or found, as suggested in the Copyright Office's third report? If so, then right now, even independent of generative AI, we would have a strengthened fair use risk mitigation factor when doing digital projects for orphan works.

In the meantime, we will continue to be at the mercy of commercial, political, and technical forces that none of us can control. If the past is prologue, then hold onto your hats (and your wallets). It will be a wild ride.

11 Changing Copyright Law
What You Can Do

It's inescapable. If you're an archivist, you've been pulled into the copyright business, a business that preempts your purpose as archivist and interferes with your mission. That's why there's an individual and a profession-wide need for us to work together to modify copyright's exclusive rights regime to reduce the barriers it places on our mission and the public use of archives.

Advocacy on policy matters has long been called for as an essential responsibility of archivists.[1] Now we need to embrace that role to address a law that is long overdue for amendments to meet our archival needs. Actual legislative change requires both focused advocacy and lobbying, which Kathleen D. Roe has identified as more concentrated steps that must be preceded by awareness-building.[2]

Indeed, an improved copyright law is a very ambitious objective that will require substantial organizational resources and time. That's the focus of Chapter 12. However, to build a foundation for that advocacy, there are essential roles for individual archivists. Primary among them is to broaden the public understanding of the value of archives while also educating the public about the ways the current copyright law frustrates archives users from obtaining the value they seek from our collections. This work is closely connected to the basic public advocacy work that is a critical need of the profession, and there are essential actions that individual archivists can and should take. In fact, it could be argued that the general need to build a broad public constituency in support of archives might be a higher immediate priority for individual archivists than the substantive legislative changes. Those changes are better understood as the province of our professional organizations and institutions.

So, what can we as individuals do to work toward the bigger changes? Before starting we must understand that the very nature of records and their use calls for us to play at least four roles in the copyright business. First, we are trustees for the authors and creators who hold copyright in many of the works in our repositories. Second, we are responsible for informing all users about the presence and the nature of exclusive rights in what they find of value in our archives. Third, we need to assist those users in understanding copyright's constraints as well as the law's nooks and crannies that might allow them to use archivally held copyrighted works. A fourth role arises from the tension between having to fulfill the first three roles while carrying out our mission as archivists. That fourth role, in other words, is to use every interaction with users as an opportunity for advocacy.[3]

Box-11.1 "Advocacy in Every Encounter"

"Every time we respond to a reference question in person or on the telephone, every time we talk with a director, a university treasurer, a state legislator, board chairperson, county representative, or other resource allocator, we advocate or fail to do so. Every time we work with a donor, a county or town clerk, with a probable customer—a teacher, film maker, novelist, scientist or medical person, for example—we advocate or we do not. Every time we talk to the passerby who may eventually be the legislator, donor, or user-beyond-the walls, we establish, for good or bad, our public relations" (Elsie Freeman Finch quoted in Roe, *Advocacy and Awareness*, 113.)

As this book has shown, our work places us in the crosshairs of copyright. That's why it is essential for all of us—individual archivists and the profession as a whole—to have a clear agenda for changes needed in copyright policy. For instance, a careful reading of Chapter 4, the survey of US copyright law, makes it clear that there is a range of tasks commonly completed by archivists for which copyright law does not provide clear legal support. These include:

- making multiple digital back-up preservation copies to guard against loss, deterioration, or system failures;
- making digital copies of preserved works available beyond the premises of the archives;

- circumventing passwords or other access controls on electronic records;
- transmitting copies of photographic, musical, or audiovisual works still under copyright to off-site users.

The risk of legal exposure in these activities may be limited because we usually do them on a case-by-case basis. They are actions that can be systematically assessed in an almost routine way in relation to criteria in our basic risk-management policy. They are, in fact, the type of activities that seem like basic common sense to us, but they may not be in strict adherence to the current law. That's why they all point to issues that need to be addressed through copyright reform.

Archival work, of course, must also be directed toward society-wide use. This means a case-by-case approach may not work. The more that a public activity is involved, the more risk there is of legal exposure. This means all of our mission-driven work related to facilitating and promoting the use of archival materials by both internal users and the public at large can expose us to copyright risks. Work supporting such use, of course, is central to the very purpose of archives. It is, after all, the reason we take the time to select, arrange, describe, and preserve materials. For this reason, the public use of our materials must be the major focus of our policy advocacy. This is another reason that we need to call for changes in the law—to deliver needed research material to users, whether to enable them to assert their rights, to pursue social justice, or to understand and explain history itself.

11.1 Areas Needing Advocacy Attention

Copyright law presently contains some allowance for use- and user-related exceptions to its exclusive rights (see Chapter 4, sections 4.1.7, 4.1.8, 4.1.9, and 4.1.10). However, these exceptions are narrowly framed, often difficult to understand, and not applicable for all types of materials and uses. Section 108's provisions, for instance, do not allow archives to make copies for remote user requests if the work is musical, pictorial, graphical, or audiovisual. Section 109's exemption allowing the owner of a lawfully obtained copy of a work to transfer or donate the work to another party (e.g., an archives) only applies to analog, not digital works. Section 110's exceptions for performances of works are severely constrained by a welter of conditions that limit its application, and its impenetrable exceptions for use of works in online instruction are inoperable. Furthermore, none of these exceptions are relevant for materials held in secure digital systems. Such a constricted working space shows why we need a dedicated bright-line general exception for archivists and users of archival materials, an exception that covers the variety of materials and uses that reflect the reality of archives.

On first glance, § 107—Fair Use—would seem to be that broad exception, but rather than providing clarity, such as that found in the § 108 exceptions, fair use is a balancing test that is only definitively determined through a court ruling for each particular case. Unfortunately, as documentary film makers have discovered, even a solid four-factor argument is rarely sufficient to convince an editor or publisher to approve uses of the work beyond short, limited quotations.[4] The utility of fair use for archivists and users of archival materials will remain very limited if we are expected to meet commercial market standards for inherently non-market materials. As far as the copyright system is concerned, these kinds of materials are orphans.

The very mission of archives is to preserve and make available substantial numbers of unpublished works that were not created for commercial exploitation, were never registered for copyright, and are lacking in identifiable or traceable copyright owners. That's why an orphan works exception should be at the center of not only our organizational but also our individual advocacy. For instance, you might suggest to users that what we need is an exception enabling an archivist who applies reasonable criteria to establish that an item is a copyright orphan, which then could be held in trust in the permanent custody of the archives. On that basis, the exception would allow the archivist to make the work available to the public under the terms of a Creative Commons license. Educating our various constituencies about the orphan works problem is absolutely essential. Promoting a solution is something we as individual archivists can and should do immediately.

11.2 What You Can Do Now to Advocate for Better Copyright

If you think that there is little an individual archivist can do in the face of well-heeled lobbyists or the publication industry itself, you're wrong. There are many day-to-day actions that you as an individual can take to build a foundation for a consensus on the need for reforms. After all, who better than you as an archivist to gather stories that can be used as evidence to show our communities and society the impact resulting from use of our holdings? Who better to explain the copyright barriers that block people from the fullness of their heritage and that impede citizens from exercising their rights? It's archivists, individually and collectively, who can and must educate their constituencies. It may take some time, but we should work one by one to create a basis for something like the wide public activism described in Chapter 9 that frustrated PIPA, SOPA, and ACTA. Not only will this work make clear that archives do not belong in copyright's monetary universe, but those same points will also advance the critical policy agenda of convincing the public that archives matter to society, as former SAA President David Gracy and his successors have advocated.

Here are several examples of how you as an individual archivist can begin to build a foundation to effect change:

- The most obvious first act in individual advocacy is to never miss an occasion to contact your elected representatives. If election season is approaching, reach out to candidates who are just beginning to test the waters. Attend candidate and issue forums to raise the problems created by the overreaching copyright monopoly. Raise the issue in letters to the editor and social media forums. Who knows, the candidate may be so relieved to get a question on something other than immigration, the climate crisis, or any other "wedge issue" that they actually stop to think about what's at stake. To capture the attention of lawmakers and their staff, keep your comments very brief and focus only on the heart of the issue—it can be unhelpful to provide either a long explanation of the need or any qualifying conditions you would accept.
- As an archivist, you have a tremendous asset in the one-on-one or small group conversations you have every day with archives users. Let them hear about the challenges that the current copyright law poses to education, citizen rights, or the building of community identity. Educating our users will only help when the time comes to have hundreds, or more, of people contact their legislators about potential changes to the copyright law. The personal stories you hear will also help you provide the anecdotes needed for our professional organizations to mitigate the shopworn tales and tropes from industrial lobbyists. If you are lucky, the archives user who hears your story might just have an in-law or other relative who is a key advisor for an up-and-coming elected official.

- Conventional archives outreach activities, such as exhibits, blogs, lectures, or class visits, should be adjusted to draw attention to archival copyright problems. Small steps may include having exhibit, blog, and social media captions and citations draw attention to the copyright constraints on the materials displayed or quoted. Thus, the rights statements discussed in Chapter 8, section 8.3.1 are not only good administrative practice, but they also drive home the pervasiveness of copyright's smothering of culture and knowledge. Increasing the awareness of our supportive audiences is important because, despite their enthusiasm with what they find in archives, they often have little idea about the copyright limits on what they and we can do with these gems. Rather than just listing the date of the document you are displaying, make a point of noting the year the work will finally enter the public domain. Given the excessive length of copyright, that alone could be a real eye-opener to copyright's absurd stranglehold on archival materials.
- Any time you limit one of your internet postings to just short quotes because of a work's still-in-copyright status, you should add an explicit reference to copyright as the reason the viewer cannot see the full original regardless of the work's age or non-commercial nature. Furthermore, if you have a general social media policy to avoid placing online photos created after a specific date because of rights concerns, consider periodically posting a notice about that policy and how changes to copyright law would allow you to put up more recent images.
- As some of our copyright librarian colleagues have done, join with local colleagues to celebrate Public Domain Day every January with online and in-person activities identifying authors and works in your own collection which have only just emerged from copyright's shackles.
- Given how often new copyright lawsuits appear in the popular press, your public commenting on these stories is an opportunity to raise relevant issues in the cases that connect to your work, your collections, and your users. An important additional benefit—it helps your community and your public see that archives materials and work are not just tied to the dusty past, but they matter right now and deserve public policy attention.

All of the above actions are within your reach. To pursue them, it will be essential to be well informed about basic archival copyright matters as well as newly evolving intellectual property issues.[5] Online advocacy organizations, such as the Access to Knowledge Coalition (A2K), Electronic Frontier Foundation (EFF), Library Copyright Alliance (LCA), and Program on Information Justice and Intellectual Property (PIJIP) can keep you abreast of the latest policy issues and provide inspiration for new ways to make the case for why archivists and our users need copyright reform.

Every archivist needs to be involved in advocacy. As Kathleen Roe said in her 2015 SAA presidential address on archives advocacy, "'Each of us' means precisely that—every single one of us can and must contribute in some way. It will take work—and we need to step up and do that work, make that commitment for ourselves and in our professional organizations. It is not somebody else's to do."[6]

12 Changing Copyright Law
It Takes an Organization

You've done the hard work to learn about copyright, and you've helped your archives users learn about copyright's mysteries and absurdities. The stories they have told you have re-energized you about the importance of being a professional archivist. So, what more can archivists do to obtain a more responsive copyright law? That requires legislative change, and that means the substantial work that can only be undertaken through professional associations, especially ones at the national level.

In any field, only such associations are in a position to provide focused and sustained attention to policy matters that are as entrenched as copyright. Only they will have the stature and some of the resources needed to engage in and maintain advocacy as well as the standing to speak with national policymakers on behalf of individual practitioners. No doubt, legislative advocacy in these organizations can be overshadowed by the typical work of an association—member services, organizing conferences, and maintaining publication and education programs. However, a core role for any national professional association should be identification of the standards that make their members professionals as well as practitioners. When the standard is a law that undermines basic professional goals, however, the organization needs to engage in advocacy and lobbying to change the law. Thus, when a profession's core mission is impeded from fulfilling its mission by arcane and outdated laws, the related associations should use their collective weight to obtain better laws.

In many organizations, the resources needed for full-time legislative advocacy staffing or even having a professional lobbyist on a continuing retainer can be beyond reach. That should not preclude the professionals within the organization and its governing officers from identifying policy matters that call for advocacy in the organization's strategic plan. Once this advocacy is made a strategic objective, specific policy positions and long-term goals can be developed by policy-specialist members within the organization, even one with limited resources.

As an example, the Society of American Archivists (SAA), the largest and most broadly based US archival organization, has a record of pursuing public policy concerns and advocacy, including on copyright matters via the work of concerned members and governing and executive leadership. It has been particularly active by itself, as well as with coalition partners, over more than three decades when the implications of digital media, global intellectual property action, and online networks became increasingly important. In a team-based approach, SAA's governing Council monitors and acts on copyright policy issues aided by its Intellectual Property Working Group. Attention has been given both to the positive changes we want to achieve as well as to responsive action when others, whether in allied or competing fields, have proposed changes that would make the work of archivists harder. Success has been mixed, but the readiness of the organization to call attention to the effect that copyright law has on citizens has brought positive recognition to the importance of archives and archivists as a whole.

Copyright change is a "long game" and our needs are multiple. That is why the development and evolution of policy stances since the early to mid-1990s has put the SAA and its members in a better position to make a difference. SAA's advocacy has enabled archivists' concerns to be heard despite the great disproportion of our resources when compared to those of the copyright industries. Continued progress can only be enhanced by individual archivists broadening their engagement with individual users to obtain the stories (as discussed in Chapter 11) that can be used to make the SAA's message more compelling in organization-based advocacy. Copyright advocacy should be treated by professional organizations as an ongoing program rather than just a limited-term project.

As the omnibus national organization of archivists, SAA is the logical professional body to lead in tracking and representing archival interests in copyright, but there is a strong network of regional and local archival organizations, as well as other records-related organizations, with which SAA is already working on other policy issues. That's why it is essential that all SAA members, as well as other US archival professionals, acquire a deeper and broader understanding of copyright. More attention should be paid to intellectual property topics in formal archival education, especially on specific archival problems resulting from a law designed for protecting commercial markets rather than promoting learning and culture. Archivists also need more focused continuing education offerings on intellectual property. SAA, and regional and local archival associations, already have packed conference programs. However, considering that all archivists are affected by copyright law on a daily basis, they should provide more opportunity for general discussion of copyright and related intellectual property issues.

Archivists and archival associations cannot accomplish all of this on their own. We need to look for alliances with organizations and individuals with shared needs, interests, and concerns. This outreach should include law professors, technology innovators, and humanities scholars as well as the more immediately obvious allies in libraries and museums. At the same time, we need to remember that, as important as allies are, their priorities, publics, and needs will differ at times from ours, so we will sometimes need to make clear to our partners why and how our and their advocacy priorities might not always align tightly.

Especially important will be proactive work to engage with professional organizations to which many archives users already belong. After all, it's our users who are the people most severely caught between the rock of exclusive rights and the hard place of needing to use material so far out of commerce as to provide no means for obtaining permission. Academic historians, genealogists, public historians, historic preservationists, and journalists are the most obvious potential allies to seek, but to that list we might add film makers, podcasters, documentarians, and those in the creative arts. Whether archives users are "traditional" or "non-traditional," our first challenge is to convince user groups to adopt our understanding that everyone's stake in copyright is broader than just protecting the exclusive rights in their own works. We need our allies to have the conviction that everyone has a clear stake in obtaining a copyright law with a reasonably limited duration and comprehensible and balanced exceptions. Clearly, the breadth of archival materials and the policy changes needed are so great that we need to remember that every reference question we receive and answer we provide offers an opportunity to gain new partners and new stories. That's how we can build the strongest cases for the copyright policy changes we need.

Another reason that copyright advocacy needs to be part of the strategic priorities of archival associations is to make sure there is an advance plan for dealing with the most critical issues while also being prepared for action on topics that arise in other parts of the intellectual property spectrum. Having these separate archival policy issues identified in advance will support developing and obtaining agreement on future policy position statements. Then, with positions already in place, full position papers can be developed expeditiously. These steps have helped SAA in recent decades to make clear and compelling statements on relatively short notice. However, we need to be honest and acknowledge that, given the limited size of SAA, even with collaboration with the regional archival associations, advocacy at the national level requires resources beyond what existing dues and revenue streams provide. Even if we accept the idea of not having an ongoing lobbying presence, we are further challenged by the need to have a continually renewing cadre of copyright specialist members able to invest the time needed to track the issues and develop policy positions for the SAA to advance on its own leadership or through its coalition partners. The financial challenge for ongoing contracted representation and the challenge of sustaining engaged expert members with the institutional foundation for them to dedicate time to the advocacy are substantial. Thus, we need to be realistic about how much the SAA can accomplish beyond having clear policy positions.

Even if the resources may not be available to do all that we would like, the need for changes is very broad. Because not all matters can be pursued at once, it is even more important that we be aware of the major areas of copyright law that should be prioritized. The following is a survey of topics needing attention as resources become available or occasions arise where the archivist voice needs to be heard in response to legislative initiatives by others.

12.1 Specific Legislative Issues for Organization-Centered Advocacy

The following are the most relevant changes needed in the copyright law to support archives. They are based on the archival functions and activities that law should support.

- Eligibility for Archives Exceptions, § 108(a), should be amended to expand the scope of eligible heritage repositories to include museums in what are currently called "library and archives" exceptions.

- Preservation Copying Exceptions, § 108(b) and (c): The number of allowable copies for preservation purposes should be changed from just three to something along the lines of "whatever number is necessary" to ensure future availability of a complete and authentic copy that could serve as a replacement of the original. The allowance for an open-ended number of preservation copies is needed in the digital era to preclude loss in the event of compounded system failures.
- Availability of Preservation Copies, § 108(b): The limitation on making digital preservation copies available only on the premises of the eligible institution should be removed for unpublished materials and replaced with remote availability when a user makes a formal request to the repository.
- Availability of Preservation Copies of Older Works, § 108(h): The exception that allows libraries and archives to make available digital preservation copies of works in the last 20 years of their copyright term should be expanded to also include unpublished works in the scope of this exception.
- Works Not Eligible for Archives to Supply Copies, § 108(i): The exclusion of graphical, pictorial, musical, and audiovisual works from what an archives can reproduce and distribute to remote users should be eliminated so that those works would also benefit from the "user service" exceptions in § 108(d) and (e). Alternatively, the current exclusion should be made applicable only if the intended use would be for commercial purposes.
- First Sale Right, § 109: Provisions that allow the legal owner of an analog copy of a work to transfer ownership to another should be amended to make this "first sale" right apply to digital materials as well.
- Exceptions for Performance, § 110 (2): The performance exceptions for use of works in online instruction should be made less restrictive to allow instructional performance of all types of works and entire works rather than just short segments. It should also be applicable to all forms of online educational presentations whether part of a formal curriculum or use in basic archival outreach activities.
- Technological Locks and Anti-circumvention, § 1201 through § 1203: These measures should be tempered by creation of exceptions for archives, libraries, and museums to allow access to technologically protected works for preservation and fair use purposes.

Archival advocacy attention is also needed to ensure there is no erosion of the flexibilities currently in the law, whether in the statute or in court rulings. Relevant areas include:

- Most importantly, we need to monitor any proposals for amendments to § 107 or §108 and be prepared to dedicate resources to protecting the allowances these two sections provide for archival work, even if we find these two sections less than ideal in their current state.
- Copyright Term, § 302 through § 304: No additional years should be added to copyright's already long term.
- Registration Requirements, § 411(a): At least in the case of unpublished works, this section's requirement that works be registered for copyright as a prerequisite to litigation must be maintained.
- Registration and Remedies for Infringement, § 412 (1): The prohibition on the award of statutory damages or attorney fees for infringement prior to an unpublished work's registration should remain unaltered.
- Statutory Damages for Infringement, § 504(c) (2): The law's current safe harbor providing relief to libraries and archives from statutory damages when acting with a reasonable expectation of fair use should be extended. It should be revised to cover more than just infringements involving the making of copies. It should also cover the distribution and creation of derivative works.

12.2 Court Cases Matter

Beyond legislative matters, there are the courts. We should be prepared to file or join in filing amicus/amici briefs regarding fair use cases, even those not centered on archival or library materials. We need to support a broad application of fair use for transformative activities that arise in the normal course of archival work even if the argument for a transformative character is narrowed when there is a commercial purpose. We should especially support a flexible interpretation of the legitimacy of fair use when the use involves an unpublished work. As with legislative matters, filing cases and creating *amicus* briefs requires resources, both financial and members able to dedicate time when issues arise. However, through sustained relations with other cultural, civil society, and public interest organizations, there often arise opportunities to join in *amicus* briefs on court cases.

12.3 Who Knows What the Future Holds

Artificial Intelligence (AI) has attracted great attention in the popular media, higher education, and in collective bargaining and professional organizations, but its copyright implications are yet to be sorted out. The issues pull in directions quite different from what we are used to seeing in copyright "battles" of the past several decades. On the one hand, there is the matter of copyrighted works being copied and manipulated in Large Language Model AI systems, often without permission. On the other hand, AI's ability to generate new works presents theoretical challenges to what is copyrightable as well as whether these new products infringe on the § 106 (2) derivative works exclusive right.[1]

Regardless of the variety of what AI-related legislative and regulatory proposals emerge, it would be consistent with copyright and conventional archival practice to advocate that any archival content ingested into AI systems should include the capacity to generate and supply metadata to support full attribution to the original creator and full citation of the archival source. Based on some of the AI industry comments referenced in the Copyright Office's report, *Copyright and Artificial Intelligence Part 3: Generative AI Training*, discussed in Chapter 10, this need may meet resistance from the industry. However, this point emanates from traditional archival practice and research standards as well as from the need to respect the authors' rights entitlement to attribution. What priority the profession should give to this issue in our advocacy work will not be possible to determine until some of the current dust settles and we see what other AI-related archival needs arise. Only then can we have clarity to develop a professional consensus for effective advocacy.

Just as over three decades ago, when public policy concerns turned to the emergent World Wide Web, the new AI technology promises to offer a mix of complications and opportunities for archival content and practice as well as for how we relate to our users. Its consumer and industrial opportunities are not yet fully predictable. However, if the past history of intellectual property has taught us anything, it is that the general societal benefits of new technology will end up being in tension with the ways technology can override an individual's rights. This new technology will also, inevitably, drive interest in state-enforced protections for corporate entities wishing to exploit technology in ways that may end up limiting the benefits it otherwise could provide to individual citizens. Indeed, regular news accounts of the close connection between government and the technology sector seem to only underscore that history is repeating itself.

Given the historical dynamic between information technology innovations and information policy, new issues and priorities beyond AI are sure to arise over the many decades before this book's own copyright expires. Just as in the past, there's every reason to expect that litigation and legislative amendments will provide new challenges for archivists. That's why we must constantly monitor the landscape and be prepared to assert that archives-based needs must be incorporated into public policy. Our collections and the communities we serve deserve nothing less than for us to be bold and knowledgeable advocates. We may encounter roadblocks along the way, but copyright is too important an issue—not just for us, but especially for those who use the records and heritage we steward. What we do truly matters to society.

Appendix 1: Copyright Fair Use Checklist*

Introduction

This checklist for fair use is intended to serve two fundamental purposes. First, it should help educators, librarians, and others to focus on factual circumstances that are important to the evaluation of fair use as it may apply in a given set of circumstances. A reasonable fair use analysis is based on four factors set forth in the fair use provision of copyright law, Section 107 of the U.S. Copyright Act. The application of those factors depends on the particular facts of your situation; changing one or more facts may alter the outcome of the analysis. The checklist is based on the four factors and judicial decisions interpreting and applying them.

A second purpose of the checklist is to provide an important means for recording your decision making process. Maintaining a record of your fair use analysis could be critical to establishing your reasonable and good faith attempts to apply fair use to meet your educational objectives. Section 504 (c)(2) of the U.S. Copyright Act offers some protection for educators and librarians who act in good faith. Once you have completed your application of fair use to a particular need, keep your completed checklist in your files for future reference.

As you use the checklist and apply it to your situation, you might often check more than one box in each column and even check boxes across columns. Some checked boxes will *favor fair use*, and others may *oppose fair use*. A key concern is whether you are acting reasonably in checking any given box; the ultimate concern is whether the cumulative weight of the factors favors or opposes fair use. The checklist is a guide; you still need to bring your knowledge and reasonable perspective to the task.

---

*With permission from, Kenneth D. Crews, *Copyright Law for Librarians and Educators: Creative Strategies and Practical Solutions*, (American Library Association, 2020. ProQuest Ebook Central).

The checklist for fair use originated in 1998 as a task undertaken by Kenneth Crews, while then on the faculty of Indiana University, working closely with Dwayne Buttler in the university's Copyright Management Center. Since then, many colleges, universities, libraries, primary and secondary schools, companies, governmental organizations, and others have adopted and used it. Some users have accepted it without change; others have revised and adapted it to distinct needs. The version here is revised in small measure from the original. As with all advice and information about fair use, you should look closely at whether it serves your particular needs and whether you should make any changes.

Copyright Checklist: Fair Use

Name: ____________________ Date: ____________________

Project: ____________________ Institution: ____________________

Prepared by: ____

Purpose

Favoring Fair Use

- ☐ Teaching (including multiple copies for classroom use)
- ☐ Research
- ☐ Scholarship
- ☐ Nonprofit educational institution
- ☐ Criticism
- ☐ Comment
- ☐ News reporting
- ☐ Transformative use (alters the original work in a creative manner)
- ☐ Transformative use (uses the work for a purpose other than the original purpose)

- ☐ Restricted access (for only students or other appropriate group)
- ☐ Parody

Opposing Fair Use

- ☐ Commercial activity
- ☐ Profiting from the use
- ☐ Straight reproduction (copying without modification)
- ☐ Nontransformative use
- ☐ Entertainment
- ☐ Bad-faith behavior
- ☐ Denying credit to original author

Nature

Favoring Fair Use

- ☐ Published work
- ☐ Factual or nonfiction based
- ☐ Important to favored educational objectives

Opposing Fair Use

- ☐ Unpublished work
- ☐ Highly creative work (art, music, novels, films, plays)
- ☐ Fiction
- ☐ Consumable work (e.g., worksheets and standard exam forms)

Amount

Favoring Fair Use

- ☐ Small quantity
- ☐ Portion used is not central or significant to entire work
- ☐ Amount is tailored to meet the educational or other favored purpose

Opposing Fair Use

- ☐ Large portion or whole work used beyond the favored purpose
- ☐ Portion used could interfere with a reasonable market for the use (e.g., multiple chapters from a single book)
- ☐ Portion used is central to work or "heart of the work"

Effect

Favoring Fair Use

- ☐ User owns lawfully acquired or purchased copy of original work
- ☐ Few or modest number of copies made
- ☐ No significant effect on the market or potential market for copyrighted work
- ☐ No similar product marketed by the copyright holder
- ☐ Lack of a reasonable licensing mechanism for the work and the intended use

Opposing Fair Use

- ☐ Straight copying that is not transformative
- ☐ Portion used could interfere with a reasonable market for the use or derivatives (e.g., multiple chapters from a single book)
- ☐ Reasonably available licensing mechanism for the use of the copyrighted work
- ☐ Affordable permission available for using work
- ☐ Numerous copies made
- ☐ Posted to the Internet or otherwise made widely accessible
- ☐ Repeated or long-term use

Appendix 2: How to Use Risk Assessment Tables

To illustrate how Chapter 8's risk assessment and risk rating tables function, this appendix includes collection descriptions for two real-life collections from the archives I directed for many years. Using the risk assessment rating forms included in Chapter 8 as Tables 8.1, 8.2, and 8.3, I have presented here an actual assessment of two sample collections to show how I would arrive at a risk-management-based decision on whether to move forward on a hypothetical project for digitization and web display. The resultant decisions are then examined for an indication of how confident I should be in proceeding. These examples may not be exhaustive of the risk issues you face, and the collections may not be typical. However, the samples are meant to show how you might use Chapter 8's discussion and tables to structure your decision-making process and preserve evidence of due diligence in case there is ever a question.

N.B.: Because of space considerations, I have condensed the risk attributed inventory (Table 8.1) to show only the scores I believe best describe the nature of the sample material. To see the full table, be sure to look back to Chapter 8, sections 8.4.1 and 8.4.2.

Each example is followed by narrative comments that explain my assessment of the risk level and reasoning for deciding whether to proceed on each of the sample collections. For the "Decision on a Course of Action" and "Level of Confidence in Risk Assessment" (Tables 8.2 and 8.3), this appendix merely reproduces the blank form from Chapter 8, but I have provided a brief narrative explanation of how I arrived at confidence level for a decision on the hypothetical project.

A.2.1 Descriptions of Sample Collections

SAMPLE COLLECTION A:

D. H. Lloyde Photograph Album, 1909–14

Volume: 0.3 cubic feet (one letter-size document case).

Description: Photograph album containing 390 postcard-size prints taken by University of Illinois alumnus and local commercial photographer D. H. Lloyde (1835–1922). Images include campus scenes and buildings, student activities (including push ball, hobo band, Maypole dances, theatrical productions, track, football, baseball, student class broadsides, electrical engineering show, military reviews, band), fraternity and sorority houses, and public buildings in Urbana and Champaign, and related subjects.

SAMPLE COLLECTION B:

Photographic Subject File, 1868–2000s

Volume: 63.6 cubic feet (approximately 220 document cases and photograph boxes).

Summary Description: Photographic Subject File contains prints, negatives, glass plates, and digital images relating to University of Illinois administration; agriculture; alumni; athletics; buildings; campus scenes; Chicago campus; colleges; conferences and short courses; documents, memorials, and seals; engineering; events; faculty and staff portraits; housing and food services; libraries and museums; nonacademic personnel; non-university topics; physical education; presidents; research projects and services; student military activities; students and student activities (including "Hobo Parade" and minstrel shows); student organizations; trustees; and visitors. The majority of this series consists of images created by University Photographic Services, but it also includes images from other individual, institutional and private donors, and publications such as the *Urbana Morning Courier*, and the *Champaign-Urbana News Gazette*.

A.2.2 Risk Attribute Inventories

RISK ATTRIBUTE INVENTORY (from Table 8.1) for **Sample Collection A: Lloyde Photo Album**

NOTE: text in *italics* is from headings and options in Table 8.1. Text in Roman is commentary to explain rationale for rating chosen. In the interest of space, only the rating chosen is shown here.

Attribute	Risk Score	Rationale for Risk Score
Age	1.0	*1 = Date of Creation is:* 70 > 120 years ago
Heterogeneity	1.0	*1 = Multiplicity of authors is:* 1 to 3 authors present
Anonymity/ renown	2.0	*2 = Presence of authors known to have sought to benefit or actually benefited economically from their creative works* Commercial photo studio.
Cultural sensitivity	1.5	*"Subject content or function of records related to items of known cultural sensitivity, especially traditional cultural expressions, race/ethnicity, political identity"* *1 = Limited/Medium amount present* Note: Given when the images were taken and given inclusion of class rivalry broadsides and portrayal of student activities such as the "Hobo Parade" where blackface occurred, some items may be unsuitable for online access.
Personal privacy	0.0	*"Subject content or function of records related to items of personal privacy, such as educational, employment, health, sexual preference, personal finances"* Note: Given age of material and nature of images having been taken in public, privacy is not likely to be a factor.

Attribute	Risk Score	Rationale for Risk Score
Ownership/ authorship	0.0 or 4.0	*"Preponderance of works authored by the archives' 'parent' institution"* *0 = None / 4 = majority of material created by external persons* Note: Difficult to score: Commercial photographer, but he has been dead more than 70 years.
Size/Extent of collection	0.0	*"0 = ≤1.0 cubic/linear foot"*
Creative nature of content	3.5	*"Factual vs. fictional or creative (expressive) nature of material"* 3 = Largely composed of moderately creative materials 4 = Composed of highly creative material made for external circulation.
Attribute Total	**9.0 or 13.0**	

RISK ATTRIBUTE INVENTORY (from Table 8.1) **Sample Collection B: University Photographic Subject File**

NOTE: text in *italics* is from headings and options in Table 8.1. Text in Roman is commentary to explain rationale for rating chosen. In the interest of space, only the rating chosen is shown here.

Attribute	Risk Score	Rationale for Risk Score
Age	3.0	*Date of Creation* *3 = created < 30 years ago* Note: broad range of materials from late nineteenth century to early 2000s, with large bulk in 1950s through 1990s
Heterogeneity	10.0	*Multiplicity of authors* *10 = uncounted or unsampled number of authors present*
Anonymity/ renown	2.0	*2 = Presence of authors known to have sought to benefit or actually benefited economically from their creative works* Note: substantial portion is University authored images, but also many images by private citizens, external publicity agencies, or national publications

Attribute	Risk Score	Rationale for Risk Score
Cultural sensitivity	1.0	*Subject content or function of records related to items of known cultural sensitivity, especially traditional cultural expressions, race/ethnicity, political identity* *1 = Limited amount present* Note: contains some blackface and some Native American mascot images but these are in a smaller proportion than in Sample Collection A.
Personal privacy	0.5	*Subject content or function of records related to items of personal privacy, such as educational, employment, health, sexual preference, personal finances* *0 = None / 1 = Limited amount present* Note: Proportionally to size of collection, contains a few historic images of unidentified children and research subjects
Ownership/ authorship	2.8	*Preponderance of works authored by the archives' "parent" institution* *2 to 3 = mixture of "parent"-owned works-made-for-hire and externally created materials (e.g., incoming correspondence)* Note: majority of images created by University's public affairs units, Photographic Services, colleges, departments, research, extension offices, etc., but collection also includes one-off donations of images from alumni and general public, as well as publicity images created by local and national news publications and then sent to campus public affairs.
Size/Extent of collection	3.0	*3 = 40 to 100 cubic/linear feet*
Creative nature of content	2.5	*Factual vs. fictional or creative (expressive) nature of material* *2 = Mix of administrative materials and creative materials,* ***or*** *3 = Largely composed of moderately creative materials*
Attribute Total	**24.8**	

A.2.3 Deciding on Risk Level and Course of Action

Table 8.2 illustrates how eight different levels of risk should lead you to one of eight decision options based on how large the total score was on Table 8.1.

Decision on Course of Action	Risk Level
Proceed with digitization of the collection.	1
Proceed with caution.	2
Proceed on basis of a single collection-wide argument after obtaining review and concurrence of institutional risk management of this approach.	3
Conduct a systematic sampling of collection to locate sensitive materials or high-risk copyright items, then proceed with caution on expectation of viability of fair use defense and expectation of institutional support, as above.	4
Proceed with selective digitization *excluding* materials where there are known or perceived copyright holders who have exercised economic rights in their works or materials with possible cultural or personal sensitivity.	5
Proceed with selective or complete digitization but only after making a good-faith effort to locate the rights holders for persons who are known or believed to have exploited their works for economic benefit, and excluding works of those where you cannot locate or secure permission of rights holders, or where it is not feasible to complete a good-faith effort.	6
Proceed with complete digitization but with digital access limited to only onsite users.	7
Abandon project.	8

The following narrative is provided to explain risk rating and course of action and thus avoid the need to include two risk level tables in this appendix.

Sample Collection A: D. H. Lloyde Photograph Album: With a risk attribute score of 13, I would assign this collection a risk level/decision of 1—"Proceed with digitization." It is a small collection with an item level finding aid; the newest material in it is over a century old; and its creator died over 70 years ago. **Or** it could be rated as a 2—"Proceed with caution." That is, conduct the project after having reviewed the images to make sure there are none containing blackface, derogatory language, or other content that may be troubling for some viewers now if placed online today. With only 390 images, it is not burdensome to review the entire series.

Sample Collection B: University Photographic Subject File: With a risk attribute score of 24.8 for this series, and with only a summary-level descriptive control for a large collection, I would assign it a risk level/decision of at least "5"—"Proceed with selective digitization *excluding* materials where there are known or perceived copyright holders who have exercised economic rights in their works, or materials with possible cultural or personal sensitivity." Being the institutional repository should support the digitization and web posting of any University-authored photos, including images made in recent decades. Otherwise, the presence of multiple external authors, some of whom may have been commercial publishers, as well as the presence, even if limited, of culturally sensitive images, make it inadvisable to launch a project for end-to-end digitization if an administrator or financial backer insisted that all of the content be online. A recommendation for complete digitization on the condition of obtaining permission of all of the copyright holders is simply not viable because of the size of the collection and the number of external authors who would need to be tracked down. However, a reasonable approach might be to do a summary analysis to establish general risk and selection categories so that staff could proceed in a nuanced or modular fashion.

A.2.4 Last Step: How Confident Can I Be with My Decision

Table 8.3 illustrates that your confidence in deciding on a risk is tied to the quality of your knowledge of the collection and the amount of effort put into assessing the risk factors considered in Table 8.1. It is Table 8.1 that provides a foundation for how much risk there is and how confidently you can go forward or not. A quick glance at Table 8.3, however, makes clear that the sparser the archival arrangement and description, the less you can be confident that the risk attributes you inventoried in Table 8.1 by themselves provide a sufficient basis for a decision.

Table 8.3 Level of Confidence in Risk Assessment

Confidence Level	Extent of Intellectual and Physical Control of the Collection
★★★★★★	Very well arranged and described in detail, providing a high level of confidence in ratings assigned to above attributes.
★★★★★	Generally well arranged, material generally foldered by name of correspondent or with an index mechanism that identifies authors and dates/date range of documents.
★★★★	Finding aids have provided an effective means to complete the Attribute Inventory.
★★★	Names of majority of authors in the collection do not appear in the finding aid or indexing system.
★★	Poorly described with material listed only at the box level.
★	Described only at the series level.
0	Unprocessed.

For the purpose of this appendix, I believe that the Confidence Level for deciding a course of action for Sample Collection A, the Lloyde Photographic Album, should be 6 stars. The number of unknowns are few. There is an item-level finding aid, and all of the material was authored by a single individual deceased more than 70 years.

By contrast, for Sample Collection B, University Photographic Subject File, I would assign either 0 stars—Unprocessed or only 1 star—"Described only at the series level." Without looking at every image to see if it bears a photographer's name, it is really impossible to know how many copyright holders might be represented in the collection. As a legacy collection without detailed provenance information for each item, it is difficult to have confidence that we know enough to proceed other than on an image-by-image basis. The collection's heterogeneity also is too great for a single course of action.

In practice it may not be necessary to fill out this last table. Once you have gone through the steps called for in the Risk Attribute Inventory and the Risk Level/Decision tables, you would have probably reached a common-sense conclusion. However, invoking simple common sense is not always sufficient when interacting with administrative superiors or donors. That's when these risk assessment and rating tables will be particularly useful to explain why their idea for an ambitious digital project presents enough copyright challenges that they should rethink or abandon the project altogether.

Notes

Chapter 1

1 Solon J. Buck, "Let's Look at the Record," *American Archivist* 8, no. 2 (1945): 110.

2 Frank Evans, "The Many Faces of the Pennsylvania Archives," *American Archivist* 27:2 (1964) 271. "archives," *Dictionary of Archives Terminology*, (Chicago, IL: Society of American Archivists), accessed July 27, 2025, https://dictionary.archivists.org/entry/archives.html.

3 *Universal Declaration on Archives*, English version, accessed July 27, 2025, https://www.ica.org/app/uploads/2023/12/20190510_ica_declarationuniverselle_en_0.pdf.

4 Solon J. Buck, "Let's Look at the Record."

5 *Planning for the Archival Profession: A Report of the SAA Task Force on Goals and Priorities,"* (Chicago, IL: Society of American Archivists, 1986), 23.

Chapter 2

1 Kenneth D. Crews, *Copyright Law for Librarians and Educators: Creative Strategies and Practical Solutions* (Chicago, IL: American Library Association, 2020), 43–4.

2 For purposes of brevity, in most places this book hereafter will use § symbol, consistent with the law's practice, instead of the word "section."

3 This complex exception is highly dependent on the factual details of the materials and the uses in question. They will be explored via references to fair use court cases noted in Chapter 5.

4 Library of Congress, Copyright Office of the United States, *International Copyright Relations of the United States, Circular 34A*, Library of Congress, 2025, accessed July 27, 2025, https://www.copyright.gov/circs/circ38a.pdf.

5 WIPO is a United Nations agency established in 1967 and based in Geneva, Switzerland and currently includes 193 member states.

6 Interestingly, related § 412(2) provisions do not impose such a limitation on its registration requirement for a successful plaintive to receive the more significant monetary awards for infringements made prior to registration of an unpublished work.

7 17 U.S.C. § 104(a).

Chapter 3

1 Augustine Birrell, "The Origin of Copyright," in *Seven Lectures on the Law and History of Copyright in Books* (New York: G. P. Putnam's Sons, 1899), 41–2. R. R. Bowker, *Copyright, Its History and Its Law: Being a Summary of the Principles and Practice of Copyright with Special Reference to the American Code of 1909 and the British Act of 1911* (Boston, MA: Houghton Mifflin, 1912), 9.

2 Having been immersed a bit too long in modern copyright case law, I have wanted to know more about the actual "facts" of the materials and actions in the *Finnian v. Columba* dispute. One can imagine the claims and counter claims that today's attorneys might have raised in sixth-century Ireland. Might Finnian have claimed that the copy Columba had made was actually a work-made-for-hire because the abbey's employment agreement stated that Columba's duties included transcription of manuscripts? Might Columba's counsel have retorted that since Columba was a student of Finnian, the copy was actually a student work that fell under sixth-century FERPA-like rules and thus the copyright belonged to the student rather than teacher? Or was the underlying work actually in the public domain and Finnian was just testing an early form of copy protection measures presaging the 1996 WIPO treaty and the 1998 US Digital Millennium Copyright Protection Act?

3 Birrell, *Seven Lectures*, 48–49, 51. Birrell argues that the invention of printing did not result in any novel need for a copyright law to control the making or distribution of works. Rather, if there had been such a need, the underlying conditions were of long standing. Throughout the Middle Ages, there was a very active market in the making, distributing, and selling of manuscript copies long before Gutenberg. Birrell wrote: "The invention of printing, had it stood alone, was nothing more than a clever labour-saving device for multiplying copies more quickly and cheaply than by hand, nor did it involve the birth of a new property-right. The new printers pursued precisely the same plan as the old copyists. . . . Printing by itself was not the mother of author's copyright." Rather, it was the combination of censorship of the press and the monopoly of the booksellers as the source of copyright as a property right.

4 The Renaissance interplay of exclusive rights and technological advances is well covered in Neil Weinstock Netanel, "From Privileges and Printer Guilds to Copyright," in *From Maimonides to Microsoft: The Jewish Law of Copyright since the Birth of Print* (New York: Oxford University Press, 2016), Chapter 2.

5 Joseph Loewenstein, *The Author's Due: Printing and the Prehistory of Copyright* (Berkeley, CA: University of Chicago Press, 2002).

6 L. Ray Patterson and Stanley W. Lindberg, *The Nature of Copyright: A Law of Users' Rights* (Athens, GA: University of Georgia Press, 1991) 27.

7 L. Ray Patterson, *Copyright in Historical Perspective* (Nashville, TN: Vanderbilt University Press, 1968), 145.

8 If a work published in the period of 1978 to March 1, 1989 appeared without notice, it still could be entitled to copyright if it were registered within 5 years of publication.
9 Caution! The purpose of the above summary of the evolution of the types of works eligible for copyright, the length of copyright term, or the threshold requirements for copyright to apply, is merely to provide an impression of the general continuity and progression of the law from the early eighteenth century. It should *not be your only or final source* for answers when making important decisions about the application of copyright's rules to any particular use of any given work in the archives. Those are complicated questions that will be discussed in the review of the current law in Chapters 4 and 5.
10 Bowker, *Copyright: Its History and Its Law*, "Chronological Table," 653–75.
11 Barton Beebe, "An Empirical Study of U.S. Copyright Fair Use Opinions Updated, 1978–2019," *New York University Journal of Intellectual Property & Entertainment Law* 10, no. 1 (Fall 2020): 1–39. See also Barton Beebe, "An Empirical Study of U.S. Copyright Fair Use Opinions, 1978–2005," *University of Pennsylvania Law Review* 156, no. 3 (January 2008): 549–624.
12 Barton Beebe, "An Empirical Study of U.S. Copyright Fair Use Opinions, 1978–2005," 621–2.

Chapter 4

1 For a deeper sense of the legislative maze, compare one of the more concise subsections, (§ 106 (4)) on the public performance of motion pictures) to TEACH Act's labyrinth of conditions for an exception to use motion pictures in online teaching (§ 110 (2) (D) (ii) (I) (bb)). That complex maze is what happens when Congress tries to catch up with technology while holding hands with industry lobbyists.
2 ". . . the Act never explicitly defines 'author' in the definitions section, 17 U.S.C. §101 or elsewhere." J. Thomas McCarthy, *McCarthy's Desk Encyclopedia of Intellectual Property* (Bureau of National Affairs, Inc., 1991): 24. McCarthy does offer the following definition: "author—either the real person who creates a copyrightable work or the real person or corporate employer of a person who creates a copyrightable work within the scope of employment." He references a definition in the Supreme Court ruling in *Burrow-Giles Lithographic Co. v. Sarony*, 111 U.S. 58 (1884) stating "He to whom anything owes its origin; originator, maker; one who completes a work of science or literature." As to a "work of authorship," the genres and formats listed in § 102 (a) provide a sense for what Congress had intended by using this phrase in the 1976 Copyright Act.
3 Library of Congress, Copyright Office, "Copyright Registration Guidance: Works Containing Material Generated by Artificial Intelligence," accessed July 4, 2025,

https://www.copyright.gov/ai/ai_policy_guidance.pdf. With regard to the question of "authorship," it should be noted that, based on its analysis of the Constitution and multiple court opinions, the Copyright Office will not register a work for copyright unless it has been authored by a human. The issue has arisen in relation to a monkey having taken a "selfie" as well as an attempt to register copyright in something produced by an Artificial Intelligence system. See Chapter 10, Section 10.2.

4 "§ 5.12 Governmental Works: Judicial Opinions and Statutes," and "§ 5.14 Works of State Governments." Melville B. Nimmer and David Nimmer *Nimmer on Copyright*, LexisNexis, Release 123 April, 2025. Hereafter cited as "*Nimmer on Copyright*."

5 The fact that a copyright owner's exclusive right of performance of a sound recording is applicable only for digital transmission is a reflection of the long and strange history of copyright law's inability to adapt to the technological innovation of audio recordings. The courts in the early 1900s could justify piano rolls as meeting the Constitution's authorization of exclusive rights for "writings" because the rolls consisted of holes punched on paper. However, the recording of sound waves on wax cylinders or shellac disks was beyond the imagination of Congress when they revised the copyright law in 1909. After radio developed and became dominant a few decades later, other means of managing and enforcing the market for performance of sound recordings over the airwaves developed in anti-competition laws at the state level. A 1971 law established that all sound recordings made after February 14, 1972 would be subject to federal copyright, but that left previous sound recordings in limbo. It was not until the 2018 Music Modernization Act that pre-1972 sound recordings were brought sufficiently within copyright law that fair use and library and archives exceptions could be applied to them (see 4.1.14 below). Meanwhile, in the mid-1990s, Congress came to understand the market issues involved in high-quality digital transmission of audio records so it moved to establish an exclusive right in performance of sound recordings when done by digital means. The passage of the Digital Performance Right in Sound Recordings Act of 1995 covered this specific type of performance, but left the older market model of mandatory licensing compensation in place for analog radio AM and FM radio transmission.

6 US House of Representatives, 94th Congress, 2nd Session, *Copyright Law Revision*, Historical and Revision Notes, House Report no. 94–1476, September 3, 1976, p. 65, accessed July 15, 2025, https://www.copyright.gov/history/law/clrev_94-1476.pdf.

7 Peter B. Hirtle, "Research, Libraries, and Fair Use: The Gentlemen's Agreement of 1935," *Journal of the Copyright Society of the USA* 53, no. 3–4 (Spring 2006–Summer 2006): 545–601.

8 *Schmid Brothers, Inc. v. W. Goebel Porzellanfabrik 589 F. Supp. 497* (E.D.N.Y. 1984). The court noted that the drawings Sr. Hummel made for the porcelain figurines were based on her "personal" activity, not as part of the convent's official assignment of her to work on the drawing of ecclesiastical vestments.

9 "§4.3.2.1, Work Prepared by an Employee within the Scope of Employment," Paul Goldstein, *Goldstein on Copyright*. Wolters Kluwer (3rd ed. 2025–2 Supplement), hereafter cited as *Goldstein on Copyright*. In general, see American Association of University Professors, "Statement on Copyright," 1999, accessed July 15, 2025, https://www.aaup.org/report/statement-copyright. For an example at a major research university see, *General Rules Concerning University Organization and Procedure* of the University of Illinois system. It contains the following on faculty copyright in its Article III, Section 4 (a) "Ownership. Unless subject to any of the exceptions specified below or in Sections 4(b) and 4(c), creators retain copyright rights to traditional academic copyrightable works as defined in Section 2(b) above." Accessed July 15, 2025, https://www.bot.uillinois.edu/governance/general_rules.

10 *Nimmer on Copyright*, "Right of one joint owner to license the work . . . ," 6.10 [A].

11 One joint owner may transfer their interest in a joint work but cannot transfer the interest of another joint owner. "Right of One Joint Owner to Transfer the Copyright in a Work . . . ," *Nimmer on Copyright* 6.10 [A] 6.11.

12 "Village People Singer Wins a Legal Battle in Fight to Reclaim Song Rights," *New York Times*, May 8, 2012, reports an example of a successful exercise of termination rights.

13 House of Representatives, Committee on the Judiciary, *Copyright Law Revision*, 130–1, accessed July 15, 2025, https://www.copyright.gov/history/law/clrev_94-1476.pdf.

14 Library of Congress, Copyright Office, "Notices of Termination," accessed July 15, 2025, https://www.copyright.gov/recordation/termination.html. The web page also includes a link to the Copyright Office's 2,500-word Form TCS "Notice of Termination Cover Sheet."

15 Available from the Copyright Office, accessed July 15, 2025, https://www.copyright.gov/circs/circ24.pdf.

16 Library of Congress, Copyright Office, "Regulation 313.2 'Works That Lack Human Authorship,'" *Compendium of U.S. Copyright Office Practices,* 3rd edition, United States Copyright Office, accessed July 15, 2025, https://www.copyright.gov/comp3/docs/compendium-12-22-14.pdf.

17 The § 101 definition of "United States work" includes the following: "(2) in the case of an unpublished work, all the authors of the work are nationals, domiciliaries, or habitual residents of the United States, or, in the case of an unpublished audiovisual work, all the authors are legal entities with headquarters in the United States. . . ." Thus, unpublished works whose authorship does not meet this definition would not require registration before a suit can be initiated.

18 The Copyright Office makes clear that "preregistration" is intended for those "unpublished works that are being prepared for commercial distribution for types of works that . . . have had a history of pre-release infringement." Only the following kind of unpublished works are eligible for preregistration: motion pictures, sound recordings, musical compositions, literary works, computer programs, and advertising or marketing photographs. See: "Preregister Your Work," accessed July 15, 2025, https://www.copyright.gov/prereg/.

19 It would be a good idea for you to refresh your memory on the nature and number of exclusive rights you could be found to be violating. See this chapter's section 4.1.6 above and Box 4.4.

20 *Goldstein on Copyright*, at 14.3.2.2.

21 *Warner Chappell Music, Inc. v. Nealy*, 601 U.S.—(2024).

22 Information on the process for registration and a database of the currently registered ISPs institutions can be found in the Copyright Office's "DMCA Designated Agent Directory," accessed July 15, 2025, https://www.copyright.gov/dmca-directory/.

23 Jessica Litman, Chapter 9, "The Bargaining Table," *Digital Copyright* (New York: Amherst, 2001): 122–50. Litman's is a frank and quite readable account of the years leading up to the WIPO treaty and the DMCA. She has mastered the enormous amount of detail needed to understand the excruciating process by which major stakeholders jostled with each other in a process that left public interest out.

24 Interestingly, 17 U.S.C. Chapter 12 does not articulate a statute of limitations for civil actions.

25 Accessed July 15, 2025, https://ccb.gov/libraries-archives-opt-out/. The relevant part of the law (§ 1506(aa) (1)) reads: ". . . a library or archives that does not wish to participate in proceedings before the Copyright Claims Board [may] preemptively opt out of such proceedings." See discussion below relating to § 1506.

26 See: https://ccb.gov/handbook/Smaller-Claims.pdf URL verified May 20, 2025.

27 Library of Congress, Copyright Office, "Small Claims Procedures for Library and Archives Opt-Outs and Class Actions," 87 *Federal Register* / 13171 (March 9, 2022), accessed July 15, 2025, https://www.govinfo.gov/content/pkg/FR-2022-03-09/pdf/2022-04747.pdf.

28 Library of Congress, Copyright Office, *CCB HANDBOOK Opting Out*, accessed July 15, 2025, https://ccb.gov/handbook/Opting-Out.pdf.

Chapter 5

1 *Campbell v. Acuff-Rose Music*, 510 U.S. 569 (1994) at 575.

2 Barton Beebe, "An Empirical Study of U.S. Copyright Fair Use Opinions Updated, 1978–2019," *New York University Journal of Intellectual Property and Entertainment Law* 10, no. 1 (Fall, 2020): 3, footnote 4. He notes that the number of journal articles on fair use exceeds the total of 435 fair use cases from 1978 through 2019.

3 US Congress, House Committee on the Judiciary, "Historical and Revision Notes," *Copyright Law Revision*, 94th Congress, Second Session, *House Report* 94-1476 at 65 (1976). On the first insertion of "fair use" into the federal copyright law, the House Committee was unapologetic about it being a malleable rule. Its legislative note read: "Although the courts have considered and ruled upon the fair use doctrine over and over again, no real definition of the concept has ever emerged. Indeed, since the doctrine is an equitable rule of reason, no generally applicable definition is possible, and each case raising the question must be decided on its own facts."

4 Beebe, "An Empirical Study," (2020): 3–4. He cautions that when looking at the full array of lower course rulings, "the 'leading cases' do not necessarily reflect or influence everyday fair use adjudication." That does not, however, supersede the purpose of this chapter's discussion of cases as a guide to how to think about what exactly fair use means. He further notes lower courts mistakenly refer to superseded rationales and court "dicta."

5 *Campbell v. Acuff-Rose Music*, 510 U.S. at 578.

6 "The Tidal Wave of Transformative Use," and especially "The Highwater Mark: Misapplying Transformation," and "Rising Countercurrents," *Nimmer on Copyright*, at § 13F.10 [F] and § 13F.10[F][3][a] and [b]. Over the past decade, Nimmer's treatise on US copyright law has expressed growing concern about increased reliance on transformativeness as a fair use criterion that could preempt a full assessment of all four fair use factors. He has also noted "potential ambiguity" on the relation of a transformative work to how a derivative work is defined in § 101. Especially concerning was a 2013 Second Court ruling, in *Cariou v. Prince* (714 F. 3d 694 (2d Cir. 2013)) which noted that the secondary work need not comment on or critique the copied work but merely needed to create a new work.

7 *Campbell v. Acuff-Rose Music*, 510 U.S. at 584. "If, indeed, commerciality carried presumptive force against a finding of fairness, the presumption would swallow nearly all of the illustrative uses listed in the preamble paragraph of § 107. . . ." The importance of the *Campbell* decision can be seen in the way in which it is cited by later courts. Subsequently, lower courts have followed this advice; for example, in *Kelly v. Arriba Soft Corporation* (2003), the Appeals Court for the Ninth Circuit stated: "The Supreme Court has rejected the proposition that a commercial use of the copyrighted material ends the inquiry under this [character and purpose] factor." *Kelly v. ArribaSoft Corporation* 336 F.3d 811 (9th Cir. 2003) at 818.

8 Andy Warhol Foundation for the Visual Arts, Inc., 598 U.S. at 534. In the majority opinion, Justice Sotomayor wrote: "Finally, AWF used the photograph when it licensed an image of Warhol's Orange Prince to Condé Nast in 2016. Only that last use, however, AWF's commercial licensing of Orange Prince to Condé Nast, is alleged to be infringing. We limit our analysis accordingly. In particular, the Court expresses no opinion as to the creation, display, or sale of any of the original Prince Series works."

9 *Harper & Row v. Nation Magazine*, 471 U.S. 539 (1985) at 562. "The crux of the profit/nonprofit distinction is not whether the sole motive of the use is monetary gain but whether the user stands to profit from exploitation of the copyrighted material without paying the customary price."

10 *Harper & Row v. Nation Magazine*, 471 U.S. at 563 and 564, respectively.

11 *New Era Publications International v. Henry Holt Co.*, 873 F.2d 576, 593 (2d Cir. 1989).

12 *Wright v. Warner Books, Inc.*, 953 F.2d 731 (2d Cir. 1991) at 740.

13 *Sundeman v. Seajay Soc'y, Inc.*, 142 F.3d 194 and *Chicago Bd. of Educ. v. Substance, Inc.*, 354 F.3d 624 (2003) at 628. However, note Barton Beebe's comment: "since 1992, only eight opinions have explicitly alluded to the added statement regarding unpublished works as informing their fair use analysis." He also noted that three of these opinions ruled against fair use. Beebe, "An Empirical Study," (2020) 6.

14 *Sundeman v. Seajay Soc'y, Inc.*, 142 F.3d 205.

15 *Maxtone-Graham v. Burtchaell*, 803 F.2d 1253, 1260 (2d Cir. 1986), cert. denied, 481 U.S. 1059.

16 *Campbell v. Acuff-Rose*, 510 U.S. at 586–87.

17 *Campbell v. Acuff-Rose*, 510 U.S. at 578. The Court also said, "No 'presumption' or inference of market harm that might find support in *Sony* is applicable to a case involving something beyond mere duplication for commercial purposes" (*Campbell v. Acuff-Rose*, 510 U.S. at 591).

18 *Twin Peaks Prods., Inc. v. Publ'ns Int'l, Ltd.*, 996 F.2d 1366 (2d Cir. 1993).

19 *Suntrust Bank v. Houghton Mifflin Co.*, 268 F.3d 1257 (11th Cir. 2001).

20 *Bond v. Blum*, 317 F.3d 385 *cert. denied* 540 U.S. 820, full text accessed July 27, 2025, https://caselaw.findlaw.com/court/us-4th-circuit/1361728.html. This is an instance where a court's formal ruling is an example of truth seeming stranger than fiction.

21 "Fair Use Index," Library of Congress, Copyright Office, accessed July 27, 2025, https://www.copyright.gov/fair-use/.

22 *Nimmer on Copyright* § 13F.11[B][4].

23 Credit for this observation about the dearth of actual cases belongs to Peter Hirtle, who since 2007 has introduced his periodic Society of American Archivists' copyright update presentations with the good news/bad news observation that while few archivists have been sued, the lack of cases leaves us without much direct guidance from the courts.

24 Indeed, monitoring lobbying and legislation and being prepared to act quickly on potential changes in the law is a key part of the public policy agenda that archivists should be pursuing both individually and as members of professional organizations. See below, Chapters 11 and 12, especially sections 11.1 and 12.1.

Chapter 6

1 United States Patent and Trademark Office, "Patent Public Search," accessed July 20, 2025, https://www.uspto.gov/patents/search/patent-public-search.

2 United States Patent and Trademark Office, "Relationship Between Design Patent, Copyright, and Trademark," *Manual of Patent Examining Procedure*, Chapter 1500,

Section 1512, accessed July 20, 2025, https://www.uspto.gov/web/offices/pac/mpep/s1512.html.

3 "Copyright Protection for Patentable Subject Matter," 2A.07[A], and "Subsequent Rejection" 2A.07[C][3][f], *Nimmer on Copyright.* Unfortunately, whatever clarity might have been achieved by the change of rules in 1995 may have since been blurred by the 2010 to 2021 *Google v. Oracle* saga in which Google's unauthorized use of Oracle's computer code, seemingly eligible for a utility patent, was ultimately decided on the basis of copyright law.

4 An updated and slightly different drawing of the bottle was registered in 1977 by Coke Cola as a trademark and is still in force. Coca Cola Corporation, *History of the Coca-Cola Contour Bottle*, accessed July 20, 2025, https://www.coca-colacompany.com/about-us/history/the-history-of-the-coca-cola-contour-bottle.

5 *Mattel Inc. v. Walking Mountain Productions*, 353 F.3d 792 (9th Cir. 2003). See also: "Significance: *Mattel, Inc. v. Walking Mountain Productions*," *Artists Rights*, accessed July 20, 2025, https://www.artistrights.info/mattel-inc-v-walking-mountain-productions.

6 National Conference of Commissioners on Uniform State Laws, *Uniform Trade Secrets Act with 1985 Amendments*, 1985, accessed July 20, 2025, https://www.uniformlaws.org/HigherLogic/System/DownloadDocumentFile.ashx?DocumentFileKey=e58f19a0-6a5e-c90f-67c1-ac1f747ad47b&forceDialog=0. Its definition of "trade secret" provides a narrower scope than other kinds of information which an archives receives and manages as restricted material (e.g., personnel evaluations, health information, student records, etc.). Given the critical nature of a trade secret, it seems logical that any information of such core business necessity as to be considered a trade secret would be effectively "defined" by the special steps essential to their protection. The Uniform Act also notes, "Finally, reasonable efforts to maintain secrecy have been held to include advising employees of the existence of a trade secret, limiting access to a trade secret on 'need to know basis', and controlling plant access."

7 Trade secrets acts following a national model have been enacted in 48 states plus the District of Columbia, Puerto Rico, and the US Virgin Islands. *Trade Secrets Act,* "Enactment Map," Uniform Law Commission, accessed July 20, 2025, https://www.uniformlaws.org/committees/community-home?communitykey=3a2538fb-e030-4e2d-a9e2-90373dc05792.

8 Society of American Archivists, "Code of Ethics for Archivists," accessed July 20, 2025, https://www2.archivists.org/statements/saa-core-values-statement-and-code-of-ethics.

9 Samuel Warren and Louis Brandeis, "The Right to Privacy," *Harvard Law Review* IV no. 5 (1890): 193, 195, and especially 205.

10 Wendy J. Gordon, "Copyright Owners' Putative Interests in Privacy, Reputation, and Control: A Reply to Goold," *Virginia Law Review Online* 103 (2017): 47.

11 This was illustrated in the 2004 Supreme Court decision in *National Archives and Records Administration v. Allan J. Favish* 541 U.S. 157. The court found that the privacy of the surviving family would have been violated if death scene photographs of a suicide were released, stating "They seek to be shielded by the exemption to secure their own refuge from a sensation-seeking culture for their own peace of mind and tranquility, not for the sake of the deceased."

12 Gordon, "Copyright Owners," 47.

13 J. Thomas McCarthy, *The Rights of Publicity and Privacy* (Thomson Reuters, 2015), v. He adds that liability is not precluded by principles of free press or free speech and that implication of endorsement, commercial source, or celebrity status are not needed to create liability.

14 A good example of how publicity rights could lead to a restriction on speech arose in the "cease and desist" letter which the *Atlanta Journal-Constitution* received saying that their music critic, Bill Wyman, had to cease using his name since it was the same name as the Rolling Stones' former bassist Bill Wyman (born William George Perks). The action was settled with an out-of-court agreement that the journalist would include a disclaimer on his name whenever he wrote about the Stones, but the experience must have been unsettling. Joe Garofoli, "Can Bill Wyman be Bill Wyman? No, says Bill Wyman" *San Francisco Chronicle*, November 21, 2002, p. A2.

15 Jennifer E. Rothman, *The Right of Publicity: Privacy Reimagined for a Public World* (Cambridge, MA: Harvard University Press, 2018). Rothman calls into question the traditional hard line distinction between privacy's "appropriation prong" and publicity as a separate right. She also explores blurred lines cases where copyright may or may not preempt publicity rights. Supplementing her excellent summation of pivotal differences in how states have defined the rights (see especially page 3) is her excellent website, "Rothman's Roadmap to the Right of Privacy," which allows one to see how individual states have addressed core issues, such as term of post-mortem rights, scope of coverage, remedies and damages, exceptions, and reliance on common law in the absence of a publicity statute. Accessed July 20, 2025, https://rightofpublicityroadmap.com.

16 Alyssa J. Devine, "Why You Should Care About a Federal Right of Publicity" IPWatchdog, December 15, 2023, accessed July 20, 2025, https://ipwatchdog.com/2023/12/15/why-you-should-care-about-a-federal-right-of-publicity/id=170583/.

17 *Tennessee Code Annotated*, § 47-25-1104 (a) provides for a complex term. Publicity rights endure for 10 years after death, but under subsection (b), commercial exploitation will continue to be protected but will be terminated by proof of non-use for a period of two years following the initial 10.

18 Ind. Code § 32-36-1-1(a) (2024). The Indiana publicity statute reads "This chapter applies to an act or event that occurs within Indiana, regardless of a personality's domicile, residence, or citizenship."

19 "Limitations on the Right of Publicity," and § 17.20.2.2, "The Role of the Fair Use Defense in Right of Publicity Cases," *Goldstein on Copyright* § 17.20.2.

20 Pierre N. Leval, "Fair Use or Foul?" *Journal of the Copyright Society of the U.S.A.* 36 (April 1989): 169. Judge Leval wrote, "Copyright is not a moral or natural right vested in an artistic creator. It is a pragmatic measure by which society confers monopoly exploitation benefits on the artist or author with the objective of thereby obtaining intellectual enrichment for itself." This exchange nature was central to Judge Leval's argument to "rescue" fair use from a precedent that would have severely curtailed the use of unpublished works.

21 While not formally part of US copyright law, the Creative Commons licenses make attribution, i.e., giving credit to the creator, a central piece to its framework of model licenses as seen in the fact that the "BY" component appears in its six primary examples of licenses. "About CC Licenses," Creative Commons, accessed July 20, 2025, https://creativecommons.org/share-your-work/cclicenses/.

22 *Berne Convention for the Protection of Literary and Artistic Works*, September 9, 1886, as amended September 28, 1979, accessed July 20, 2025, https://www.wipo.int/wipolex/en/text/283693.

23 Berne Convention, "Article 6bis: Moral Rights," accessed July 20, 2025, https://www.wipo.int/wipolex/en/text/283698#P119_19081. It reads: "(1) Independently of the author's economic rights, and even after the transfer of the said rights, the author shall have the right to claim authorship of the work and to object to any distortion, mutilation or other modification of, or other derogatory action in relation to, the said work, which would be prejudicial to his honor or reputation."

24 Peter Jaszi, "Toward a Theory of Copyright: The Metamorphoses of 'Authorship,'" *Duke Law Journal* (April 1991): 497.

25 Register of Copyright, *Authors, Attribution, and Integrity: Examining Moral Rights in the United States* (Washington, DC: US Copyright Office, 2019), accessed July 20, 2025, https://www.copyright.gov/policy/moralrights/full-report.pdf. First Amendment concerns were noted by a number of the respondents to the Copyright Office's 2017 call for public comment on moral rights, but a number also argued for amending the copyright act to make moral rights of attribution and integrity explicit.

26 Samuel G. Freedman, "Who's to Say Whether a Playwright is Wronged?," *New York Times*, December 14, 1984, Section 4, p. 6. Martin Garbus and Gerald E. Singleton, "Whose Play Is It Anyway?" *New York Law Journal*, Friday December 28, 1984, p. 1. For the Paris incident see "People" *International Herald Tribune,* October 14, 1988, p. 20. "Actualité: À la Comédie Française Roland Bertin joue Beckett," *Avant-Scene Théâtre,* December 1–15, 1988, pp. 100–1. For a more general analysis of the Cambridge incident, see: Jon Garon, "Director's Choice: The Fine Line Between Interpretation and Infringement of an Author's Work," *Columbia-VLA Journal of the Law & the Arts* 12, no. 2 (1987–8): 277–306.

27 For the purpose of this Chapter, I use "Native American" in the broad sense used in the *Protocols for Native American Archival Materials* (citation below), whose glossary states that Native American "Refers to Indian (First Nations), Eskimo (Inuit), and Aleut individuals and communities in the United States and Canada as well as to Native Hawaiians." To ease the flow of the text, I will also use the term "indigenous" to refer to the same individuals and communities.

28 United States, *Federal Register*, 88, no. 238, December 23, 2023, 43 CFR Part 10.5 page 86470, column 1, accessed July 20, 2025, https://www.govinfo.gov/content/pkg/FR-2023-12-13/pdf/2023-27040.pdf. Despite public comments on the "Final Rule" for NAGPRA, the Department of Interior declined the request, arguing that the change in scope "would be inconsistent with the Act." Subsequently, it has been argued that Congress should enact new legislation to fill this gap perhaps through copyright or data security law. See: Jiaying Jessie Zhang, "Battle in the Digital Sphere: the Repatriation of Digitized Native American Cultural Properties," *AIPLA Quarterly Journal* 52, no. 2 (Spring 2024): 403–34.

29 First Archivist Circle, *Protocols for Native American Archival Materials*, 2007, accessed August 3, 2025, https://www2.nau.edu/libnap-p/protocols.html. Note: page references are to the PDF version, accessed July 20, 2025, https://www2.nau.edu/libnap-p/PrintProtocols.pdf. The *Protocols* were endorsed as an external standard by the Society of American Archivists in 2018.

30 "Glossary," *UNESCO Convention on the Means of Prohibiting and Preventing the Illicit Import, Export and Transfer of Ownership of Cultural Property*. 1970, accessed July 20, 2025, https://www.wipo.int/tk/en/resources/glossary.html. Note: UNESCO's use of "State" refers to nation state members of the United Nations.

31 "Indigenous Knowledge," Inuit Circumpolar Council, accessed July 20, 2025, https://www.inuitcircumpolar.com/icc-activities/environment-sustainable-development/indigenous-knowledge/.

32 UNESCO, *Text of the Convention for the Safeguarding of the Intangible Cultural Heritage*, 2003, accessed July 20, 2025, https://ich.unesco.org/en/convention.

33 World Intellectual Property Organization, "Traditional Knowledge, Resources, Glossary" accessed July 20, 2025, https://www.wipo.int/tk/en/resources/glossary.html#48.

34 World Intellectual Property Organization, "Glossary," accessed July 20, 2025, https://www.wipo.int/tk/en/resources/glossary.html#49.

35 Boatema Boateng, *The Copyright Thing Doesn't Work Here: Adinkra and Kente Cloth and Intellectual Property in Ghana* (Minneapolis, MN: University of Minnesota Press, 2011). She also presents a quite useful discourse (pp. 12–13) on what she sees as inherent weaknesses and prejudices in such terms as "folklore," "indigenous knowledge," and "traditional knowledge."

36 Terri Janke as quoted in *Protocols for Native American Archival Materials*, accessed July 20, 2025, https://www2.nau.edu/libnap-p/PrintProtocols.pdf, p. 14.

37 *Protocols*, p. 5.

38 Society of American Archivists, "SAA Council Endorsement of Protocols for Native American Archival Materials," accessed July 20, 2025, https://www2.archivists.org/statements/saa-council-endorsement-of-protocols-for-native-american-archival-materials.

39 *Protocols*, p. 9.

40 *Protocols*, see: pp. 9–10 (relating to access) as well as pp. 5–6 (relating relations with native communities) and p. 8 (relating to acquisition and curation).

Chapter 7

1 Aprille C. McKay, "Managing Rights and Permissions," in *Rights in the Digital Era*, ed. Menzi L. Behrnd-Klodt and Christopher J. Prom (Chicago, IL: Society of American Archivists, 2015), 217.

2 Paul Goldstein, "Work Prepared by an Employee Within the Scope of Employment," 4.3.2.1, *Goldstein on Copyright*. He explains: "Because of the traditions of independence and judgment that are commonly associated with professional activities, the fact that the individual who prepared the work is a professional, such as an architect or university professor, will weigh heavily toward a finding that he, rather than his employer, is the author of any works that he creates while in the other's employ." For example, the University of Illinois *General Rules Concerning University Organization and Procedure* (Article III, Section 4 (a)) state: "Unless subject to any of the exceptions specified . . . creators retain copyright rights to traditional academic copyrightable works. . . ." accessed July 28, 2025, https://www.bot.uillinois.edu/governance/general_rules.

3 The inability to obtain copyright should not be a per se barrier to acquisition, but the more encumbered the exclusive rights, the more problematic will be the ongoing management and usefulness of the collection, reducing their overall value to the archives.

4 While arrangement and description following the More Product/Less Process model might be a budgetary necessity, its lighter touch approach can leave collections less prepared for digitization projects until time is later invested in copyright investigation. One institution has developed a processing workflow that goes in the opposite direction by calling for detailed tracking of authors, prospective owners, and related rights within a collection to facilitate both prospective digitization as well as ongoing copyright issues that may arise with use. For a review of the Emory University Rose Library's rationale and a view of the revised processing workflow see: Carrie Hintz, Melanie T. Kowalski, Sarah Quigley, and Jody Bailey, "Finding Balance Copyright: Case Study Emory University Libraries," 2023, accessed July 28, 2025, https://opentext.ku.edu/findingbalance/chapter/case-study-emory-university-libraries/.

5 Ronald L. Becker, "On Deposit: A Handshake and a Lawsuit," *American Archivist* 56, no. 2 (1993): 320–8. Becker's account of a dispute over *Partisan Review* materials illustrates how a deposit agreement can become unraveled.

6 Library of Congress, Copyright Office, "§ 201.14 Warnings of copyright for use by certain libraries and archives," Library of Congress, Copyright Office, accessed July 28, 2025, https://www.copyright.gov/title37/201/37cfr201-14.html.

7 Note: throughout this section on permission requests, I have used "publisher(s)" as the agents requesting researchers and others to obtain written permissions. I am using that term generically to refer to any type of intermediary who might be taking the works created by a researcher to a public audience, such as a music or motion picture production company, a dance or theater troupe, museum, website, or a radio or television station. Any of these intermediaries might be very cautious lest their use of a work infringes the original creator.

8 Of course, as noted above in discussing § 107, the archivist should not make a declaration that the proposed use is a fair use but merely direct the user's attention to fair use resources for them to make their own decision.

9 Society of American Archivists, "Orphan Works: Statement of Best Practices," 2009, accessed July 28, 2025, https://www2.archivists.org/sites/all/files/OrphanWorks-June2009.pdf.

10 Peter B. Hirtle, "Archives or Assets?" *American Archivist* 66, no. 2 (2003): 235–47. The path-breaking challenge in Hirtle's Presidential Address has been followed by Jean Dryden's provocative "Copyfraud or Legitimate Concerns Controlling Further Uses of Online Archival Holdings," *American Archivist* 74, no. 2 (2011): 522–43 and Michelle Light's informative case study of why her institution moved away from charging fees; see "Controlling Goods or Promoting the Public Good: Choices for Special Collections in the Marketplace," *RBM: A Journal of Rare Books, Manuscripts, and Cultural Heritage*, 16, no. 1 (2015): 48–63.

11 Peter B. Hirtle, Emily Hudson, and Andrew T. Kenyon, *Copyright and Cultural Institutions: Guidelines for Digitization for U.S. Libraries, Archives, and Museums* (Ithaca, NY: Cornell University Library, 2009), accessed July 28, 2025, https://ecommons.cornell.edu/bitstreams/73163724-80d4-4542-a155-c7e8f274f2c1/download, Sections 10.5 and 10.6 (pages 202–12). *Copyright and Cultural Institutions* provides a thoughtful and extensive treatment of work flows and decision trees for digitization projects, and it describes practical steps for minimizing risk.

12 There's no single answer to the best approach, and all projects should consider using more than one, but strategic decisions on the level of assessment will make the best use of your resources and likely be most helpful in managing risk.

13 A useful screening device to differentiate the options for the status of works to be examined could be adopted from the variety of rights statements at http://rightsstatments.org (accessed July 28, 2025). Although those were developed for how you should cite ownership of materials placed online, they could be adapted to provide elements of a front-end assessment tool.

14 Two examples of takedown notices and instructions are those of New York University, accessed July 28, 2025, https://library.nyu.edu/about/policies/notice-takedown-policy/and of the University of Illinois, Urbana-Champaign, accessed July 28, 2025, https://www.library.illinois.edu/geninfo/takedown-procedure-for-university-of-illinois-library/.

15 Three sources for online tutorials are: Columbia University Library's "Copyright Quick Guide," at https://copyright.columbia.edu/basics/copyright-quick-guide.html; Harvard University's "CopyrightX," at https://pll.harvard.edu/course/copyrightx?delta=0; The University of Texas Library's "Copyright Crash Course," at https://guides.lib.utexas.edu/copyright (all accessed: July 28, 2025).

Chapter 8

1 Thomas A. Lipinski, *The Complete Copyright Liability Handbook for Librarians and Educators* (New York: Neal-Shuman, 2006). At approximately the same time, the potential usefulness of a risk management strategy for library digitization projects in the United Kingdom was suggested by: Nicholas Joint, "Risk Assessment and Copyright in Digital Libraries," *Library Review* 55, no. 9 (2006): 543–46 and Nicholas Joint, "Applying General Risk Management Principles to Library Administration," *Library Review* 56, no. 7 (2007): 542–51.

2 Laura Clark Brown, Judy Ruttenberg, and Kevin L. Smith, "Intellectual Property Rights Strategy for Digitization of Modern Manuscript Collections and Archival Record Groups," Triangle Research Libraries Network (TRLN) (June 2011); Kevin Smith, "Copyright Risk Management: Principles and Strategies for Large-Scale Digitization Projects in Special Collections," *Research Library Issues* (RLI 279) (June 2012): 17–23; Kevin Smith and Susan Davis, "Copyright in a Digital Age: Conflict, Risk, and Reward," *The Serials Librarian* 64 (2013): 57–66.

3 David Hansen, *Digitizing Orphan Works: Legal Strategies to Reduce Risks for Open Access to Copyrighted Orphan Works*, Kyle K. Courtney and Peter Suber, eds., Harvard Library, 2016, accessed: July 28, 2025, http://nrs.harvard.edu/urn-3:HUL.InstRepos:27840430.

4 David Bearman, "Archival Methods," *Archives and Museum Informatics Technical Report #9* (Pittsburgh, PA: Archives and Museum Informatics, 1989). David Bearman, "Archival Strategies," *American Archivist* 58 (Fall, 1995): 380–3.

5 Richard Pearce-Moses, *A Glossary of Archival & Records Terminology* (Chicago, IL: Society of American Archivists, 2005), 348. More recently, "risk management" has retained its connection with preservation, as seen in the chapter "Risk Management: A Programmatic Approach" in Elizabeth Joffrion and Michèle V. Cloonan, *Advancing Preservation for Archives and Manuscripts* (Chicago, IL: Society of American Archivists, 2020), 128–38. Note that SAA replaced the *Glossary* in 2020 by *Dictionary of Archives Terminology* which retains the main elements of the 2005 definition. Accessed July 28, 2025, https://dictionary.archivists.org.

6 Peter B. Hirtle, Emily Hudson, and Andrew T. Kenyon. *Copyright and Cultural Institutions: Guidelines for Digitization for U.S. Libraries, Archives, and Museums* (Ithaca, NY: Cornell University Library, 2009). Heather Briston, "Managing Copyright in

Archives: Risk Management" in "Module 4: Understanding Copyright Law" by Menzi L. Behrnd-Klodt and Christopher J. Prom, eds., *Rights in the Digital Era* (Chicago, IL: Society of American Archivists, 2015). Meanwhile, risk management was soon embraced for archival preservation assessment as seen in Mary Lynn Ritzenthaler, *Preserving Archives & Manuscripts*, 2nd edition (Chicago, IL: Society of American Archivists, 2010).

7 Mark Greene quoting Dennis Meissner, in Mark Greene, "MPLP: It's Not Just for Processing Anymore," *American Archivist* 73, no. 1 (Spring/Summer 2010): 197, footnote 62. "Zero risk is not an acceptable real-world model. [We] need to significantly elevate our risk tolerance as archivists. We are not responsible for ideal outcomes; we are only responsible for reasonable processes."

8 Hansen, *Digitizing Orphan Works*, 12.

9 "Risk Management," *Dictionary of Archives Terminology,* accessed, July 28, 2025, https://dictionary.archivists.org/entry/risk-management.html.

10 "Terms and Definitions," *Risk Management Guidelines,* International Organization for Standardization, https://www.iso.org/obp/ui/#iso:std:iso:31000:ed-2:v1:en;"Risk management—Guidelines," *Electropedia: The World's Online Electrotechnical Vocabulary*, International Electrotechnical Commission https://www.electropedia.org/iev/iev.nsf/display?openform&ievref=903-01-07 (URLs accessed: July 28, 2025).

11 OCLC Research, "Well-intentioned practice for putting digitized collections of unpublished materials online," OCLC Research, 2010, accessed July 28, 2025, https://www.oclc.org/content/dam/research/activities/rights/practice.pdf. See also: Society of American Archivists, "Preface prepared by SAA's Intellectual Property Working Group," accessed July 28, 2025, https://www2.archivists.org/groups/intellectual-property-working-group/well-intentioned-practice-for-putting-digitized-collections-of-unpublished-materials.

12 Victoria Stobo, with Ronan Deazley and Ian G. Anderson, "Copyright & Risk: Scoping the Wellcome Digital Library Project," CREATe Working Paper No. 10, Centre for Regulation of the Creative Economy, December 2013, accessed July 28, 2025, http://zenodo.org/record/8380/files/CREATe-Working-Paper-2013-10.pdf.

13 Stobo et al., "Copyright & Risk," Section 7.3 WL Archive Risk Criteria.

14 "Copyright Term and the Public Domain," Cornell University Library, Copyright Services, accessed July 28, 2025, https://guides.library.cornell.edu/copyright/publicdomain. Web searches on "public domain status" will turn up other sites from libraries and law schools pointing to further web tools, although there is often considerable overlap or duplication. Two particularly helpful ones are those from the University of Virginia Library, accessed July 28, 2025, https://www.library.virginia.edu/copyright/user-rights-and-responsibilities/determining-the-copyright-status-of-a-work. Also see the University of Texas Library public domain LibGuide, accessed July 28, 2025, https://guides.lib.utexas.edu/pd.

15 Hansen, *Digitizing Orphan Works*, 30–1.

16 Ibid., 46.

17 The condition on who can bring an action is reinforced by §501(b), which indicates that it is the "legal or beneficial owner of an exclusive right" who is entitled to bring action.

18 Jean Dryden, "Copyfraud, or Legitimate Concerns? Controlling Further Uses of Online Archival Holdings," *American Archivist* 74, no. 2 (2011): 539–43; Jason Mazzone, "Copyfraud," *New York University Law Review* 81, no. 3 (June 2006): 1034–8, 1084–5. Mazzone acknowledges that actual criminal prosecutions are uncommon.

19 Meanwhile, keep in mind that the § 411 and § 412 provisions do not provide a safe harbor from damages that could be awarded through the Copyright Claims Board.

20 Crews, *Copyright Law for Librarians and Educators*,186. Crews cautions that the § 504(c)(2) exemption from statutory damages may not be as good news as it may first seem. He writes "the exception for librarians and educators does not cover all possible uses of copyrighted materials. It only explicitly addresses reproducing the work in copies or phonorecords." However, "No court yet has had the need to test the meaning or extent of this law."

21 Hansen, *Digitizing Orphan Works*, 87–8.

Chapter 9

1 Emily Dickinson, *Further Poems of Emily Dickinson: Withheld from Publication by Her Sister Lavina*, eds., Martha Dickinson Biaichi and Alfred Leete Hampson (Boston, MA: Little, Brown, and Company, 1929). The punctuation and use of upper and lower case is as presented in the 1929 publication. Later critical editions issued by Harvard Press include all of the same words in the same order but use slightly different capitalization and punctuation.

2 In many ways, archivists may be of the same mindset as Emily Dickinson reflects in her last stanza. We want to be the "Merchant/Of the Heavenly Grace"—i.e., the ones who enable others to see the output of inspired creators but without having to impose the "Disgrace of Price." In other words, her vision foreshadows how our mission to provide access to creative works is constrained by economic and political structures that care little about creators, culture, or heritage—except as the source of a guaranteed income stream to intermediaries with only limited returns to the creators themselves.

3 Mark Rose, *Authors and Owners: The Invention of Copyright* (Cambridge, MA: Harvard University Press, 1993), 142. Rose adds, "It is also an institution built on intellectual quicksand: the essentially religious concept of originality, the notion that certain extraordinary beings called authors conjure works out of thin air."

4 For example, Edward Samuels, *The Illustrated History of Copyright* (New York: St. Martin's Press, 2000).

5 Laura R. Ford, *The Intellectual Property of Nations: Sociological and Historical Perspectives on a Modern Legal Institution* (Cambridge: Cambridge University Press, 2021) 413.

6 Anne W. Branscomb, *Who Owns Information?: From Privacy to Public Access* (New York: Basic Books, 1994).

7 Rosemary J. Coombe, *The Cultural Life of Intellectual Properties: Authorship, Appropriation, and the Law* (Durham, NC: Duke University Press, 1998). Two key articles are: "Contesting Paternity: Histories of Authorship," *Yale Journal of Law and the Humanities* 6 (1994): 397–422. "Left out on the Information Highway," *Oregon Law Review* 75, no. 1 (Spring 1996): 237–48.

8 Coombe, *Cultural Life of Intellectual Properties*, 254–55.

9 Jessica Litman, *Digital Copyright: Protecting Intellectual Property on the Internet* (Amherst, NY: Prometheus, 2001).

10 William Patry, *Moral Panics and the Copyright Wars* (New York: Oxford University Press, 2009), 164.

11 Patry, *Moral Panics and the Copyright Wars*, 10.

12 For example: "The problems—such as the decline in sales of CDs and DVDs—are the result of the copyright industries' many and considerable failures to focus on satisfying consumers' desires as opposed to stifling those desires out of a woefully misguided view that copyright equals control and that control equals profits." Patry, *Moral Panics*, 198.

13 Jessica Litman, "Real Copyright Reform," *Iowa Law Review* 96, no. 1 (November 2010): 39. For example, she notes: "The copyright system currently offers incentives to copyright owner intermediaries that are so substantial that they spend millions of dollars to lobby Congress to preserve and shore up the status quo."

14 Margaret Chon, "Intellectual Property and Critical Theories," in *Handbook on Intellectual Property Research: Lenses, Methods, and Perspectives*, eds. Irene Calboli, Maria Lillà Montagnani (Oxford: Oxford University Press, 2021), 764–60.

15 Victoria Smith Ekstrand, Andrew Famiglietti, Cynthia Nicole, "The Intensification of Copyright: Critical Legal Activism in the Age of Digital Copyright," *IDEA: The Intellectual Property Law Review* 53, no. 3 (2013): 291–322.

16 Jessica Litman, "What We Don't See When We See Copyright as Property," *Cambridge Law Journal* 77, no. 3 (Summer 2018): 536–55.

17 Litman, "What We Don't See," 554.

18 Ibid., 557.

19 In a sense, the attention Litman calls to the implications of works being property, and her reference to the Dawes Act's use of the right of private property to eliminate the Native American tradition of communal ownership, suggests a "thought experiment" for an archival solution to the orphan works problem. Perhaps a small group of archivists and legal scholars might develop a legislative approach. After establishing reasonable criteria for what constitutes an archival orphan work, the law should be amended to declare that any such orphan works in the permanent custody of a publicly accessible archives are thenceforth a special type of property—an intellectual property—that is owned by the archives but held in trust to be made available to a public intellectual commons for use under terms of a Creative Commons license, e.g., CC BY-NC.

20 Glynn S. Lunney Jr., "Copyright and the 1%," *Stanford Technology Law Review* 23, no. 1 (Winter 2020): 1–70.
21 Lunney, "Copyright and the 1%," especially, 31–2 and 69.
22 Ibid., 42.
23 Robert F. Brauneis, "Copyright, Music, and Race: The Case of Mirror Cover Recordings," in *The Cambridge Handbook of Intellectual Property and Social Justice*, ed. Steven D. Jamar and Lateef Mtima (Cambridge: Cambridge University Press, 2024).
24 Brauneis, "Copyright, Music, and Race," 184.
25 Reebee Garofalo, "Crossing Over: From Black Rhythm & Blues to White Rock'n'Roll," in *R&B: Rhythm and Business—The Political Economy of Black Music*, ed. Norman Kelley (New York: Akashic Press, 2002), 123.
26 *Supreme Records v. Decca Records*, 90 F. Supp. 904 (S.D. Cal. 1950) at 912.
27 Russell Sanjek, *American Popular Music and Its Business. III, From 1900 to 1984: The First Four Hundred Years* (New York: Oxford University Press, 1988), 325. See also, Brian Ward, *Just My Soul Responding: Rhythm and Blues, Black Consciousness and Race Relations* (Berkeley and Los Angeles, CA: University of California Press, 1998), 42–6.
28 Randall C. Jimerson, "Archives for All: Professional Responsibility and Social Justice," *American Archivist* 70 (Fall/Winter, 2007): 252–81; Randall C. Jimerson, *Archives Power: Memory, Accountability, and Social Justice* (Chicago, IL: Society of American Archivists, 2009).

Chapter 10

1 To move beyond all the imprecision in the public and professional usage of "AI," this chapter explores a few definitions from differing quarters to provide a foundation for discussions within the archival profession. It also reviews a few recent Copyright Office pronouncements and studies to show how that standards-setting agency is beginning to sketch out lines that may end up defining the landscape for the types of works that parallel the works held in archives.
2 Stuart J. Russell and Peter Norvigand PeterNorvig, *Artificial Intelligence: A Modern Approach*, 4th edition (Hoboken, NJ: Pearson, 2021), 7–8.
3 James Boyle, *The Line: AI and the Future of Personhood* (Cambridge, MA: MIT Press, 2024), 3, cf. 285, footnote 8.
4 National Artificial Intelligence Initiative of 2020, 15 U.S. Code § 9401(3). The NAIIA was incorporated into the William M. (Mac) Thornberry National Defense Authorization Act for Fiscal Year 2021, P.L. 116–283.
5 Library of Congress, Copyright Office, "Artificial Intelligence and Copyright: Notice of Inquiry," 88 *Federal Register*, 59942 (August 30, 2023).
6 "Artificial Intelligence and Copyright," 59948.

7 Library of Congress, Copyright Office, "Copyright Registration Guidance: Works Containing Material Generated by Artificial Intelligence," accessed July 29, 2025, https://www.copyright.gov/ai/ai_policy_guidance.pdf.

8 Library of Congress, Copyright Office, *Copyright and Artificial Intelligence, Part 1: Digital Replicas*, iv, 2, 57, accessed July 29, 2025, https://www.copyright.gov/ai/Copyright-and-Artificial-Intelligence-Part-1-Digital-Replicas-Report.pdf.

9 Library of Congress, Copyright Office, *Copyright and Artificial Intelligence Part 2: Copyrightability*, ii–iii, cf. 41, accessed July 29, 2025, https://www.copyright.gov/ai/Copyright-and-Artificial-Intelligence-Part-2-Copyrightability-Report.pdf.

10 Library of Congress, Copyright Office, *Copyright and Artificial Intelligence Part 3: Generative AI Training* pre-publication version, accessed July 29, 2025, https://www.copyright.gov/ai/Copyright-and-Artificial-Intelligence-Part-3-Generative-AI-Training-Report-Pre-Publication-Version.pdf.

11 "White House fires head of Copyright Office amid Library of Congress shakeup," *Washington Post*, May 11, 2025. Indeed, observers did not miss the coincidence that it was on the day immediately after the Register's firing when Part 3 of the Office's *Copyright and Artificial Intelligence* reports was issued as a "Pre-Publication Version." The Copyright Office's website states, "A final version of Part 3 will be published in the future, without any substantive changes expected in the analysis or conclusions." However, in these uncertain times, that remains to be seen. Likewise, based on two footnotes in the "Part 3" report, at least one further study/report ("Part 4") apparently was planned, but the Office's "Copyright and Artificial Intelligence" webpage (https://www.copyright.gov/ai/, accessed July 29, 2025) makes no reference to a further report or study.

12 Those concerns from the "creative sector" triggered the Copyright Office to pronounce the old chestnut that the wonder of copyright is that it has been able to adapt to prior introductions of innovative technologies, such as photography, sound recordings, and the internet. That is partially true, but legal modifications have too often been cumbersome at best, and barely intelligible and unfriendly to civil society (e.g., § 110 (b) and § 114, and much of Chapter 12) at the worst.

13 *Copyright and Artificial Intelligence Part 3: Generative AI Training*, 26.

14 *Copyright and Artificial Intelligence Part 3: Generative AI Training,* 32.

15 *Copyright and Artificial Intelligence Part 3: Generative AI Training*, 107, cf. 74.

16 *Copyright and Artificial Intelligence Part 3: Generative AI Training*, 71. Emphasis added. This emerges in the context of the report's analysis of a situation that could equally describe the world of archives: "Administrative or transactional costs can pose particular challenges when works are created outside of professional creative industries or are not intended to be monetized, or when ownership is diffuse."

17 William Patry, *Moral Panics and the Copyright Wars* (New York: Oxford University Press, 2009): xviii, 135, 138.

18 "Reply Comments of Songwriters Guild of America (SGA), Society of Composers & Lyricists (SCL), and Music Creators North America (MCNA), December 6, 2023," 8, accessed July 29, 2025, https://downloads.regulations.gov/COLC-2023-0006-10291/attachment_1.pdf.

19 "Reply Comments of Meta Platforms, Inc.," December 6, 2023, 5, accessed July 29, 2025, https://downloads.regulations.gov/COLC-2023-0006-10332/attachment_1.pdf.

20 Carys Craig, "The AI-Copyright Trap," 100 no. 1 (2025) *Chicago-Kent Law Review*, 139. Craig's position is reinforced by Mark Lemley's argument that the classic copyright concepts of idea/expression and substantial similarity are ill-suited as tools in deciding whether works generated by AI have or have not infringed existing works. Mark A. Lemley, "How Generative AI Turns Copyright Upside Down," *Columbia Science & Technology Law Review* 25, no. 2 (Spring 2024): 190.

21 Craig, "AI-Copyright Trap," 126.

22 Ibid., 134.

23 Ibid., 130. Emphasis in the original.

Chapter 11

1 David B. Gracy II, "Our Future Is Now," *American Archivist* 48, no. 1 (Winter 1985): 12–21.

2 Kathleen D. Roe, *Advocacy and Awareness for Archivists* (Chicago, IL: Society of American Archivists, 2019), 4–10. Roe provides an up-to-date practical handbook of the breadth of activities to build awareness and conduct advocacy.

3 Elsie Freeman Finch, "Archival Advocacy: Reflections on Myths and Realities," *Archival Issues* 20, no. 2 (1995): 116.

4 Lawrence Lessig, "Re-Crafting a Public Domain," *Yale Journal of Law & the Humanities* 18, no. Supplement–Special (2006): 61.

5 Stanford University Libraries' "Copyright and Fair Use" website (https://fairuse.stanford.edu) provides excellent updates and commentaries on fair use. It also is a good way to stay current on pending legislation (https://fairuse.stanford.edu/whatsnew?tab=legislation) and is convenient for staying up to date on decisions in copyright cases (https://fairuse.stanford.edu/case, accessed July 29, 2025).

6 Kathleen Roe, "Why Archives," *American Archivist* 79, no. 1 (Spring/Summer 2016): 11.

Chapter 12

1 Mark A. Lemley, "How Generative AI Turns Copyright Upside Down," *Columbia Science & Technology Law Review* 25, no. 2 (Spring 2024): 190–212. Lemley argues persuasively that generative AI content frustrates the conventional criteria used by courts to determine infringement—the idea/expression dichotomy and substantial similarity.

Bibliography

Bearman, David. "Archival Methods." *Archives and Museum Informatics Technical Report #9*. Pittsburgh, PA: Archives and Museum Informatics, 1989.

Bearman, David. "Archival Strategies." *American Archivist* 58 (Fall 1995): 380–3.

Becker, Ronald L. "On Deposit: A Handshake and a Lawsuit." *American Archivist* 56, no. 2 (1993): 320–8.

Beebe, Barton. "An Empirical Study of U.S. Copyright Fair Use Opinions, 1978–2005." *University of Pennsylvania Law Review* 156, no. 3 (January 2008): 549–624.

Beebe, Barton. "An Empirical Study of U.S. Copyright Fair Use Opinions Updated, 1978–2019." *New York University Journal of Intellectual Property & Entertainment Law* 10, no.1 (Fall 2020): 1–39.

Birrell, Augustine. *Seven Lectures on the Law and History of Copyright in Books*. New York: G. P. Putnam's Sons, 1899.

Boateng, Boatema. *The Copyright Thing Doesn't Work Here: Adinkra and Kente Cloth and Intellectual Property in Ghana*. Minneapolis, MN: University of Minnesota Press, 2011.

Bowker, R. R. (Richard Rogers). *Copyright, Its History and Its Law: Being a Summary of the Principles and Practice of Copyright with Special Reference to the American Code of 1909 and the British Act of 1911*. Boston and New York: Houghton Mifflin, 1912.

Boyle, James Boyle. *The Line: AI and the Future of Personhood*. Cambridge, MA: MIT Press, 2024.

Branscomb, Anne W. *Who Owns Information?: From Privacy to Public Access*. New York, NY: Basic Books, 1994.

Brauneis, Robert F. "Copyright, Music, and Race: The Case of Mirror Cover Recordings." In *The Cambridge Handbook of Intellectual Property and Social Justice*, edited by Steven D. Jamar and Lateef Mtima. Cambridge: Cambridge University Press, 2024, 183–207.

Briston, Heather. "Managing Copyright in Archives: Risk Management." In *Rights in the Digital Era*, edited by Menzi L. Behrnd-Klodt and Christopher J. Prom. Chicago, IL: Society of American Archivists, 2015.

Brown, Laura Clark, Judy Ruttenberg, and Kevin L. Smith. "Intellectual Property Rights Strategy for Digitization of Modern Manuscript Collections and Archival Record Groups." Triangle Research Libraries Network, June 2011.

Buck, Solon J. "Let's Look at the Record." *American Archivist* 8, no. 2 (1945): 109–14.

Chon, Margaret. "Intellectual Property and Critical Theories." In *Handbook on Intellectual Property Research: Lenses, Methods, and Perspectives*, edited by Irene Calboli and Maria Lillà Montagnani. Oxford: Oxford University Press, 2021, 764–60.

Coombe, Rosemary J. "Contesting Paternity: Histories of Authorship." *Yale Journal of Law and the Humanities* 6 (1994): 397–422.

Coombe, Rosemary J. *The Cultural Life of Intellectual Properties: Authorship, Appropriation, and the Law*. Durham, NC: Duke University Press, 1998.

Coombe, Rosemary J. "Left out on the Information Highway." *Oregon Law Review* 75, no. 1 (Spring 1996): 237–48.

Cornell University Library, Copyright Services. "Copyright Term and the Public Domain." Accessed May 24, 2025, https://guides.library.cornell.edu/copyright/publicdomain.

Craig, Carys. "The AI-Copyright Trap." *Chicago-Kent Law Review* 100, no. 1 (2025): 107–39.

Crews, Kenneth D. *Copyright Law for Librarians and Educators: Creative Strategies and Practical Solutions*. Chicago, IL: American Library Association, 2020.

Devine, Alyssa J. "Why You Should Care About a Federal Right of Publicity." IPWatchdog, December 15, 2023. Accessed July 18, 2025, https://ipwatchdog.com/2023/12/15/why-you-should-care-about-a-federal-right-of-publicity/id=170583/.

Dickinson, Emily. *Further Poems of Emily Dickinson: Withheld from Publication by Her Sister Lavinia*. Edited by Martha Dickinson Bianchi and Alfred Leete Hampson. Boston, MA: Little, Brown, 1929.

Dryden, Jean. "Copyfraud or Legitimate Concerns Controlling Further Uses of Online Archival Holdings." *American Archivist* 74, no. 2 (2011): 522–43.

Ekstrand, Victoria Smith, Andrew Famiglietti, and Cynthia Nicole. "The Intensification of Copyright: Critical Legal Activism in the Age of Digital Copyright." *IDEA: The Intellectual Property Law Review* 53, no. 3 (2013): 291–322.

Electronic Frontier Foundation. "*RIAA v. The People: Five Years Later*." (2008). Accessed May 25, 2025, https://www.eff.org/wp/riaa-v-people-five-years-later.

Evans, Frank. "The Many Faces of the Pennsylvania Archives." *American Archivist* 27, no. 2 (1964): 269–83.

Finch, Elsie Freeman. "Archival Advocacy: Reflections on Myths and Realities." *Archival Issues* 20, no. 2 (1995): 115–27.

First Archivist Circle. *Protocols for Native American Archival Materials*. 2007. Accessed May 22, 2025, https://www2.nau.edu/libnap-p/protocols.html or https://www2.nau.edu/libnap-p/PrintProtocols.pdf.

Ford, Laura R. *The Intellectual Property of Nations: Sociological and Historical Perspectives on a Modern Legal Institution*. Cambridge: Cambridge University Press, 2021.

Garon, Jon. "Director's Choice: The Fine Line Between Interpretation and Infringement of an Author's Work." *Columbia-VLA Journal of the Law & the Arts* 12, no. 2 (1987–88): 277–306.

Goldstein, Paul. *Goldstein on Copyright*. Alphen aan den Rijn: Wolters Kluwer. 3rd edition, 2025–2 Supplement.

Gordon, Wendy J. "Copyright Owners' Putative Interests in Privacy, Reputation, and Control: A Reply to Goold." *Virginia Law Review Online* 103 (2017): 47.

Gracy, David B., II. "Our Future Is Now." *American Archivist* 48, no. 1 (Winter 1985): 12–21.

Greene, Mark. "A Critique of Social Justice as an Archival Imperative: What Is It We're Doing That's All That Important?" *American Archivist* 76, no. 2 (2013): 302–34.

Greene, Mark. "MPLP: It's Not Just for Processing Anymore." *American Archivist* 73, no. 1 (Spring/Summer 2010): 175–203.

Hansen, David. *Digitizing Orphan Works: Legal Strategies to Reduce Risks for Open Access to Copyrighted Orphan Works*. Kyle K. Courtney and Peter Suber, eds., Harvard Library, 2016. Accessed May 24, 2025, http://nrs.harvard.edu/urn-3:HUL.InstRepos:27840430.

Hirtle, Peter B. "Archives or Assets?" *American Archivist* 66, no. 2 (2003): 235–47.

Hirtle, Peter B. "Research, Libraries, and Fair Use: The Gentlemen's Agreement of 1935." *Journal of the Copyright Society of the USA* 53, no. 3–4 (Spring 2006–Summer 2006): 545–601.

Hirtle, Peter B., Emily Hudson, and Andrew T. Kenyon. *Copyright and Cultural Institutions: Guidelines for Digitization for U.S. Libraries, Archives, and Museums*. Ithaca, NY: Cornell University Library, 2009. Accessed May 23, 2025, https://ecommons.cornell.edu/bitstreams/73163724-80d4-4542-a155-c7e8f274f2c1/download.

International Council on Archives. *Universal Declaration on Archives*. https://www.ica.org/app/uploads/2023/12/20190510_ica_declarationuniverselle_en_0.pdf.

Jaszi, Peter. "Toward a Theory of Copyright: The Metamorphoses of 'Authorship.'" *Duke Law Journal* 2 (April 1991): 455–502.

Jimerson, Randall C. "Archives for All: Professional Responsibility and Social Justice." *American Archivist* 70 (Fall/Winter 2007): 252–81.

Jimerson, Randall C. *Archives Power: Memory, Accountability, and Social Justice*. Chicago, IL: Society of American Archivists, 2009.

Jimerson, Randall. "Embracing the Power of Archives." *American Archivist* 69, no. 1 (2006): 19–32.

Joffrion, Elizabeth, and Michèle V. Cloonan. *Advancing Preservation for Archives and Manuscripts*. Chicago, IL: Society of American Archivists, 2020.

Joint, Nicholas. "Applying General Risk Management Principles to Library Administration." *Library Review* 56, no. 7 (2007): 542–51.

Joint, Nicholas. "Risk Assessment and Copyright in Digital Libraries." *Library Review* 55, no. 9 (2006): 543–46.

Lemley, Mark A. "How Generative AI Turns Copyright Upside Down." *Columbia Science & Technology Law Review* 25, no. 2 (Spring 2024): 190–212.

Lessig, Lawrence. "Re-Crafting a Public Domain." *Yale Journal of Law & the Humanities* 18, no. Supplement – Special 2006 (2006): 56–83.

Leval, Pierre N. "Fair Use or Foul?" *Journal of the Copyright Society of the U.S.A.* 36 (April 1989): 167–81.

Library of Congress, Copyright Office. "Artificial Intelligence and Copyright: Notice of Inquiry." 88 *Federal Register*, 59942 (August 30, 2023).

Library of Congress, Copyright Office. *Authors, Attribution, and Integrity: Examining Moral Rights in the United States*. Washington, DC: US Copyright Office, 2019. Accessed May 22, 2025, https://www.copyright.gov/policy/moralrights/full-report.pdf.

Library of Congress, Copyright Office. *CCB HANDBOOK: Opting Out*. Accessed July 15, 2025, https://ccb.gov/handbook/Opting-Out.pdf.

Library of Congress, Copyright Office. *Compendium of U.S. Copyright Office Practices*. 3rd edition. United States Copyright Office, December 22, 2014. Available from Copyright Office. Accessed May 20, 2025, https://www.copyright.gov/comp3/docs/compendium-12-22-14.pdf.

Library of Congress, Copyright Office. *Copyright and Artificial Intelligence, Part 1: Digital Replicas*, iv, 2, 57. Accessed July 4, 2025, https://www.copyright.gov/ai/Copyright-and-Artificial-Intelligence-Part-1-Digital-Replicas-Report.pdf.

Library of Congress, Copyright Office. *Copyright and Artificial Intelligence Part 2: Copyrightability*. Accessed July 4, 2025, https://www.copyright.gov/ai/Copyright-and-Artificial-Intelligence-Part-2-Copyrightability-Report.pdf.

Library of Congress, Copyright Office. *Copyright and Artificial Intelligence Part 3: Generative AI Training pre-publication version*. Accessed July 4, 2025, https://www.copyright.gov/ai/Copyright-and-Artificial-Intelligence-Part-3-Generative-AI-Training-Report-Pre-Publication-Version.pdf.

Library of Congress, Copyright Office. "*Copyright Registration Guidance: Works Containing Material Generated by Artificial Intelligence.*" Accessed July 4, 2025, https://www.copyright.gov/ai/ai_policy_guidance.pdf.

Library of Congress, Copyright Office. *International Copyright Relations of the United States Circular 34A*. Washington DC: Library of Congress, 2025. Available at: https://www.copyright.gov/circs/circ38a.pdf.

Library of Congress, U.S. Copyright Office. "§ 201.14 Warnings of Copyright for Use by Certain Libraries and Archives." Library of Congress, Copyright Office. Accessed May 23, 2025, https://www.copyright.gov/title37/201/37cfr201-14.html.

Light, Michelle. "Controlling Goods or Promoting the Public Good: Choices for Special Collections in the Marketplace." *RBM: A Journal of Rare Books, Manuscripts, and Cultural Heritage* 16, no. 1 (2015): 48–63.

Lipinski, Thomas A. *The Complete Copyright Liability Handbook for Librarians and Educators*. New York: Neal-Shuman, 2006.

Litman, Jessica. *Digital Copyright*. Amherst, NY: Prometheus Books, 2001.

Litman, Jessica. "Real Copyright Reform." *Iowa Law Review* 96, no. 1 (November 2010): 39.

Litman, Jessica. "What We Don't See When We See Copyright as Property." *Cambridge Law Journal* 77, no. 3 (Summer 2018): 536–55.

Loewenstein, Joseph. *The Author's Due: Printing and the Prehistory of Copyright*. Chicago, IL: University of Chicago Press, 2002.

Lunney, Glynn S. "Copyright and the 1%." *Stanford Technology Law Review* 23, no. 1 (Winter 2020): 1–70.

Mazzone, Jason. "Copyfraud." *New York University Law Review* 81, no. 3 (2006): 1026–100.

McCarthy, J. Thomas. *McCarthy's Desk Encyclopedia of Intellectual Property*. Washington, DC: Bureau of National Affairs, Inc., 1991.

McCarthy, J. Thomas. *The Rights of Publicity and Privacy*. Toronto: Thomson Reuters, 2015.

McKay, Aprille C. "Managing Rights and Permissions." In *Rights in the Digital Era*, edited by Menzi L. Behrnd-Klodt and Christopher J. Prom. Chicago, IL: Society of American Archivists, 2015.

Netanal, Neil Weinstock. *From Maimonides to Microsoft: The Jewish Law of Copyright since the Birth of Print*. New York: Oxford University Press, 2016.

Nimmer, Melville B., and David Nimmer. *Nimmer on Copyright*, Lexis-Nexis, Release 123 May 2025.

OCLC Research. "Well-Intentioned Practice for Putting Digitized Collections of Unpublished Materials Online." Accessed May 24, 2025, https://www.oclc.org/content/dam/research/activities/rights/practice.pdf.

Patry, William. *Moral Panics and the Copyright Wars*. New York: Oxford University Press, 2009.

Patterson, L. Ray (Lyman Ray). *Copyright in Historical Perspective*. Nashville, TN: Vanderbilt University Press, 1968.

Patterson, L. Ray (Lyman Ray), and Stanley W. Lindberg. *The Nature of Copyright: A Law of Users' Rights*. Athens, GA: University of Georgia Press, 1991.

Ritzenthaler, Mary Lynn. *Preserving Archives & Manuscripts*. 2nd edition. Chicago, IL: Society of American Archivists, 2010.

Roe, Kathleen D. *Advocacy and Awareness for Archivists*. Chicago, IL: Society of American Archivists, 2019.

Roe, Kathleen Roe. "Why Archives." *American Archivist* 79, no. 1 (Spring/Summer 2016): 6–13.

Rose, Mark. *Authors and Owners: The Invention of Copyright*. Cambridge, MA: Harvard University Press, 1993.

Rothman, Jennifer E. *The Right of Publicity: Privacy Reimagined for a Public World*. Cambridge, MA: Harvard University Press, 2018.

Russell, Stuart J., Peter Norvig, Ming-Wei Chang, Jacob Devlin, Anea Dragan, David Forsyth, Ian Goodfellow, et al. *Artificial Intelligence: A Modern Approach*, 4th edition. Hoboken, NJ: Pearson, 2021,

Samuels, Edward. *The Illustrated History of Copyright*. New York: St. Martin's Press, 2000.

Sanjek, Russell. *American Popular Music and Its Business. III, From 1900 to 1984: The First Four Hundred Years*. New York: Oxford University Press, 1988, 325.

Smith, Kevin. "Copyright Risk Management: Principles and Strategies for Large-Scale Digitization Projects in Special Collections." *Research Library Issues* 279 (June 2012): 17–23.

Smith, Kevin, and Susan Davis. "Copyright in a Digital Age: Conflict, Risk, and Reward." *The Serials Librarian* 64 (2013): 57–66.

Society of American Archivists. *Dictionary of Archives Terminology*. Chicago, IL: Society of American Archivists, 2020. Accessed May 24, 2025, https://dictionary.archivists.org; dictionary.archivists.org/entry/archives.html.

Society of American Archivists. "Orphan Works: Statement of Best Practices." 2009. Accessed May 24, 2025, https://www2.archivists.org/sites/all/files/OrphanWorks-June2009.pdf.

Society of American Archivists. *Planning for the Archival Profession: A Report of the SAA Task Force on Goals and Priorities*. Chicago: Society of American Archivists, 1986.

Society of American Archivists, Intellectual Property Working Group. "Guide to Implementing Rights Statements from RightsStatements.org." 2016. Accessed May 24, 2025, https://www2.archivists.org/sites/all/files/RightsStatements_IPWG%20Guidance.pdf.

Stobo, Victoria, with Ronan Deazley and Ian G. Anderson. "Copyright & Risk: Scoping the Wellcome Digital Library Project." CREATe Working Paper No. 10. Centre for Regulation of the Creative Economy. December 2013. Accessed July 11, 2025, http://zenodo.org/record/8380/files/CREATe-Working-Paper-2013-10.pdf.

U.S. House of Representatives, 94th Congress, 2nd Session, *Copyright Law Revision*, Historical and Revision Notes, House Report no. 94–1476, September 3, 1976, p. 65. Available from Copyright Office. Accessed May 20, 2025, https://www.copyright.gov/history/law/clrev_94-1476.pdf.

United Nations. *UNESCO Convention on the Means of Prohibiting and Preventing the Illicit Import, Export and Transfer of Ownership of Cultural Property*. 1970.

Ward, Brian. *Just My Soul Responding: Rhythm and Blues, Black Consciousness and Race Relations*. Berkeley, CA: University of California Press, 1998.

Warren, Samuel, and Louis Brandeis. "The Right to Privacy." *Harvard Law Review* IV, no. 5 (1890): 193, 195, and especially 205.

Writers Artists and Their Copyright Holders. Accessed May 23, 2025, https://norman.hrc.utexas.edu/watch//.

Zhang, Jiaying Jessie. "Battle in the Digital Sphere: The Repatriation of Digitized Native American Cultural Properties." *AIPLA Quarterly Journal* 52, no. 2 (Spring 2024): 403–34.

Index

About the Author

William Maher has 45 years of experience as an archivist at the University of Illinois Urbana-Champaign, starting as Assistant University Archivist, followed by 28 years as Director of the Archives and University Archivist. Throughout his career, he selected, organized, and promoted a broad array of records and external collections, including a near encyclopedic array of special topics ranging from advertising and architecture to international sport, and information and physical science.

Over the past 20 years, Maher has regularly taught workshops on copyright law for archivists on behalf of the Society of American Archivists (SAA). He is also co-chair of the SAA's Intellectual Property Working Group. Since 2011, he has been the Head of Delegation in representing SAA at the World Intellectual Property Organization and its Standing Committee on Copyright and Related Rights.

Beyond the university, he has served as Chair of the International Council on Archives (ICA)'s Section on Archives of Universities and Research Institutions and a member of ICA's Executive Board. He served as elected Treasurer and later as Vice-President / President of the Society of American Archivists (SAA). Previously he had served as elected Secretary-Treasurer and President of the Midwest Archives Conference. He also has served as a Program Officer related to library and archives projects at the National Endowment for the Humanities. His publications include *The Management of College and University Archives* as well as over 100 articles and conference presentations on archives and history, cultural heritage, university archival administration, and copyright law. He holds degrees from Case Western University, Washington University (St. Louis), and University of Illinois Urbana-Champaign.

www.ingramcontent.com/pod-product-compliance
Ingram Content Group UK Ltd.
Pitfield, Milton Keynes, MK11 3LW, UK
UKHW021851130926
475466UK00003B/68